SHAKESPEARE'S TRAGIC FRONTIER

Shakespeare's Tragic Frontier

The World of His Final Tragedies

By Willard Farnham

University of California Press

Berkeley and Los Angeles

1950

UNIVERSITY OF CALIFORNIA PRESS
BERKELEY AND LOS ANGELES
CALIFORNIA

❖

CAMBRIDGE UNIVERSITY PRESS
LONDON, ENGLAND

PRINTED IN THE UNITED STATES OF AMERICA
BY THE UNIVERSITY OF CALIFORNIA PRESS

Foreword of Acknowledgment

THE STUDIES that went to the making of this book were begun and carried much of the way toward completion during a year's tenancy of a research fellowship at the Henry E. Huntington Library and Art Gallery, San Marino, California. For aid and privileges given me by the Huntington Library, not in one year only but through many years, I am deeply grateful.

W. F.

Berkeley, California
January 5, 1949

Contents

Chapter I

TAINTS AND HONORS

WITHIN the larger world of Shakespearean tragedy, *Timon of Athens, Macbeth, Antony and Cleopatra,* and *Coriolanus* make up a world of their own. In chapters to follow I consider these four plays as parts of the world they constitute. I take them to be Shakespeare's final tragedies. Their world is well defined and is set off against a world equally well defined which appears in *Julius Caesar, Hamlet, Othello,* and *King Lear,* the other tragedies of Shakespeare's maturity.

When the death of Antony is announced to Octavius in *Antony and Cleopatra,* Maecenas and Agrippa become a chorus and comment upon the hero of the tragedy. Maecenas says:

> His taints and honours
> Wag'd equal with him.

Agrippa caps the comment:

> A rarer spirit never
> Did steer humanity; but you, gods, will give us
> Some faults to make us men.   (V, i, 30–33)[1]

It is rare spirits deeply tainted that Shakespeare places at the center of his last tragic world. The faults given them to make them men are not only great enough to "wage equal" with their virtues but are also pervasive, and yet these spirits are noble. Their nobility, as we shall find, is one of life's mysteries, for it seems to issue from ignoble sub-

---

[1] For notes to chapter i see pages 265–267.

stance. In his presentation of this mystery Shakespeare is greatly daring, not merely in risking loss of sympathy for his tragic heroes but in other ways as well. He takes up an advanced position in a realm of late Renaissance tragedy where new refinements of tragic truth are to be discovered in paradox but where the tragic emotions and the essential simplicities of tragic understanding are in constant danger of being overwhelmed by paradox. Here he occupies a country of the mind that may be called his tragic frontier. Here he finds marches of tragedy beyond which he cannot go without deserting tragedy.

II

Though the chronology of Shakespeare's plays has not been determined exactly, the general course of his development as a dramatist is plain. We may think of a part of that development as producing an early tragic world, a middle tragic world, and a last tragic world.

The early tragic world is that of *Richard III, Titus Andronicus, Romeo and Juliet,* and *Richard II.* There is little to indicate the order in which these plays were written, but the order may well be that in which they are here named.[2] It is certain that all were written before the publication in 1598 of Meres's *Palladis Tamia,* since all are mentioned in that omnium-gatherum of literary references. Shakespeare's early tragic world is without settled form, and in its variations and inconsistencies it is a microcosm of the world of early Elizabethan tragedy, a world built tentatively upon medieval and Senecan heritages that were often difficult to reconcile.[3] Especially is Shakespeare's early tragic world without settled form in what it has to show of human faults and their place in a scheme productive of human suffering. The Shakespeare whom Meres knew in 1598 had developed no tragic manner, however much he had developed a poetic style. His tragedies had been a series of diverse experiments, and one measure of their diversity had been the wide variation in their heroes, from the strong to the weak and from the villainously guilty to the piteously unfortunate.

With the writing of *Julius Caesar* Shakespeare found a tragic manner. It appears that he wrote *Julius Caesar* in 1599, and there is no need to doubt that it is the first of the four plays which make up his middle tragic world. The other three of these four he apparently wrote in this order: *Hamlet* (*ca.* 1600), *Othello* (*ca.* 1604), *King Lear* (*ca.* 1605).[4]

Julius Caesar is a landmark not merely in the history of Shakespearean tragedy but in the history of English tragedy. Before Brutus there had been no tragic hero on the English stage whose character had combined noble grandeur with fatal imperfection. Heroes fatally imperfect there had been, as interest in tragic justice had grown and the medieval picture of a disorderly mortal scene ruled by Fortune had faded, but many of them had been villains or weaklings and all of them had been incapable of arousing profound admiration. Though Marlowe's Tamburlaine had achieved grandeur, it was of a kind not to be called noble, and he had achieved it by being free from any fatal imperfection except a mortal nature and thus by being a dubious tragic hero. In Brutus, then, Shakespeare discovered the noble hero with a tragic flaw. By that discovery he made it possible for English tragedy to reach a greatness hitherto attained only by Greek tragedy. All his tragedies written after *Julius Caesar* benefited by the discovery.

The heroes of *Julius Caesar, Hamlet, Othello,* and *King Lear* are blood brothers in their nobility. With all their faults they are nothing if not admirable characters. Shakespeare lavishes poetic power upon them to magnify them and give them an appeal to our hero-worshiping faculties, and we find that even Lear, though old age has had a sad effect upon his majesty, possesses that which commands esteem.

Probably the most significant thing one may say about these four heroes as admirable characters is that, however difficult it is to probe the meanings of their tragedies, it is not at all difficult to understand the hold their humanity has upon us. When they arouse our admiration, they do not leave us uncertain why they do so. Moreover, they arouse some measure of admiration in all of us who know them; no one of them creates among us a camp of condemners as well as a camp of praisers, for they are noble spirits in a simple sense of the word. If good and evil are mighty opposites in the finite universe, as Shakespeare often makes them in his tragedies, then Brutus, Hamlet, Othello, and Lear can be placed on the side of good, without debate and without involved justification. Each has plainly a bent toward good. Brutus and Hamlet have a consuming desire to further the cause of right, and Othello and Lear suffer the tortures of remorse when they realize the wrong they have done.

Because these heroes of Shakespeare's middle tragic world are at heart incorruptible, their tragic flaws do not reach into the centers of their characters. They are not deeply flawed, even though their flaws are fatal. The flaws of Brutus and Hamlet do not lead either hero to the doing of evil—that is, to the doing of evil according to the light in which their dramas are written. Shakespeare does not put Brutus in a class with Judas and make him worthy of a place in deepest Hell for treacherous betrayal of a master, as Dante does. In *Julius Caesar* the high-minded hero tries dutifully to do right, even by means of assassination, which for him is a form of judicial execution, and comes to ruin because of fatal mistakes in judgment growing out of faulty wisdom. Nor does Shakespeare make Hamlet guilty of sin in the seeking of a private revenge forbidden by God, as he might have made him. Hamlet, too, tries dutifully to do right, even by means of assassination, which in his case is enjoined by a primitive code of honor. Hamlet speaks of God's setting a canon against self-slaughter, but neither he nor anyone among his associates speaks of God's setting a canon against the kind of villain-slaughter which, after a tragic struggle, he finally succeeds in perpetrating. Thus the Hamlet problem, involved as it is, is not so involved as it might be. The flaws of Othello and Lear, unlike those of Brutus and Hamlet, do lead their possessors into the doing of evil. We may look upon Lear as less guilty than Othello, and yet we are meant to accept, I think, Kent's judgment that Lear's actions are evil when he gives away his throne and not only metes out rank injustice to the too honest Cordelia but also confers destructive power upon her evil sisters. Kent's judgment procures his banishment because it is put in such naked terms as these:

> Revoke thy gift;
> Or, whilst I can vent clamour from my throat,
> I'll tell thee thou dost evil.   (I, i, 167–169)

But both Othello and Lear lend themselves to evil largely in the way of ignorance, for Othello's evil action is put upon him by his unwise faith in Iago, and Lear's by his unwise faith in his two evil daughters. Consequently, Othello and Lear are shown to have faulty substance in them to which evil can be attached, rather than faulty substance that evil can penetrate.

The natural evil not found in the noble heroes of Shakespeare's middle tragic world is found in the villains. In each of the plays that make up this world there is definite villainy working in general against good and in particular against the hero. Cassius and Claudius, it is true, are not such thoroughgoing villains as Iago and Lear's evil daughters. As Shakespeare proceeds with the creation of his middle tragic world he deepens the villainy in it and increases the effective power of evil. Evil comes to have a dramatic character such as it has in the medieval moral play. In *Othello* it makes a masked assault upon the hero to deceive and destroy him, much as though it were proceeding by sleight against a medieval Mankind. Iago is a Renaissance descendant of the medieval Vice, in whom the Vice's irreverent humor has grown profoundly grim and the Vice's power to corrupt turned Machiavellian. *Lear* shows evil that works not only by sleight but also by brutal direct action, even by force of arms, and in this tragedy the assault of evil upon the hero and upon good brings a din of universal thunder.

III

The opinion of A. C. Bradley that *Timon* came immediately after *Lear* and immediately before *Macbeth* is well known.[5] So is the opinion of Sir Edmund Chambers that it is the last of Shakespeare's tragedies and shows an explosive ending of his tragic inspiration.[6] Agreeing with Bradley that, all things considered, verse tests included, the most likely position in which we can place *Timon* is between *Lear* and *Macbeth,* I take *Timon* to have been written about 1605 and to be the first of the four plays that make up Shakespeare's last tragic world. Whether it is wholly Shakespearean has been a long-standing question. It bears strongly the impress of the mature Shakespeare in many of its scenes, as no critic has ever doubted, but is a very imperfect and uneven play. The belief of Sir Edmund Chambers that Shakespeare wrote all of *Timon* but left it unfinished is gaining adherents. It is clear that if Shakespeare did not write all of *Timon,* he wrote enough of it to control its tragic implications and its spirit.[7] The plays that join with *Timon* in the constitution of Shakespeare's last tragic world seem to have been written in the following order under the influence of a sustained special inspiration: *Macbeth* (*ca.* 1606), *Antony and Cleopatra* (*ca.* 1607), *Coriolanus* (*ca.* 1608).[8]

Unlike the heroes of the middle tragic world those of the last tragic world are deeply flawed. No one of them is a doer of duty, like Brutus or Hamlet, or an unselfish repenter for wrong done, like Othello or Lear. Macbeth has a conscience that brings him to despair at the end of his tragic course, but, as we shall find, this conscience leaves something to be desired because, like himself, it is deeply flawed. Each of these heroes has faulty substance reaching to the very center of his character. Timon's glowing love for his fellow men turns out to be in reality a form of selfishness, for as soon as he learns that his fellows have never had love for him, but only love for his money, this glowing love becomes searing hate. Macbeth gives himself to evil in order to gain worldly position, and gives himself completely, realizing that he does so. Antony knows that Cleopatra is destructive of his honor as a man and a soldier, and at the opening of his tragedy we find him breaking his "strong Egyptian fetters" so that he will not lose himself in dotage; but he quickly chooses that these fetters shall be forged again, and there is then no more question of his leaving Cleopatra. Coriolanus, the warrior aristocrat, is so thoroughly blinded by regard for himself that he embraces treason, the crime *par excellence* for a warrior aristocrat bred to fight for his state. Coriolanus embraces treason not once, but twice, and yet he never comes to know what treason really is. It is plain that these four heroes are self-centered individualists.

In the last tragic world there is less of the medieval drama of good and evil than in the middle tragic world. In *Timon* and *Antony and Cleopatra* there are no villains, and the heroes are so much bent upon involving themselves in tragedy through the flaws in their characters that they seem to need no villains to help in the work of entanglement.

In *Coriolanus* the tribunes and Aufidius take on villainous roles when they work against the hero underhandedly, but Coriolanus also seems to need no help in making his tragic end certain. In *Macbeth,* however, the witches, who are greater than merely human villains in the hierarchy of evil, do villain's work upon the hero and are by no means a supernumerary part of the tragedy. Of these four plays, *Macbeth* alone presents a fearsome struggle between representatives of good and representatives of evil that is reminiscent of *Othello* and *Lear*. Yet this is a struggle with a difference. It is to be remembered that in *Othello* and *Lear* the heroes are never truly brought over to the side of evil, though in their confusion they for a time join its ranks. In *Macbeth* the soul of the deeply flawed hero is securely won by evil at the beginning of the action.

Timon, Macbeth, Antony, and Coriolanus all have a power, such as the heroes of the middle tragic world do not have, to draw from us reactions that vary widely between profound antipathy and profound sympathy. Along with sympathy they can inspire admiration. Each, because of his deeply flawed nature, can compel from some of us severe condemnation. Each, despite his deeply flawed nature, can compel from others of us high praise. Probably in most who observe their tragedies, antipathy and sympathy for these heroes tend to be strangely mixed and any admiration for them tends to be tempered by a knowledge that it cannot easily be explained. There is nobility to be found in Timon, Macbeth, Antony, and Coriolanus, but in the main it seems inseparable from their flaws, and an admirer of that nobility may wonder whether he is not admiring the flaws themselves even while he sees that they are flaws.

In Macbeth, guilty of atrociously inhuman crimes, we find most to repel us, and yet, in capacity to make us feel something other than repulsion, he is certainly not the least of these four heroes. Shakespeare comes perilously close to cutting Macbeth off from our sympathy and then triumphantly saves him from that isolation. It is an amazing feat. Shakespeare accomplishes it by giving Macbeth a noble greatness of spirit that reveals itself even in the motions of evil-willing and evil-doing. Of the ways in which it reveals itself I intend to speak later.

Thus there is in Macbeth a paradoxical nobility—paradoxical because it seems to be of a piece with, and even to spring from, the very opposite of nobility. Macbeth has a similarity to the Satan of Milton's *Paradise Lost* because there is in both characters a fusion of baseness and nobility. Whether the Satan of *Paradise Lost* is or is not to be called the hero of the poem, he is certainly to be called nobly heroic. That which has made him first among angels makes him first among devils. As for Macbeth, that which makes him great as a doer of evil is the stuff of greatness wherever greatness is found, on the side of evil or that of good. One feels that the world needs such greatness even at the cost of having it go astray in a Macbeth.

Each in his own way, as we shall find, the other heroes of the last tragic world show paradoxical nobility, and by the side of Antony stands Cleopatra as a companion study in deeply flawed yet somehow admirable humanity. Shakespeare seems willing to make it hard for us to admire, even while he asks us to admire, these tragic individualists who as they impel themselves toward catastrophe are totally self-absorbed, Timon and Coriolanus blindly, Antony and Cleopatra willfully. All are children of folly. All are at times made ridiculous, and all are frequently enough subjected to ridicule at the hands of associates. Because of the blind folly of Timon and Coriolanus and their subjection to ridicule, Professor O. J. Campbell, in *Shakespeare's Satire,* presents their dramas as tragical satires.[9] But when we do admire these children of folly, we remember that though they are ridiculed in their dramas, they are also praised, and praised in no mean terms. Taints and honors "wage equal" with them, and despite their faults they are counted rare spirits.

IV

Shakespeare's last tragic world is of the age in which it was created, though it is distinctively Shakespearean. The age was one in which the English Renaissance came to full maturity and found as it searched for new truth that knowledge could be confounded with knowledge. It was one in which the medieval temper was unmistakably yielding to the modern, though the medieval still had strong expression in many quarters. About the beginning of the seventeenth century, English tragedy, not the tragedy of Shakespeare alone, became capable of the analysis of deeply flawed human greatness in a subtly mixed spirit of detachment and sympathy that was utterly different from any spirit it had shown even a few years before. For centuries the Christian tradition had known the separation of sin and the sinner through which there could be hate for the one and charitable sympathy for the other; but here was a spirit that could extend sympathy to the sinner or the faulty character in a mood far more complex than that of medieval charity, for it could represent serious shortcomings as apparently inseparable from the heroic greatness for which it had sympathy, yet without letting its sympathy minimize the shortcomings.

Because of their sympathetic concern with deeply flawed but noble-spirited tragic figures, Chapman and Webster help us, more than any others of the dramatists who were fellows of Shakespeare in the seventeenth century, to understand the Jacobean quality in Shakespeare's last tragic world. They do so in characteristic plays, Chapman in *Bussy D'Ambois* and *Charles Duke of Byron* (the latter being one tragedy in two plays), and Webster in *The White Devil*. A period of perhaps no more than five years covered the writing of these three tragedies and the creation of Shakespeare's last tragic world. Within that period, as I shall now try to make plain by an examination of the three tragedies, Chapman and Webster gained a common ground with Shakespeare. Shakespeare, Chapman, and Webster occupied that common ground each in his own manner.

Bussy was first printed in 1607 and was probably written some few years earlier, perhaps in 1604. In history, Louis de Clermont d'Amboise, Seigneur de Bussy (b. 1549), played a minor role. He was a gallant figure at the French court, with a reputation as a swordsman and a lover, and after an adventurous life of thirty years was trapped and killed by the Count of Montsoreau at an assignation with Montsoreau's countess. Just where Chapman found the story of his career we do not know. On this "homme de sang et de feu" the imagination of Chapman worked strangely; for Chapman's Bussy appears as a greatly noble spirit, one of the titans among human beings. He is a Jacobean extension of Marlowe's Tamburlaine.[10] In him the grandiose Scythian shepherd becomes sophisticated and stalks through a polite European court, instead of riding in triumph through the cities of Asia. At the beginning of *Bussy* the hero is taken up as a favorite by Monsieur, the brother of the French king, who recognizes in him a daring spirit and thinks that he can use him. But Bussy is not of the stuff that can be used by another man; he is too much the indomitable individualist. Through half of the play he rises. He flouts the Duke of Guise by pretending openly to court his duchess, proves himself a matchless swordsman in a fray between courtiers, wins not only the king's pardon for his taking of lives in this fray but also the king's admiration and favor, and gains the love of Tamyra, the Countess of Montsurry. Then comes the turning point in his fortunes. Monsieur agrees with the Duke of Guise that Bussy flies too high and must be checked. Monsieur himself is in love with Tamyra. The Court of Montsurry is informed of a meeting between Bussy and the countess, and Bussy, whose largeness of spirit makes him incapable of defending himself successfully by devious "policy," is lured to his death at the hands of murderers. He dies as bravely as he has lived.

There is a more essential difference between Marlowe's Tamburlaine and Chapman's Bussy than that between a barbaric Scythian and a courtly Frenchman. Whatever we ourselves may think of Tamburlaine, Marlowe presents his greatness as utterly without flaw except for the flaw of mortality that is common to humanity. Nothing could be simpler and less questioning than the spirit in which Marlowe writes of him. No opponent finds the greatness of Tamburlaine to be vulnerable. Zenocrite has momentary fears that he may be subject to the Fortune whom he defies and may fall from the top of her wheel, but they turn out to be groundless. He dies, but is not overcome by weakness in himself any more than by strength in another. He makes no errors. The flamboyance in his actions and in his "working words" can at times seem ludicrous to us, but they never become ludicrous to those whom Marlowe makes Tamburlaine's companions, and clearly never to Marlowe himself. There is no sign that Marlowe ever has his tongue in his cheek when he writes Tamburlainean bombast. We feel that he gives himself to Tamburlaine passionately and uncritically. But when we come to Bussy, we feel that though Chapman is giving himself to his hero passionately, he is far from giving himself uncritically. Among the shortcomings of Bussy there is a characteristic ability to make his high mightiness ludicrous, and this is searchingly recognized in the play. Chapman strikes a balance between sympathetic praise of Bussy and sharply adverse criticism of him.

It is Monsieur who searches the character of Bussy for the faults that make him ludicrous. He analyzes those faults eloquently and with malicious shrewdness upon an occasion when the two men have agreed to dissect each other's natures unsparingly. Bussy is a wild horse or tiger, says Monsieur—as daring, headstrong, and bloody. He would

serve a butcher and cut men's throats, though he would stop
at killing the king. In his quarreling he can run as mad as
Ajax. In his valor he is

> like other naturals,
> That haue strange gifts in nature, but no soule
> Diffus'd quite through, to make them of a peece.[11]

Moreover, in that valor he is

> more ridiculous and vaine-glorious
> Than any Mountibancke; and impudent
> Than any painted bawde.[12]

When Monsieur speaks thus, he has turned against Bussy.
Earlier in the play, he has been the first to praise the greatness of Bussy and has found in him a heart that will not
down, a heart like the sea, filled with natural ardor and
power and "bristled with surges," one that never will be
won

> To make retreat into his setled home,
> Till he be croun'd with his owne quiet fome.[13]

A consideration of all that is said in the play about Bussy's
greatness gives us a fairly clear idea of the heroic quality
we are meant to see in Bussy. It is no more than a fairly clear
idea because Chapman has a tendency to drown his thought
in swirls of intellectual passion. We may gather that Bussy
is somehow the admirable natural man raised to the ultimate degree. He possesses to the full a glorious primitive
force of being, though he lives in a world grown effete and
corrupt. The king speaks of him as

> A man so good, that only would vphold
> Man in his native noblesse, from whose fall
> All our dissentions rise; that in himselfe

(Without the outward patches of our frailtie,
Riches and honour) knowes he comprehends
Worth with the greatest.[14]

The king goes on to say, with fine disregard of his own
vested interests, that kings would never have dominated
other men if all had kept the spirit and state of D'Ambois,
nor would the golden age of Saturn have come to an end
and evils have come into the world

Had all beene held together with the nerues,
The genius and th'ingenuous soule of D'Ambois.[15]

But when a natural man like Bussy, who has "worth with
the greatest," lives in a corrupted world, he finds, it would
seem, that his great virtue can be a great flaw, though it does
not cease to be admirable as virtue. For the natural greatness of a Bussy is not to be contained. It overflows and does
what is called wrong in a world too small and mean to subjugate such genius with its laws. A Bussy thinks of himself
as his own law and stands on what he regards as his special
rights. Bussy makes this plain in what he says to the king
when he asks for pardon after the combat between the
courtiers:
                                Since I am free,
(Offending no iust law) let no law make
By any wrong it does, my life her slaue:
When I am wrong'd and that law failes to right me,
Let me be King my selfe (as man was made)
And doe a iustice that exceedes the law.[16]

Thus we see why, when Tamyra talks of a conscience bur-
dened with sin and fear after an adulterous meeting with
Bussy, her lover replies that sin is a coward and that it only

insults weakness. He himself, law unto himself that he is, is beyond being terrified by such "faulty apprehensions," and scorns the "Puritan spice" in what she has said.

Bussy goes to his death because he is the lover of Tamyra. It is a simple, worldly matter: a wronged husband takes revenge. The world can destroy with its laws of right and wrong the natural man who is too big for those laws. In this, as Monsieur says just before Bussy's death, there is profound irony, for Nature gives with a lavish hand to make a "whole man," who will not wind in the crooked ways of the servile world, and by the very lavishness of her giving exposes him to all the force of the winds of Fortune. Those winds blow through empty men and merely make them dance, but the whole men, whose fullness offers resistance, they blow down.

All this can of course be called "sympathizing with sin" on Chapman's part, and has been called so.[17] Yet from what we know of Chapman generally, we must conclude that he was not one to think of himself as against all morality. He seems to have thought of himself as an earnest champion of a special morality higher than that recognized by the common herd of humanity. So far as Bussy is concerned, the essence of Chapman's special morality seems to lie in a comment on Bussy made by Tamyra:

> For though his great spirit something ouerflow,
> All faults are still borne, that from greatnesse grow.[18]

These words imply something utterly different from the medieval idea of forgiveness for sin. No repentance is called for, and there never is any repentance, in Bussy.

Greatness of spirit such as Bussy's involves serious faults, according to the world's view of things, faults grave enough to lead to sin and catastrophe, but it is full of a saving grace that in the end denatures those faults. Apparently we are to admire in him a magnificent virtue and never think of it is separable from his faults, since his faults are part of it. Indeed, it seems that we are even to admire the faults themselves because they are those of a man truly great.

Thus, because Chapman gives to Bussy a paradoxical nobility, there is a certain similarity between Bussy and the heroes of Shakespeare's last tragic world. But unlike any of those Shakespearean heroes, Bussy is open to the accusation that he rationalizes the indulgence of his passions by creating, to suit himself, a system of extra-morality. Chapman can therefore be accused of "making vice virtuous" or "sympathizing with sin" through a tragic hero, as Shakespeare cannot. We are given to understand by Chapman that if Bussy's natural genius were spread through humanity it would regenerate the world and give it new goodness. After we get away from Chapman's poetry and consider the matter coolly, we may doubt the validity of Chapman's idea. But we can easily see that great good has gone to waste in the heroes of Shakespeare's last tragic world. Their nobility is a profounder paradox by far than Bussy's.

Chapman himself discovered a more profound paradox in deeply flawed nobility when he came to writing the two plays which were published together in 1608 as *The Conspiracie, and Tragedy of Charles Duke of Byron, Marshall of France*. He probably finished his work on these plays early in 1608. They are based upon *A General Inven-*

torie of the History of France (1607), a work by Edward
Grimeston which in large part is a translation of Jean de
Serres's *Inventaire général de l'histoire de France* (1603).[19]
We know that in the spring of 1608 Chapman and a group
of players got into trouble because the French ambassador
protested against the acting of certain matter that Chapman had put into his dramatization of Byron's career.[20]
Offending passages were stricken out when the work was
published. Chapman was dealing with very recent French
history, for the historical Duke of Biron had been executed
in 1602. What Chapman found in Grimeston's *General
Inventorie* was a hero ready-made to his taste, another
tumultuous spirit capable of "overflowing" and dying
tragically in an attempt to be king unto himself. Byron,
one might say, had already been given almost all his Chapmanesque qualities before Chapman made drama out
of him. Chapman was able to versify whole passages of
Grimeston much as Shakespeare versified passages of
North in *Antony and Cleopatra*. He was fortunate in finding a subject who was spiritually akin to Bussy but who
had left a much deeper mark on the world and was in all
ways a greater tragic figure.

Grimeston describes Biron's character thus:

This Marshall had goodly parts, communicable to fewe, his Valour
was admirable, and happy in all his incounters; of an inuincible
Courage, infatigable and neuer tired with any toyle, continuing
ordinarily fifteene dayes together on Horse-backe. He was not in-
clined to Voluptuousnesse, nor much to the loue of Women, sober
ynough, the which began to quench that furious humour, as In-
temperancy & greatnesse increased, or that Rest did moderate his
boyling passions. He was extremely Vaine-glorious, yea sometimes he

would refuse his meate, and content himselfe with little to feede his Fantasie with Glory and Vanity. He was of a meane stature, Blacke, reasonable grosse, hollow eyd, and rough in speech and conuersation. He was aduenturous in War, Ambitious beyond all measure. The excesse of his Ambition made him to braue it without iudgement. He became so presumptuous, as he thought that the King, nor *France* could not subsist without him. He was become ill-tounged, speaking ill of all the Princes, threatning the Parliaments, and the Officers of Iustice, some with death, and to dispossesse others of their places. He was aduanced from the meanest to the highest degrees of Honour; of a simple Souldiar, hee became a Captaine, then a Colonell, afterwards Admirall and Marshall, and in the ende Lieutenant of the Kings Armies, and in his Heart he aspired to be Duke of *Burgundy,* son in Lawe to the Duke of *Sauoy,* and Nephew to the King of *Spaine.*[21]

We find also that the duke was even accused of having royal ambitions.[22] The tragical fall which brought him to a traitor's death was due to a pride so extreme that it made him forget God and "mocke at all Religion." Says Grimeston: "Without God we hold all things indifferent, the Law folly, Iustice frenzie, and Faith a fantasie; we hold the words of vertue and vice to be idle."[23] Thus the duke was incapable of making proper moral distinctions. He was utterly blind to his faults and crimes and considered himself beyond measure meritorious. At his execution he raged like a man possessed because of what he thought to be gross injustice done him, and only by trickery could the executioner get him into position to receive the stroke that beheaded him. He was a great spirit. Again to quote Grimeston: "You shall see few of these great Spirits, that die by their owne confessions, although they be found guiltie. Some confesse the Fact, but they hold it no Cryme."[24] What Grimeston says of Biron certainly leaves no impression that he was a Machiavellian villain, knowingly and cynically choosing to do evil. The description of his death stamps him finally and most plainly as a man who held himself to be beyond good and evil. Chapman had only to surround him with a peculiar sympathy and a peculiar philosophy to make him completely Chapmanesque.

Chapman's Byron is a man who is "great, not good," as we find in the prologue to his drama:

> And see in his reuolt, how honors flood
> Ebbes into ayre, when men are Great, not Good.[25]

When the action opens, he has reached a height of honor as the savior of France from the ruin of civil war; he is a newly created duke. He has "toucht heauen with his lance" and has not yet been "toucht with hellish treacherie." The first play, *Byron's Conspiracie,* shows the duke being worked upon by enemies of the French king; yielding to thoughts that his greatness should know no limits of aspiration because, for him at least, what is high is right; asking for control of one of the key citadels of France and being refused by the suspicious king; thereupon flying into a mighty anger and even offering to draw his sword against the king; finally, kneeling to the king and gaining a pardon. The second play, *Byron's Tragedie,* shows him turning again to traitorous plots, and now thinking of "plucking out" the king and having a new creation of state and government; refusing to go to court at the command of the king after he has been betrayed by an associate; suddenly yielding to and facing the king; denying hotly that he is in any way guilty; going to his execution in a spiritual turmoil of anger at the king, faith that the king must surely pardon him, and conviction that what is done to him is outrage.

Like Bussy, Byron is so deeply flawed that he can be ludicrous. Probably Chapman knows quite well what he is doing to his hero when, in Act III of the *Conspiracie,* he makes him turn with a madman's fury upon an astrologer who tells him he is of noble parts and could be a king were it not for an action that will make him lose his head. In reply to the astrologer, Byron rants, declaring that he is of nobler substance than the stars and that the baser stuff shall not overrule the better; he is above all law, even the law of fate. And certainly Chapman knows to the full what he is doing to his hero in the last act of the *Conspiracie,* a finely conceived climax to the play in which Byron's request for control of an important citadel is refused by the king. Byron's tumbling flood of words poured out after this refusal, words about lack of recognition for his merit ("I alone" did this, "onely my selfe" did that—"married to victory"), conclude with a wild shout of "I will be mine owne King." But the king does not rage in return. He laughs! With a "Ha ha ha," he makes an exit. Byron is beside himself. Reduced to gibbering futility, he demands to know what is awful on earth if his "rage be ridiculouse," and struggles, in the arms of a restraining courtier, to draw his sword. The greatness of Byron could hardly be more cruelly dealt with.

That Chapman would have us greatly admire Byron's nobility, no matter how paradoxical that nobility may reveal itself to be, is beyond question. Even as Byron struggles to draw his sword against the king, the restraining courtier calls him "mighty Spirrit." Byron is like Bussy in having plenty of supporters to second his high opinions of his own worth. The king himself at one time praises him as formed of stuff that is "great, and gratious," though he later pronounces him a damnable traitor. The nobility that Chapman gives to Byron is by long odds more convincing than the nobility he gives to Bussy. Byron, though he has something of Bussy's raw indomitable vitality, is not suspended like Bussy in vague theorizing about the power of natural passion, unharnessed and undirected, to save the world. Byron can at least talk, as he does in Act I of the *Tragedie,* about working to reshape the scheme of things, about sitting on chaos to brood up another world, and about ruining his country only to re-advance it. We can well believe that he might show creative force as a leader of men.

In the last act of the second Byron play, Chapman achieves his finest statement of the irony and paradox that lie in his tragedies of deeply flawed human greatness. Just before Byron goes to his death one of the courtiers comments:

> O of what contraries consists a man!
> Of what impossible mixtures? vice and vertue,
> Corruption, and eternnesse, at one time,
> And in one subiect, let together, loosse?
> We haue not any strength but weakens vs,
> No greatnes but doth crush vs into ayre:
> Our knowledges, do light vs but to erre,
> Our Ornaments are Burthens.[26]

Another courtier adds:

> O reall goodnesse if thou be a power!
> And not a word alone, in humaine vses,
> Appere out of this angry conflagration,

Where this great Captaine (thy late Temple) burns,
And turne his vicious fury to thy flame:
Let pietie enter with her willing crosse,
And take him on it; ope his brest and armes,
To all the Storms, Necessity can breath,
And burst them all with his embraced death.[27]

The first of these two speeches gives depth to an idea expressed in *Bussy* that the whole man is ironically blown down by the winds of Fortune just because he is lavishly endowed with excellent substance and does not allow those winds to blow through him as the hollow man does. The second speech is a remarkable expression of the idea that great viciousness has in it something that can be used by great goodness—has, indeed, a certain potentiality for great goodness—since the force of character that makes viciousness great is equally capable of making goodness great.

In the creation of Byron's character and the handling of his tragedy Chapman comes as close to Shakespeare as he ever succeeds in doing. As we shall see in a later chapter, Byron has a notable spiritual kinship with Shakespeare's Coriolanus, though his pride and the treason to which it leads him are different from the pride and treason of Coriolanus. But Chapman's approach to the tragedy of deeply flawed nobility may easily be distinguished from Shakespeare's, whether Chapman makes Bussy or Byron his hero. Chapman is a revolter against the morality of his day, which is based on the orthodox Christian distinction between good and evil. This morality he sees as that of the vulgar herd. He tends to be a special pleader for a deeply flawed hero and to justify his pleading by an idiosyncratic

scheme of ethics. Shakespeare, on the other hand, is not a
revolter ethically any more than religiously or politically;
he does not tend to be a special pleader for a deeply flawed
hero, though he makes other characters praise that hero;
and he has no idiosyncratic scheme of ethics. Instead of
fitting the hero into a new order of things, Shakespeare lets
the hero's tragedy expose new depths of subtlety in the old
order.

Mr. Wyndham Lewis, agreeing with Swinburne that
Chapman has a "taste for extravagance of paradox and
shocks of moral surprise" which often leads him to put into
the mouths of chief characters in his plays "some defence of
the most preposterous and untenable proposition, some
apology for the most enormous and unpopular crime that
his ingenuity can fix upon for an explanation or excuse,"
thinks that this shows in the poet an "ethical negation"
something like "nihilism."[28] That it shows something different, namely, Chapman's faith in himself as a reformer
of ethics, seems to me to be borne out in his nondramatic
poems. Chapman appears to mean quite earnestly what he
says when he proposes, in a commendatory poem published
with Ben Jonson's *Sejanus* in 1605, to join Jonson in a war
to uphold virtue:

> And so good Friend, safe passage to thy Freight,
>   To thee a long Peace, through a vertuous strife,
> In which, lets both contend to Vertues height,
>   Not making Fame our Obiect, but good life.[29]

In this connection, the most revelatory of all his poems is
the ingenuous *Andromeda Liberata, or the Nuptials of Perseus and Andromeda* (1614), a work in which he takes it

upon himself to defend his patron Robert Carr, Earl of Somerset, and Somerset's bride, the former Countess of Essex, from the attacks of scandalmongers. The marriage of this ill-famed pair, after the countess had obtained a divorce from Essex, was a scandal even before they were tried and found guilty of the cruel murder of Sir Thomas Overbury in the Tower. Overbury had worked against the marriage. He died of slow poisoning on September 15, 1613, and the marriage took place on December 26, 1613. The murder did not come to light until 1615, but when Chapman published his poem, in 1614, the characters and actions of Somerset and his countess had already attracted much moral condemnation. Even Mr. Havelock Ellis, with all his sympathy for the mind and art of Chapman, judges that the author of *Andromeda Liberata* made an unhappy choice in taking an "infamous marriage" as a poetic subject.[30] Chapman could hardly have made a worse choice of hero and heroine for his own very special kind of moral glorification. For one thing, supremely ironic misfortune resulted from the high-flown passage in which, while arguing that he who loves is dead and only in his lover moves, the defender of Somerset and his bride condemns all lovers who are "churlish homicides." Because the murdered Overbury was in the background, this passage had natural appeal for gossips and was much talked about. There were other good reasons why Chapman felt called upon to write a labored justification of the poem.

In *Andromeda Liberata* Chapman pictures Somerset (Perseus) as freeing his bride (Andromeda) from a barren rock to which she has been chained and rescuing her from

a monster which represents the vulgar multitude. Andromeda is an innocent and spotless virgin, and her rescuer by
his heroic deed shows the way to a "Persean victorie" which
shall put down in the land all

> foule Barbarisme, and all
> His brood of pride, and liues Atheisticall.[31]

Chapman's manner in this poem is certainly not that of a
man who is merely complimenting his patron with a pretty
concoction. He writes like one who is fighting in deadly
earnest for a moral cause and would rally to his banner a
select body of followers. He opens his dedicatory preface
with these lines:

> As nothing vnder heauen is more remou'd
> From Truth & virtue, then *Opinions* prou'd
> By vulgar *Voices:* So is nought more true
> Nor soundly virtuous then things held by few:
> Whom Knowledge (entred by the sacred line,
> And gouernd euermore by grace diuine,)
> Keepes in the narrow path to spacious heauen.[32]

And he opens the poem itself with the cry:

> Away vngodly Vulgars, far away,
> Flie ye prophane, that dare not view the day.[33]

Turning from Chapman to Webster, we find that in
The White Devil, which was published in 1612 but may
have been written as early as 1609, Webster does something
that Chapman never attempts; he finds in a woman, Vittoria Accoramboni (b. 1559), the paradox of deeply flawed
nobility and makes her the protagonist of a tragedy. By
what course Vittoria's story came to Webster is not known,

but it is obvious that he changed some of its details in order
to create a heroine who would win sympathy and admiration. His Vittoria well deserves to be called a white devil,
and it is not only in the title of the play that he puts her
fair-seeming into words. Vittoria's enemy Monticelso, the
cardinal, says of her:

> If the deuill
> Did euer take good shape behold his picture.[34]

Even her lover, Brachiano, speaks of her in a phrase that
echoes the title:

> How long haue I beheld the deuill in christall?[35]

The instinct of Webster tells him that Vittoria would be
lacking as a tragic figure were she made to appeal to our
sympathies merely through her beauty, in purely sentimental fashion. He gives her character fire and dynamic
energy. We are moved by the sacrifice of such personal
force in tragedy as we could never be moved by the sacrifice
of beauty alone.

The handling of Vittoria's guilt is delicate in the highest
degree, but we cannot say that her guilt is minimized. She
suggests to Brachiano that he must make away with her
husband and his own wife, and it is plain enough that by
her suggestion she becomes, in fact though not in deed, responsible for murder. Her faithlessness to her husband is a
moral shock to her mother, and this moral shock is presented sympathetically. Moreover, the murder of Brachiano's wife is presented in a way that invites sympathy for
the victim. Like Chapman, Webster can dare much in risking loss of our sympathy for a deeply flawed protagonist.

That Vittoria is to Webster a great spirit though "not good," as Bussy or Byron is to Chapman, we need not doubt. She is, of course, no Jacobean female Tamburlaine. She is a womanly woman. But more than once we are called upon to see in her a "masculine" heroic force, which is the womanly counterpart of the self-confident personal power of Bussy and Byron. Its most authoritative expression comes in the trial scene, in which, as she herself says, she tenders her "modesty and womanhood" to her judges but in her defense finds herself compelled to "personate masculine vertue to the point." In this scene the guilty Vittoria is not brazen, but has the eloquence and strength of one who is deeply convinced that outrage is being done to her. When she and her Machiavellian brother Flamineo meet death together, he praises her in words that remind us of what she has said of her masculine personation in the trial scene. Flamineo says:

> Fare thee well.
> Know many glorious woemen that are fam'd
> For masculine vertue, haue bin vitious.[36]

Mr. F. L. Lucas thinks that in this praise of the vicious Vittoria "the voice of Webster is heard."[37] Certainly the words are given emphasis as a final comment on Vittoria, and their spirit is in accord with that of the tragedy as a whole; for Webster does find viciousness in his heroine and along with that viciousness a valorous excellence, which is fused with the viciousness and even expressed in it.

The ability of Webster's Vittoria to arouse sympathy and admiration, guilty as she is, may be gauged by a comment upon her by Mr. Lucas: "Webster has mixed such a power

of beauty and intellect, of pride and passion and indomitable will, that we forget the blood on her hands and the
wrongs of the kindly Isabella; and when in the trial scene
she stands at bay against both worlds, against the power of
State and Church, of Florence and Rome, we cry 'not
guilty,' despite ourselves and the truth."[38] Miss M. C. Brad-
brook states this guilty-and-not-guilty paradox in another
way: "There is, as it were, a subordinate side of Vittoria
which is innocent. Actually she is guilty, but there is a
strong undercurrent of suggestion in the opposite direction.
It never comes to the surface plainly but it is there. Her
character is a 'reconciliation of opposites.' "[39] Mr. Lucas is
quite right when he says that in *The White Devil* Webster
faced and solved the same problem of making faithless and
pitiless murderers into profoundly tragic figures that Shakespeare faced and solved in *Macbeth;* he is also quite right
when he says that in the love of Webster's Vittoria and
Brachiano there is something of the same power to turn the
edge of condemnation that is in the love of Shakespeare's
Antony and Cleopatra.[40] But in *The White Devil* Webster
is very much himself. He is the same Webster who is capable of taking the pitifully persecuted Duchess of Malfi as
a tragic heroine, and because he is that same Webster he can
show the murderous Vittoria as pitifully persecuted.

v

In the opening years of the seventeenth century the Renaissance vogue for the formal paradoxical exercise in praise of
some supposedly unworthy subject or in defense of some
supposedly indefensible proposition led Sir William Corn-

wallis (the younger) to find paradoxical good in two characters that had been condemned as vicious by history and legend. One of the formal paradoxes in his *Essayes of Certaine Paradoxes* (published in 1616 after the death of the author) is "The Prayse of Richard the Third," and one in his *Essayes or rather Encomions* (published in the same year) is "The Prayse of the Emperour Iulian the Apostata." What Cornwallis has to say about the extraction of virtue from vice as he makes an apology for choosing the Emperor Julian as one of his subjects is a noteworthy piece of argument. In part, this is his contention:

But at the worst, Vertue is not so proud as not to extract what may bee made good, out of ill: for there is a spirit in vice, that being cunningly drawne out, will serue euen the best: so ful it is of a quick and peircing vigour: he hath a poore Library to behold, that reades onely the good; let him turne ouer all, that desires to be profound; let him earne Vertue with digging it out of vice, and he will keepe it the better: let him fetch it out of the entrals of ill, that will glory of his conquest.[41]

But among nondramatic writers of the early seventeenth century in England it is John Donne, a friend of Cornwallis's, who with the authority of genius expresses the late Renaissance spirit that would confound knowledge with knowledge and would find truth in a paradox after the fashion of the tragedies with which we are concerned. He takes to himself, and makes part of him, both the paradox that is a statement or tenet contrary to received opinion and the paradox that is apparently a self-contradiction or self-revealed absurdity. It is well recognized that there is a certain affinity of mind between Donne, Chapman, and

Webster and that Webster paid Donne the compliment of imitation.[42] The sympathetic presentation of deeply flawed nobility in tragedies of Shakespeare, Chapman, and Webster is of the age that produced Donne's *Paradoxes and Problems* (published in 1633 but probably written at various times between 1599 and 1607), his unfinished *Progresse of the Soule* (1601), and his *Biathanatos* (published about 1646 but probably written at some time between 1606 and 1609).[43]

Donne's *Paradoxes and Problems* contains, in part at least, the earliest of his prose work. Slight and often flippant though it is, it offers much challenging thought looking toward his other work. Paradox V, "That all things kill themselves," demands comparison with his argument in *Biathanatos* that suicide "is not so naturally sinne that it may never be otherwise." Paradox XI, "That the gifts of the Body are better than those of the minde," with its contention that without the body the mind, and therefore the soul, would not be enabled to see the beauties of the world, is a defense of the body which, though it makes a case at all costs, has relationship with ideas expressed in his sermons concerning the dignity of the body and the relationship of the soul and the body. In these two paradoxes Donne suggests that old distinctions between right and wrong and between higher and lower elements of man have been too easily made. Paradox IV, "That good is more common than euill," also has a relationship with Donne's sermons. Here Donne holds to the distinction between good and evil, but sees in them, just as he sees in soul and body, a capacity to be closely joined together. He finds that goodness prevails not merely because it can overwhelm evil, but also because it can link itself to evil and make evil a part of its design. In this idea there is a foreshadowing of such later ideas of Donne's, expressed in his sermons, as that evil serves good just as poisons conduce to physic and discord to music, and that the essential goodness of God is so diffusive that there is nothing in the world which does not participate in it.[44] Says Donne in Paradox IV:

I have not beene so pittifully tired with any *vanity,* as with silly *old Mens* exclaiming against these times. . . . *Good* is as euer it was, more plenteous, and must of necessity bee *more common than Euill,* because it hath this for *nature* and *perfection* to bee *common.* It makes *Loue* to all *Natures,* all, all affect it. . . . And as *Imbroderers, Lapidaries,* and other *Artisans,* can by all things adorne their workes; for by adding better things, the better they show in *Lush* and in *Eminency;* so *Good* doth not onely prostrate her *Amiablenesse* to all, but refuses no end, no not of her vtter contrary *Euill,* that she may be the more *common* to vs. . . . All *faire,* all *profitable,* all *vertuous,* is *good,* and these three things I thinke embrace all things, but their vtter contraries; of which also *faire* may be *rich* and *vertuous;* poore, may bee *vertuous* and *faire; vitious,* may be *faire* and *rich;* so that *Good* hath this good meanes to be *cōmon,* that some subiects she can possesse entirely; and in subiects poysoned with *Euill,* she can humbly stoope to accompany the *Euill.*[45]

In his *Paradoxes and Problems* Donne does not go so far as to discover the tragical paradox of the deeply flawed, and even criminal, great spirit who has the force and genius to be a beneficial leader of humanity. In his somberly suggestive poem *The Progresse of the Soule* he does make that discovery. The last stanza of this fragmentary work pays tribute to the cursed race of Cain for its gifts to humanity and ends with a conception of good and evil as being so

fused together in the world that the human mind can judge
them only by opinion:

> Who ere thou beest that read'st this sullen Writ,
> Which just so much courts thee, as thou dost it,
> Let me arrest thy thoughts; wonder with mee,
> Why plowing, building, ruling and the rest,
> Or most of those arts, whence our lives are blest,
> By cursed *Cains* race invented be,
> And blest *Seth* vext us with Astronomie.
> Ther's nothing simply good, nor ill alone,
> Of every quality Comparison
>   The onely measure is, and judge, Opinion.[46]

Biathanatos is an extended paradoxical discussion which
often deals with ethical problems worthy of tragic presentation. The subtitle of the work describes it as "A Declaration
of that Paradox, or Thesis, that Selfe-homicide is not so
naturally Sinne, that it may never be otherwise." One may
entertain a suspicion that in *Biathanatos* Donne often
meant to see how far he could go with a clever argument
in partial justification of suicide, which for many Christian
generations had been regarded with horror as one of the
soul-killing sins. But it is difficult, knowing what we do of
Donne's mind in general, to dismiss this rather ambitious
book as entirely a *tour de force*. Seemingly there is in it
something that came from his heart. After he had become
a Doctor of Divinity, he desired that it should be preserved,
written though it was "by *Jack Donne,* and not by D.
Donne," but he forbade giving it to the press, apparently
because of its misinterpretable character.[47]

The weight of faith and authority against him Donne
recognizes in the opening sentences of *Biathanatos* when he

speaks of "this SELF-HOMICIDE: which to be sinne everybody hath so sucked, and digested, and incorporated into the body of his Faith and Religion, that now they prescribe against any opposer; and all discourse in this point is upon the degrees of this sinne, and how farre it exceeds all other: So that none brings the metall now to the test, nor touch, but onely to the balance."[48] The weight of all that is against Donne stimulates him to lay a firm foundation for his argument. Before he puts the medieval metal of suicide to a Renaissance test, he puts the medieval metal of sin in general to such a test. For, says he, any dealing with the three laws of Nature, of Reason, and of God, and with their precepts, is veritably "a Chymick work," since the precepts are "compos'd and elemented and complexion'd" with great subtlety. But the chemic work must not be done "by the torture and vexation of schoole-limbicks, which are exquisite and violent distinctions."[49]

One thing not duly recognized by the old faith and the old philosophy, Donne implies, is the way in which a sin that on its face is evil according to all three laws of Nature, Reason, and God can under certain circumstances take on the character of good and elevate the committer in human estimation. Donne makes this point by referring to those circumstances in which the killing of a parent, which is commonly a sinful action that arouses extreme horror, has an aspect of virtuous action:

And the Honour due to Parents is so strictly of all these Laws, as none of the second Table more. Yet in a iust warre a Parricide is not guilty; yea by a law of *Venice,* though *Bodin* say, it were better the Towne were sunk then ever there should be any example or president therein; A sonne shall redeeme himselfe from banishment by killing his Father being also banished. And we read of another state (and Laws of Civil Commonwealths may not easily be pronounced to be against Nature) where when fathers came to be of an unprofitable and uselesse age, the sons must beat them to death with clubs.[50]

In this passage on parricide Donne touches upon matters that can be the stuff of profound tragedy. The conflict of divine sanctions in the Aeschylean tragedy of Orestes— sanctions for and against the murder of a mother—is of the order of conflict between laws that Donne here presents.

As he goes forward with the main body of his argument Donne is duly cautious. His basic contention is that nothing is so naturally sin that it cannot sometimes be otherwise. Suicide is commonly sin but can sometimes be otherwise. God can even let suicide advance His glory, as when martyrs embrace death to do Him honor.

When Shakespeare wrote *Romeo and Juliet,* a paradox crossed his mind that would not be out of place in Donne's *Paradoxes and Problems.* He gave it expression in a well-known soliloquy of Friar Laurence's. As Friar Laurence gathers "baleful weeds and precious-juiced flowers" for medicinal purposes, he is led to meditate upon the ways in which nature produces not only death out of life and evil out of good but also life out of death and good out of evil. He discovers in nature not only the possibility of the corruption of good but also that of the dignification of evil:

> The earth that's nature's mother is her tomb:
> What is her burying grave that is her womb,
> And from her womb children of divers kind
> We sucking on her natural bosom find,
> Many for many virtues excellent,
> None but for some, and yet all different.

O! mickle is the powerful grace that lies
In herbs, plants, stones, and their true qualities:
For nought so vile that on the earth doth live
But to the earth some special good doth give,
Nor aught so good but strain'd from that fair use
Revolts from true birth, stumbling on abuse:
Virtue itself turns vice, being misapplied,
And vice sometime's by action dignified.

(II, iii, 9–22)

Thus, we are given to understand, vice can sometimes take on dignity through good results of its action. It can show worth and can take a place on the side of good, as poison does when it is used as medicine and cures sickness.

A world even more paradoxical than that pictured by Friar Laurence—one in which defects of human nature, including viciousness, need not always produce good results in order to dignify themselves, but can take on dignity through a quality in their very being—is the realm of tragedy for Shakespeare in *Timon, Macbeth, Antony and Cleopatra,* and *Coriolanus,* for Chapman in *Bussy* and *Byron,* and for Webster in *The White Devil.* In these tragedies the three dramatists have fellowship with Donne as they discover a measure of true worth in that defectiveness of the world which inspired medieval rejection of the world. Like Donne they know well the medieval tradition of contempt for the world. Like Donne they can at times change medieval contempt of the world into Jacobean disillusion with the world and, as they deal with the world, mix antipathy and sympathy strangely. They show concern in these tragedies to reveal a noble worth in exceptional human beings who have great defectiveness as a part of great personality. But irony as well as paradox appears in the revelation, and often enough the world which produces such noble tragic figures has much darkness and horror.

What Shakespeare, Chapman, and Webster do with tragic figures who are paradoxically noble thus has its place in a movement of the Renaissance to discover value in the world and value in the human individuality that helps to make the world. Chapman and Webster have some tendency to dramatize deeply flawed nobility in a way that glorifies individuality at the expense of the general order of life. Quite plainly sometimes they ask that such nobility be sympathized with and admired as a law unto itself. Shakespeare stands apart from Chapman and Webster in his freedom from that tendency. As he gives form to his last tragic world he keeps a subtle balance between regard for the individual and regard for that which contains the individual. In the hands of Chapman and Webster the paradox of the great spirit deeply flawed sometimes breaks the universal frame of good and evil in which the Middle Ages had placed humanity. In the hands of Shakespeare it sometimes puts pressure upon that frame but never breaks it.[51]

Chapter II

"TIMON OF ATHENS"

COLERIDGE calls *Timon of Athens* "an after vibration" of *King Lear*, "a *Lear* of domestic or ordinary life— a local eddy of passion on the high road of society."[1] In substance *Timon* has a special relationship with *Lear*. In form it has a special relationship with *Lear* and also with *Othello,* the tragedy that Shakespeare in all probability wrote immediately before *Lear.* Nevertheless, the tragic world of *Timon* is that of *Macbeth, Antony and Cleopatra,* and *Coriolanus.*

We should look at *Timon* as it is related to *Lear* and *Othello* before looking at it as one of the plays that constitute Shakespeare's last tragic world. The bond of substance between *Timon* and *Lear* is remarkable, and its existence is well recognized. The reader needs only to be reminded of its character. Each of these plays is a tragedy of atrocious human ingratitude in which repeated comparisons are made between men and beasts, and in which the idea is expressed that man is declining to a beastly state where

> Humanity must perforce prey on itself,
> Like monsters of the deep.
> (*Lear,* IV, ii, 49–50)

In each play the hero gives away large worldly possessions, finds himself dependent upon those he has benefited, trusts blindly that in their gratitude these will show generosity to him, receives cruelty from them instead of generosity, lays

---

[1] For notes to chapter ii see pages 268–270.

curses upon the human nature in which he once placed his trust, and falls into madness or insensate fury.[2]

The bond of form between *Timon, Lear,* and *Othello* is perhaps less remarkable but is no less real than the bond of substance between *Timon* and *Lear*. Structurally, *Timon, Lear,* and *Othello* are in a class by themselves among Shakespeare's tragedies.

Before the writing of *Othello,* Shakespeare had usually conceived tragedy as a pyramid of rising and falling action corresponding more or less to the full turn of Fortune's wheel in medieval tragical storytelling,[3] and for several years he had conceived tragedy in no other form. This pyramidal form of tragedy tends to make half of the action the hero's rise and half his decline and fall. In *Richard III* the rise of Richard to kingship has a dramatic development which is about equal to that of his fall from kingship. In *Romeo and Juliet* the action in which Romeo wins Juliet is of about the same length as that in which he loses Juliet. In *Julius Caesar* and *Hamlet* such pyramids of rise and fall are constructed for Brutus and Hamlet with a marked advance in skill. Steps on the slopes are delicately marked, and the slopes are almost exactly balanced. Both Brutus and Hamlet rise to a height of successful achievement which is placed by the dramatist in the third act. At this height Brutus frees Rome from Caesar, and Hamlet demonstrates the king's guilt by means of the play within the play and steels himself to take revenge upon the king. The success is of the briefest and the turning point is a knife edge. Almost immediately the hero makes a misstep, which has been prepared for by the development of his character during the rising action, and his course turns downward. The crucial misstep, Brutus's refusal to forbid Antony's oration to the mob, or Hamlet's refusal to kill the praying king, is shown in its full significance only after the descending action is developed from it and after the pyramid is made a whole. It was in the use of this pyramidal form that Shakespeare found himself as a writer of tragedy.

When he came to write *Othello,* he turned to a new form, which may be regarded as a development from that which he had given to *Richard II,* an early tragedy. *Richard II* shows the fall of its hero as beginning at the opening of the play and undergoing acceleration near the middle, at a point marked by an agony of realization on the hero's part that ruin and death press upon him. It also shows the rise of a rival as concurrent: as Richard falls from the kingship, Bolingbroke mounts toward it, and when Richard is murdered, Bolingbroke establishes himself on the throne. We thus see a man whirled down from the top of Fortune's wheel at the same time that another is whirled up to the top. We see actions of rise and fall, but not both for the hero. Richard himself characterizes the drama by means of the conventional figure of "Fortune's buckets," one bucket descending in a well while another, its counterpoise, rises (IV, i, 181–189). *Othello,* like *Richard II,* shows the fall of its hero as beginning at the opening of the play and undergoing acceleration near the middle, at a point marked by a crisis in the hero's emotions, but it does not show the concurrent rise of a rival to the position of prosperity from which the hero falls. Of *Lear* the same can be said, and also of *Timon.* But *Macbeth, Antony and Cleopatra,* and *Corio-*

lanus are built on the pyramidal scheme of rise and fall for the hero. In these three plays Shakespeare used the tragic form he had favored before he wrote *Othello*.

Let us consider the long slope of tragic decline as it appears in *Othello* and *Lear*. In each of these plays the hero is at first placed for a brief moment in prosperity. Even at this point forces are shown which are to bring about his ruin. Then, in the generous space allotted to the working of his fall, catastrophe is brought to pass by subtle gradations. The dramatic form used may be called that of a half pyramid, for the second half of the pyramid of rise and fall is taken alone to fill out a play. But the half pyramid is distorted. In the middle the line of descent is made to change its slope and become steeper than at first. The breaking of the line of descent to make its slope more precipitous is emphasized by a climactic storm of passion in the hero. This turning point midway in the tragedy corresponds to the change from rising to falling action in plays built upon the scheme of the full pyramid. In both *Othello* and *Lear* a climactic storm of passion at the turning point arises from the hero's first true realization of his tragic destiny and brings a derangement of his faculties. Just before the turning point of *Othello* the hero is still vigorously resisting his tragic fate; he looks upon Desdemona and says:

> If she be false, O! then heaven mocks itself.
> I'll not believe it.   (III, iii, 278–279)

But his resistance is finally destroyed by increased pressure from Iago, and he breaks forth with a wild vow of vengeance. Othello and his tempter kneel and thus mark the oc-

casion as the vow is made. At their first meeting thereafter,
still more pressure from the tempter draws from Othello a
mad froth of words and sends him into a trance. The turning point of *Lear* follows exactly the same dramatic pattern but is developed with even greater imaginative power.
To the end of Act II Lear resists and refuses to realize the
fate that is to be his. At the beginning of Act III he opens
his mind and heart to it. His denunciations, his subjection
to the storm on the heath which is the physical accompani-
ment of his emotional crisis, and the onset of his madness
make a grander version of the central cataclysm found in
Othello.

There is a distorted half pyramid in *Timon* which is very
plainly the same in principle as that just traced for *Othello*
and *Lear*. Timon is first shown in prosperity. Already the
forces to bring about his downfall are in existence. Before
the end of Act I we are told by his steward, Flavius, that his
coffer is empty and that his lands are all mortgaged. Timon
begins his descent but refuses to realize what is in store for
him. He persists in holding a pitiful faith in the friends to
whom he has given his wealth which is very similar to
Lear's faith that Goneril and Regan cannot both fail him,
and somewhat similar to Othello's faith in Desdemona.
(The fact that Othello struggles to keep faith in an utterly
innocent person makes some difference in the dramatic
quality of his tragedy.) At last Timon accepts his fate. The
mock-banquet scene in Act III is the stormy turning point
of the action. It brings on a more abrupt descent and is
marked by Timon's eloquent curses and his physical assault
upon his guests. True madness does not follow, but the

hero's fanatical dedication of himself to misanthropy and
his taking on of the hermit's character show derangement
in a less specific form. Alcibiades, the tough-fibered opposite of Timon, says of him after the alteration that

> his wits
> Are drown'd and lost in his calamities.
>
> (IV, iii, 88–89)

Apparently *Othello, Lear,* and *Timon* link the plays that
make up Shakespeare's middle tragic world and those that
make up his last. It appears that as Shakespeare turned, in
Timon, to the presentation of his last tragic world, he con-
cluded an exploration of human ingratitude which he had
begun just before, in *Lear,* and made final use of a tragic
form which he had worked with twice in succession just
before, in *Othello* and *Lear,* and had devised for *Othello.*

II

Timon has his place in a tragic world that also includes
Macbeth, Antony, and Coriolanus because, as I have said
in the preceding chapter, he is so deeply flawed that his
faults reach to the very center of his being and give a
paradoxical quality to whatever is noble in his nature. Like
Macbeth, Antony, and Coriolanus, and unlike Brutus,
Hamlet, Othello, and Lear, he does not win sympathy
easily and may even arouse great antipathy. The tragedy of
Timon is that of a man who has an all-consuming love for
humanity but, when he finds that he himself is not loved,
lets this love turn to all-consuming hate. His love is so
little a true forgetfulness of self, and thus so grossly imperfect, that it can change into its very opposite. Thinking to

do good by scattering his great wealth prodigally, Timon blindly lets his substance and himself be devoured by selfish flattering companions. Reduced to poverty and cast aside by those whom he has benefited, he flees to a cave in the forest and dwells there like a beast for the rest of his life. He prays that all mankind may be confounded in beastliness, and gives away new-found gold in ways that can help to bring such ruin of humanity to pass. He gladly looks forward to death, and achieves, in accord with his desires, a burial upon the seashore, away from the haunts of men, in a place where the waves can beat upon his tombstone.

Under the impact of human beastliness Lear does not himself become a beast, but Timon does. Lear has in him that which allows regeneration through suffering, but Timon has not. Here we find a profound difference between the two Shakespearean tragedies that are built upon monstrous human ingratitude. It seems that as Shakespeare goes from *Lear* to *Timon* he continues to be obsessed by the vision of a protagonist preyed upon by devouring associates who out of gratitude should love and protect him—by the vision that has made him think of Lear's daughters as "tigers," "she-foxes," or other ravenous creatures, tearing at their father's flesh. But he finds in that vision a new alignment of dramatic forces and a new tragic meaning. The evil that works against Lear is presented by Shakespeare's imagination in the guise not only of the beast but also of the fiend. It is evil on the grand scale. It has a backing of perverted spiritual greatness and at times fills us with awe because its doers reach the level of the satanic. Gloucester pictures Goneril as sticking "boarish fangs" in the flesh

of Lear. But to Albany she is devilish, nay, worse than devilish, when he says to her:

> See thyself, devil!
> Proper deformity seems not in the fiend
> So horrid as in woman.   (IV, ii, 59–61)

On the other hand, the evil that works against Timon is
presented only in the guise of the beast. It is thoroughly
petty. In its army there are no great schemers or leaders,
and its qualities are merely insensibility to good and baseness lacking perception of good. Thus in *Timon* the associates of the hero who prey upon him become much less
important in the tragic scheme of things and much less
awe-inspiring than they are in *Lear*. The hero makes up for
this by turning into something more fearsome than they—
something devil-like as well as beastlike—and by preying
bitterly on himself. All of this shows Shakespeare at work
upon the creation of a new tragic world.

In Timon there is a folly that can be highly irritating,
even to one who sympathizes with him. His folly reminds
us of Lear's but has much deeper attachment to its possessor
than Lear's. Lear has ever but slenderly known both himself and the nature of humanity in general; yet we feel that
his tragic misjudgment of his daughters comes partly from
the dotage of old age. We get glimpses of the man he has
been—a man capable of error certainly, but kingly in the
highest sense. Timon, however, makes his tragic misjudgment of human nature not when he is in his dotage, but
when he is in the prime of life and in the fullest possession
of his powers. He is so completely lacking in wisdom that
one wonders how he could ever have been useful to Athens

in a responsible position. Moreover, Timon does not even have Othello's excuse for being blind. He is not taken in by any appearance so skillfully constructed as Iago's handiwork. Shakespeare has not made those who deceive Timon into masters of pretense, but has left them very ordinary hypocrites.

How, then, may we find paradoxical nobility in Timon? It is only after he sees mankind as evil and has burning hatred instead of glowing love for it that his paradox takes full form. For Timon is truly heroic only when he pours the lava of his hate upon the evils of the world. It is Timon the man-hater that has the finest poetry of the play, and it is in this Timon, obviously, that Shakespeare found most inspiration as he shaped the tragedy. The paradox of Timon's nobility of spirit really lies in the fact that as a lover of good he lacks grandeur, but is magnificent as a hater of evil, and that he becomes a magnificent hater of evil only by becoming evil. For by the Christian standard Timon's terrible wrath is evil, not righteous, and Shakespeare's age was Christian enough to assume that the possessor of such wrath makes in gross form the error of confusing the sin with the sinner and hating the wrongdoer instead of the wrong done. In his fanatical change of spirit Timon hates not only those who have wronged him but the whole race of humanity. A man could go no farther in putting charity out of his heart. Many pre-Shakespearean writers of the Renaissance condemn the Timon of legend for his sinful and unnatural hatred of mankind. In Shakespeare's Timon there is all that these writers condemn, and it is given a new awfulness; but it is also given nobility.

Shakespeare's Timon is so deeply flawed that Professor O. J. Campbell, in a revealing examination of his character and the dramatic methods used for its presentation, finds him to be the hero of a tragical satire which in form and temper owes much to Ben Jonson's *Sejanus* and *Volpone*.[4] What one sees in Timon that is not in Sejanus and Volpone is the capacity to arouse great admiration as well as great aversion. In the comments of critics there is a violent conflict of aversion and admiration for Timon, and this conflict may be taken as a measure of the paradox in his character.

A few examples will serve to show the kind of comment that can be made by thoroughgoing scorners of Timon. William Maginn reveals detestation of him. Maginn's judgment is that "gold, and the pomps and vanities which it procures, had been to him everything"; that "when the purse was lost, he lost his senses too"; that "Apemantus was wrong when he told him he was long a madman, and then a fool.... Timon was first a fool and then a madman"; and that with or without gold the man showed his true character in his attitude toward women. "In his prosperity we do not find any traces of affection, honorable or otherwise, for women. In his curses, disrespect for the female sex is remarkably conspicuous." In short, as Maginn will have it, "Insanity arising from pride, is the key of the whole character."[5] Sir John Squire ticks Timon off with a pair of devastating phrases: "Timon is an ass in his faith and an ass in his disillusionment."[6] Mr. John Bailey thinks it impossible that we should care about him: "We see only the old spectacle of the quick parting between a fool and his money: one which never has greatly moved spectators and never will. . . . Such a figure cannot be the central figure of a great tragedy."[7]

After listening to these scorners of Timon, we are amazed to see how far some of their opponents can go. Mr. G. Wilson Knight sees in Timon not merely a great and estimable man, but a godlike creature "who aspires only to the infinite" and "chafes at the limitations of the physical." His very hate, thinks Mr. Knight, is not mere man's hate. "Apemantus and Timon hate with a difference: one, because he is less than mankind—the other because he is greater." It is even not too much for Mr. Knight to say: "We are here judging the chances of the spirit of perfected man [i.e., Timon] to embrace Fortune and find Love truly interfused in this 'beneath world': to build his soul's paradise on 'the bosom of this sphere.' Thus Timon is the archetype and norm of all tragedy."[8] Mr. Ralph Roeder and Mr. Peter Alexander have no less emphatic admiration for a divinely idealistic Timon. Mr. Roeder finds that Timon perishes of "immoderate virtues" and "the unanswerable disillusionment that attends the frustration of the most admirable human ambitions, the recognition of the cramping meanness of his mortal tether," and he adds that "tragedy can be refined no farther."[9] Mr. Alexander finds that the tragedy of Timon is the casting down of a "godlike image of man in his heart" by ordinary self-seeking men and his wakening from a "dream of restoring the golden age and all its charities in such a nest of vipers." Moreover, warns Mr. Alexander, to talk of Timon's tragedy as resulting from "kindly self-indulgence" or "easy generosity" is to talk in the vein of the legalistic and moralistic senators of Athens who, because of "their love of personal security," condemn the soldier for whom Alcibiades pleads.[10]

III

When Shakespeare made Timon into a tragic figure who could not only repel but also attract sympathy and who could even win true admiration, he went counter to the main body of tradition concerning the famous Athenian man-hater. In Timon there seems to have been a challenge for Shakespeare. Among the many writers who had built up the legend of Timon there had been small inclination to give him tragic proportions. In the classic age and in the Renaissance he was a stock example of extreme misanthropy, and when he was not condemned he was usually regarded as an inhuman curiosity.[11] Some writers who condemned him thought he was an eminent philosopher in the classic world. They had the authority of Pliny, who, in a casual reference, grants Timon distinction as one of the masters of philosophy and yet disapproves of his harshness and his effacement of all human affections.[12]

As the legend grew, condemnation of Timon took on a notable form. He was frequently pictured as a beast or as worse than a beast, and his story in some versions came to be associated with comment on the nature of beasts as compared with the nature of men. The flatterers of Timon, too, were sometimes pictured as beastlike. This beast theme that entered the story had a strong attraction for Shakespeare in ways already indicated, and we must fully understand its development within the growing legend and the use that Shakespeare made of it if we would understand the tragic world of *Timon*.

Plutarch in his *Lives* makes the first important classical contribution to the story. In his life of Alcibiades he tells very briefly of an occasion when Timon met Alcibiades walking in the midst of admirers and expressed happiness that Alcibiades was growing toward a position of power in which he would be the undoing of the Athenians. In his life of Antony, Plutarch speaks of Timon at greater length. Here he makes a digression to gather together bits of information about Timon, including the bit about his perverse liking for Alcibiades as the potential ruination of Athens. Timon as Plutarch presents him is not one to arouse sympathy, though Plutarch does imply that friends had once wronged him by failing him in time of need. He is a crusty citizen of Athens, living in the city itself and not in a wilderness, who despises his fellow men. He is willing to have the company of another man-hater named Apemantus, but not too much of that, and he is more than willing to have desperate Athenians hang themselves on a fig tree growing in his garden. His fellow citizens wonder at, laugh at, or revile him. His hate for mankind lives after his death in an epitaph written by himself, and his misanthropy is appropriately commemorated by an accident, for his tomb on the seashore is finally surrounded by water and becomes inaccessible to visitors. There is no sign that Plutarch's Timon was ever wealthy or that he ever stood high in public esteem at Athens. For all we are told, his suffering from ingratitude may have been a petty affair. As a man-hater he seems to be merely an eccentric character of a sort not unknown in other towns than Athens and in other ages than the fifth century B.C. In the telling of his story nothing whatever is said about beasts.

When Lucian takes Timon for the subject of a satiric dialogue called *Timon, or the Misanthrope,* the man-hater is made to have a certain appeal to our sympathy. But, Lucian being Lucian, the sympathetic appeal is not that of a tragic figure. The guiding purpose of the dialogue is to make sophisticated fun of the gods and to satirize hypocrisy and ingratitude among men. We are led to rejoice at the revenge Timon gets upon his untrustworthy friends more than to pity him for his woes. As the dialogue opens, we see him as a miserable laborer on an "outlying farm," dressed in dirty skins, digging with a pick, and shouting to Zeus for justice, but to a Zeus who seems lazy and weak of arm, incapable any longer of hurling shattering thunderbolts against wrongdoers. Timon, we learn, has been wealthy, has enriched many of his fellow Athenians, has impoverished himself by pouring out his wealth in generosity, and is now neglected shamefully by flatterers who once danced attendance on him. Zeus hears Timon's plaint. He has, it is true, neglected Timon because there have been things to bother him of late and because he has broken his thunderbolt hurling it at Anaxagoras, who was teaching that the gods do not count at all. But he wants to do something for Timon, who was once a fine rich gentleman, even though there is at present no thunderbolt with which to smite those who do Timon wrong. So he commands Hermes to take riches to Timon. Timon is thus put in the way of digging up a treasure of gold and of getting revenge on his old associates when they flock to him to share in his newly won treasure. These are outrageously transparent in their fawning and their trickery. Timon with grim pleasure lets them all beg and then drives them all away, beating them with his pick and throwing stones at them. Thus the dialogue ends, but what is to be Timon's manner of life after he has obtained this revenge is foreshadowed in what he says after he digs up the gold. He promises himself that he will buy the farm on which he has labored, build a tower over the treasure just large enough to live in, and have it for his tomb when he is dead. Furthermore, says he: "My life shall be solitary, like that of wolves; Timon shall be my only friend, and all others shall be enemies and conspirators . . . and the desert shall sunder me from them. . . . Timon shall keep his wealth to himself, remote from flattery and tiresome praise."[13]

Thus Lucian makes Timon express the thought that his life of enmity to mankind is to be like that of beasts in a wilderness, but the thought is merely casual. The passage is noteworthy only because of the beastlike character that Timon is to develop in the Renaissance. Lucian's Timon does not say that his life is actually to be savage and that he is to strip himself of all the appointments of civilization. He is to live alone on his outlying farm, but he is to enjoy what his gold can give him. He is still far from being a scorner of all that distinguishes man from beast.

But Timon's passing mention of wolves is not all there is in Lucian that looks forward to the beast theme in Shakespeare's play. The flatterers who have stripped Timon of his goods and abandoned him to poverty are more than once referred to as beasts of prey or birds of prey who have eaten his flesh. Timon himself calls one of them the "first of all vultures in voracity" and the hardheaded Hermes says to the somewhat sentimental Zeus that Timon has let himself be consumed by such ravenous creatures:

Well, you might say that he was ruined by kindheartedness and philanthropy and compassion on all those who were in want; but in reality it was senselessness and folly and lack of discrimination in regard to his friends. He did not perceive that he was showing kindness to ravens and wolves, and while so many birds of prey were tearing his liver, the unhappy man thought they were his friends and sworn brothers.... But when they had thoroughly stripped his bones and gnawed them clean, and had very carefully sucked out whatever marrow there was in them, they went away and left him.[14]

Hermes has only a somewhat tempered sympathy for Timon. Thus early we find Timon called a senseless fool.

About 1487, Boiardo made Lucian's dialogue into a play entitled *Timone Comoedia,* which was performed at Ferrara before Ercole I.[15] The first four acts of *Timone* follow Lucian without much alteration, but the fifth gives the story a new conclusion. Boiardo's Timon finally scorns and abandons his newly won gold, a part of which he has dug up and a part found hidden in a tomb. He resolves that for the rest of his days he will lead a savage solitary life, free from the slavery that wealth brings in its train. We are told in an epilogue that the wealth found in the tomb will be delivered to the rightful inheritor by the inheritor's servant and a companion of the servant, who have come upon Timon at the tomb, and that the wealth dug up will be taken by the servant and his companion as their own. The details of the resolution made by Timon to lead a solitary

life are arresting. He says that he will live on some mountain
or in some wild forest and will find shelter in a hollow tree
or in a cave. He will find food and drink in the wilds, but he
will have difficulty in clothing himself. This thought leads
him to compare man with other animals and to comment
upon man's disadvantage in being born poor and naked,
without natural protective covering.[16] Whether Boiardo had
some effect upon the Timon legend as it was told in Shakespeare's England is not clear, but this picture of the hermit
life which Timon is to lead makes one think of Shakespeare's Timon and his cave in the woods.[17]

A Renaissance writer who is unquestionably in the line
of contributors to what was known about Timon in Elizabethan England is the Spaniard Pedro Mexía (d. 1551). In
1540 he published at Seville the first three parts of a work
that gathered together a varied store of learning, *La silva de
varia lección*. In augmented form the book was published
again and again, and in translations it was widely read. One
of the chapters of the first part is "De la extraña y fiera
condición de Timón Ateniense, inimicísimo de todo el
género humano."[18] The *Silva* was translated into French by
Claude Gruget as *Les Diverses Leçons de Pierre Messie;* the
first three parts of the translation were published at Paris
in 1552 and were often republished in the sixteenth and
seventeenth centuries, along with additional parts. Through
the influence of this French version of the *Silva*, Timon acquired a new character in Renaissance Europe, one more
harsh and malicious than he had had before.

The Timon of Mexía was a beast worse than ordinary
beasts because he did something that one of them would

never have done: he cut himself off from his kind. In Gruget's somewhat free translation he is introduced by these condemnatory words:

> Toutes les bestes du monde s'acommodent aux autres de leur espece, & conuersent auec elles, fors le seul Timon Athenien, de l'estrange nature dequel Plutarque s'estonne en la vie de Marc Antoine: Platon & Aristofanes racōtent sa merueillieuse nature pource qu'il n'estoit homme que de la figure, au demeurant ennemi capital de tous les humains, ce qu'il confessoit librement & clairement, & les hayoit tous.[19]

This Timon, who was a man in appearance only, did not dwell in Athens, but outside the city. As Gruget goes on to say, "Il demeuroit seul en vne maissonnette aux champs," and he would go to Athens only if he had to. Apemantus ("Apemat") and Alcibiades come into the story much as in Plutarch, but Apemantus is said to have dwelt in the fields just like Timon and to have been "aspre & inhumain" also. The fig tree upon which Plutarch's Timon gladly allowed Athenians to hang themselves now changes into a real gibbet which had been erected in Timon's garden, apparently by Timon as an act of ironic charity. Finally, the burial of Timon on the seashore in such a position that the water shuts men away from his tomb becomes something that Timon planned: "Il se fit enseuelir & enterrer sur la riue de la mer, pour estre tousiours couuert des vagues qui la battaient, & s'il eust peu se faire enseuelir au profond de la mer, il l'eust fait."

Inspired by Gruget, Pierre Boaistuau found good use for the story of Timon in his *Le Théâtre du monde, où il est faict un ample discours des misères de l'homme,* which was published in 1558. There can be no doubt that Boaistuau used Gruget's translation of Mexía. Gruget's four-line French version of the epitaph said to have been written by Timon for his tomb appears without change in Boaistuau. *Le Théâtre du monde* had as a companion piece and sequel another work by the same author entitled *Un brief discours de l'excellence et dignité de l'homme,* which was published in the same year. The two works taken together form a characteristic Renaissance preachment on the medieval subject of contemning the world, in which there is an offering of old and new philosophies joined. As Boaistuau says in the older style, man is truly miserable in many ways and by contemplating the details of his earthly misery he can check his worldly pride and constrain himself to look toward Heaven, his home; but as Boaistuau says in the newer style, the pride in man that must be checked by contemplation of human miseries does have some justification in his excellences, which make a wonderful catalogue: his aspiration, his beauty of body, his courage and force of arms, his generosity, his artistic cunning, his inventive faculty (as shown in the device of printing, for example), and so forth. Before coming to a Renaissance appreciation of man's glorious effectiveness in this world, Boaistuau does so good a job with the list of man's miseries that no medieval scorner of the world could take exception to it. He offers Timon's misanthropy as an example of the extreme detestation that man's mundane condition is capable of arousing.

The first book of *Le Théâtre du monde* is much concerned with the disadvantageous state of man in nature as compared with that of the beasts. Among the authors appealed to is Pliny, because of his famous observations on that subject which are to be found in the introduction to the seventh Book of his *Natural History*. Pliny's animalitarianism, the product of a highly sophisticated age tending romantically to glorify things primitive at the expense of things civilized,[20] is of course not at all in the spirit of Christian contempt of the world, but Boaistuau makes it support his argument. Why should man have worldly pride when even pagan thinkers without benefit of Christianity saw well that as a creature of the world man has no equal, even among beasts, in misery and baseness? This, according to Boaistuau, is what Timon saw, not only along with Pliny, but also along with Heraclitus and Democritus. For Boaistuau says that among representative philosophies which show perception of man's unhappy state are those of three ancients: Heraclitus wept over, Democritus laughed at, and Timon had a particular hatred for man and all his works. "Thymon philosophe Athenien, a esté le plus affecté patriarche de sa secte."[21] Doubtless Boaistuau makes Timon into an Athenian philosopher because Pliny mentions him as one of the great philosophers in the same seventh Book that produces the comparison of man and the beasts. And so in the hands of Boaistuau the beast theme becomes more than a minor part of the Timon story. It becomes an argument to which the story must contribute.

The theme loses nothing in an English translation of Boaistuau's two works made by John Alday. This was first published without date, probably in 1566, and went into a second edition in 1581. The first edition is entitled *Thea-*

trum Mundi, The Theator or rule of the world, wherein may be sene the running race and course of euerye mans life, as touching miserie and felicity, wherin is contained wonderful examples, learned deuises to the ouerthrowe of vice, and exalting of vertue, wherevnto is added a learned, and maruellous worke of the excellencie of mankinde. In the words of Alday, Timon was a "feareful and vglye monster" with a "barbarous" voice, who "remained al his life alone in a wildernesse with the beastes, far from neighbors, for feare to be sene or visited of any"; he was a poor philosopher who, "after that he had long plunged himselfe in the contemplation of humaine miseries, had will neuer to haue bene borne, or else to haue bene transformed into the shape of some brute beast, for the great disdaine he had in mens vices." But ironically enough this man who would have been glad to be a beast had fled from the company of his fellow men as from "the companie of a fierce or cruell beast." Boaistuau improves upon Gruget's version of Mexía in the interests of a beastlike Timon, and Alday adds some improvement of his own.

In Boaistuau and Alday the garden of Timon takes on a new appearance as the result of an attempt to make him even more fanatically misanthropic than Gruget makes him. The single gibbet in his garden becomes more sumptuous furniture. In Alday's version it is said that because Timon sought the ruin of the human race and invented all the means he could to achieve that ruin, "he caused manye Gibets to be reared in his garden, to the end that ye dispaired, & those that are wearie of their liues, shoulde come thither to hang them selues."[22]

There is nothing in Boaistuau and Alday to arouse sympathy for Timon, any more than in Mexía and Gruget. There is nothing about loss of wealth by Timon. Neither is there anything about his suffering at the hands of ungrateful friends; Plutarch's hint on that score has been ignored. There is no digging up of gold. In Mexía and Gruget, the Plutarchan incidents concerning Alcibiades and Apemantus are both used in the story. In Boaistuau and Alday, Alcibiades is still present, but Apemantus has disappeared, leaving Timon without even an occasional visit from a like-minded man-hater.

In 1566, probably the year in which Alday put forth his *Theatrum Mundi,* Painter published a version of the Timon story in his *Palace of Pleasure,* with this heading: "Of the strange & beastlie nature of *Timon of Athenes* enemie to mankinde, with his death, buriall, and Epitaphe" (Novel 28). Painter's story is in the main a translation from Gruget's translation of Mexía and neglects neither Alcibiades nor Apemantus. Following Gruget's French, Painter says that "all the beastes of the worlde, dooe applie themselfes to other beastes of their kinde *Timon of Athenes* onelie excepted," and that Timon "was a manne but by shape onelie," and that "he dwelte alone, in a little cabane in the fieldes." On his own account Painter puts emphasis upon the "beastlie nature" of Timon. Gruget says of Timon's regret at not being alone when he was feasting with Apemantus: "En cela se monstroit-il vrayement fort estrange."[23] Painter changes this comment into one on Timon's beastliness: "Wherein he shewed, howe like a beaste (in deede) he was." Likewise Painter adds a touch of his own in the adjectives of the following sentence: "For like as he liued a beastlie and chorlishe life, euen so he required to haue his funerall, dooen after that maner." Nor is there anything at all in Gruget corresponding to Painter's comment that in Timon's epitaph "the qualities of his brutishe life" were described.[24] Painter has a look at, or remembers, the story in Plutarch as he goes through Gruget; he prefers the fig tree in Plutarch to the gibbet in Gruget and restores the tree to Timon's garden.

In 1579, Sir Thomas North's English translation of Amyot's French translation (1559) of Plutarch's *Lives* exhibited a Timon truly Plutarchan. Liberties taken with Plutarch's Timon story such as those of Mexía and his followers are not found in Amyot and North. Plutarch, it is to be remembered, says nothing whatever about beasts when he tells of Timon.[25]

But the beastlike Timon that Boaistuau had painted in his *Théâtre du monde* was brought again to the attention of English readers when Sir Richard Barckley published in 1598 his *Discourse of the Felicitie of Man* (second edition, 1603). Barckley made use of Boaistuau's French version of the Timon story, though he may have known Alday's English translation of Boaistuau. Barckley's *Discourse* is another religious attempt to picture the misery of the mortal world. The felicity of man of which he speaks in his title is only to be found in knowing God, both here and in the world to come. One by one he examines and punctures the supposed felicities of other sorts. At best, he says, they are only partial goods—even marriage, which goes far toward being a true felicity. Barckley, it will be seen, is no

cynic. He retells the story of Timon, as does Boaistuau, to
show what hate of the world could be like in one kind of
pagan philosopher, and he translates Boaistuau fairly
closely. Again we learn that Timon had "a great manie
gibbets in his garden" which he had placed there for the
accommodation of the despairing. And again we learn that
Timon deserted mankind and took the beasts for company.
Barckley has it that "he would neuer dwell or keepe company among men, but withdraw himselfe into the deserts,
and leade his life among beasts, that he might not be seene
of men."[26] To emphasize the moral of the story, Barckley
brings up again Pliny's comparison of beasts and men.

Probably before 1600 and perhaps between 1581 and 1590
an academic author wrote an English play on Timon.[27]
Stage directions indicate that it was put on the stage, and it
seems to have been intended for the amusement of a school
or university audience. There can be no question that the
author knew Lucian, for in certain passages he follows him
closely. But the academic play has much that is not found
in any other version of the Timon story, and it has some
features that are found elsewhere only in Shakespeare's
Timon. Like Shakespeare's play and unlike any other version of the Timon story it has a servant who is faithful to
Timon, a mock banquet given by Timon to the friends who
have failed him in his time of need, and invocations made
by Timon to the sun after misfortune has come to him.[28] It
gives much space to a comic subplot, of which there is no
need to take notice. Though it shows some serious sympathy for Timon in his suffering, it does not have a sustained spirit of tragedy. Through half the action we see

Timon in prosperity, spending money lavishly on his friends, taking pleasure in riotous drinking and foolish practical joking, and falling in love with Callimela, the daughter of a miserly citizen. Merely because Timon has wealth, Callimela promises to marry him. At the turning point, in Act III, there is a sudden and unprepared-for reversal of fortune. A sailor comes to announce that Timon's ships have been sunk and that he is now reduced to poverty. Timon is deserted by Callimela and his friends, gives the mock banquet, leaves the city with his faithful servant, digs in the fields, and uncovers gold there. The main plot has a comic ending more or less like Lucian's, with Timon scorning Callimela and his erstwhile friends and dealing them blows with his spade when they once more flock around him.

In the academic *Timon* the beast theme appears, though nothing unusual is made of it. Finding himself despised after his change of fortune, and even called a dog, Timon addresses nature in these bitter words:

> Thou, nature, take from mee this humane shape,
> And mee transforme into a dire serpent,
> Or griesly lyon, such a one as yet
> Nere Lybia or Affrica hath seene,
> Or els into a crocodile or bore,—
> What not? or with my basiliscan eies
> May I kill all I see, that at the length
> These base ingratefull persons may descende
> The pitte of hell! thus would I bee reueng'd.[29]

As in Lucian, Timon's friends are likened to devouring birds, such as vultures or crows.[30] Timon's prayer to nature to be changed into a fierce beast was almost certainly suggested by the passage in Lucian where Timon vows to become wolflike. But the author of the play seems to have taken an idea from some other version of the Timon story when he makes Timon plan to end his days in a forest wilderness, instead of in the fields as in Lucian:

> Farr from the cittie is a desart place,
> Where the thick shaddowes of the cypresse trees
> Obscure the daye light, and madge howlett whoopes:
> That as a place Ile chuse for my repose.
> Let that day be vnfortunate wherein
> I see a man.[31]

In the 1580's and 1590's, and on into the first decade of the 1600's, Elizabethan readers could find many passing references to Timon in contemporary books. As might be expected, such references usually carried on the Renaissance tradition of a detestable Timon. Robert Greene mentions Timon frequently. He calls him "currish," and specifically makes his man-hating include woman-hating; he implies in a romantic defense of women that anyone who proceeds "Tymon like, to condemne those heauenlie creatures" is a "blasphemous beast."[32] He speaks of the "Timonist" as one who abandons all good company and takes delight "onelie in solytarie life" in "the wildsome woods."[33] Thomas Lodge thinks of Timon and "Apermantus" as men who were impelled by a fiendish spirit to "waxe careles of bodie and soule, fretting themselues at the worlds ingratitude, and giuing ouer all diligent endeuor to serue the fury of their unbridled minds."[34] Lodge includes Timon and Alcibiades among examples of men undesirable in a state. "But say there be a good *Solon* in a citie," he remarks, *"Alcibiades* may royot, *Timon* may curse, *Diogenes* may bite, *Aristip-pus* may flatter: yet shall all these be but flea bytings, & may breede a spot in estates, but not the spoyle of state."³⁵ An impassioned condemnation of Timon as an adversary of both man and God occurs in *A Very Excellent and Learned Discourse, touching the Tranquilitie and Contentation of the minde...written in French by...M.I.De l'Espine, and newly translated into English by Ed. Smyth* (1592). Here Timon is said to have taken delight only in what was diseased and corrupted, and those who are as envious as he was are said to be "enemies to men, and vnto whatsoever appertaineth unto their owne prosperous estate, and also haters of God and of his glorie.... Wherein they shew themselves to be children of the devill, and make manifest that they are his heires and successours."³⁶

A condemnation of Timon much more subtle and urbane than the ordinary was to be found in Florio's translation of Montaigne's *Essays* (1603). Montaigne, writing "Of Democritus and Heraclitus," prefers the mocking scorn shown by Democritus for humanity to the pity and compassion shown by Heraclitus, because he thinks that mankind is merely inane and sottish, rather than evil and miserable, and that to make a great to-do over the imperfections of the world argues some estimation of the thing moaned and bewailed. Likewise he prefers the cynicism of Diogenes to the misanthropy of Timon. Timon took things much too hard and was thus an unbalanced philosopher, not to say a fool. As Montaigne says, in Florio's English rendering:

Even so *Diogenes,* who did nothing but trifle, toy, and dally with himself, in rumbling and rowling of his tub, and flurting at *Alex-*

ander, accoumpting vs but flies, and bladders puft with winde, was a more sharpe, a more bitter, and a more stinging judge, and by consequence more just and fitting my humour, than *Timon,* surnamed the hater of all mankinde. For looke what a man hateth, the same thing he takes to hart. *Timon* wisht all evill might light on vs; He was passionate in desiring our ruine. He shunned and loathed our conversation as dangerous and wicked; and of a depraved nature: Whereas the other did so little regarde vs, that wee could neither trouble nor alter him by our contagion; forsooke our company, not for feare, but for disdaine of our commerce. He never thought vs capable or sufficient to doe either good or evill.[37]

Montaigne's mention of Timon in connection with a discussion of Democritus and Heraclitus was probably a result of his reading in Boaistuau. A copy of Boaistuau's *Brief discours de l'excellence et dignité de l'homme* bears Montaigne's signature, and the companion piece of that work, *Le Théâtre du monde,* in which reference to Democritus and Heraclitus helps to introduce the Timon story, seems to have had an effect upon some of Montaigne's expressions.[38]

Though Montaigne has small sympathy for Timon, he nevertheless succeeds in presenting him as a character whom one might view tragically, a man who hated the evil of the world and lost his spiritual balance because he took the world so fiercely to heart. We know from *The Tempest* that Shakespeare was not unfamiliar with Montaigne, and it has been argued that he read the *Essays* extensively and closely.[39] If he read the essay "Of Democritus and Heraclitus," he encountered not only a brief hint for a tragic Timon but also a suggestive distinction made between Timon's hate for man and a professional cynic's scorn for man. The contrast drawn by Montaigne between Timon and the cynic Diogenes has some similarity to that drawn by Shakespeare between Timon and the cynic Apemantus. Shakespeare has Apemantus accuse Timon of putting on the "sour-cold habit" enforcedly, of assuming the cynic's manner not because he philosophically despises the world, but because he has been hurt by the world. Shakespeare's Apemantus is not exactly a fair critic of Shakespeare's Timon, but he makes a shrewd hit or two in his analysis of Timon's character, beginning with the lines

> This is in thee a nature but infected;
> A poor unmanly melancholy sprung
> From change of fortune.
>
> (IV, iii, 203–205)

Essentially he is the humorously scornful cynic such as Montaigne prefers to the savagely hating Timon. But there is nothing in the way of phrasing to show that Shakespeare knew the essay in which Montaigne expresses his preference for Diogenes, and Shakespeare was entirely capable of devising without aid his dramatic contrast between Timon and Apemantus.

It is plain that in Shakespeare's *Timon of Athens* there is legendary matter to which many authors contributed. The tragedy is not properly to be called Plutarchan, despite the fact that the two versions of Timon's epitaph found in North's translation of Plutarch are used in the play. The Timon who becomes a beast and finds a den for himself in the woods—the Timon who has most call upon Shakespeare's poetic power—is not in Plutarch at all. He is a creation of authors later than Plutarch.

IV

Though the beast theme of *Lear* is remarkable for its general dramatic effect, it is nothing so remarkable in this way as the beast theme of *Timon*.[40] In the beast theme of *Timon* one may perhaps find the essence of the tragedy. Shakespeare obviously put much of himself into its development, whatever portion of it he took from the Timon legend. It is of some significance that in no other of Shakespeare's plays does the word "beast" occur so often as in *Timon*.

In *Timon,* Shakespeare is mastered by the conception of a human society whose more important members either reveal themselves to have more of beasthood than of manhood in them or else turn away from manhood in disgust and embrace beasthood. After the hero of the tragedy has become a misanthrope he offers the conventional fig tree of the Timon legend to the Athenians to hang themselves upon, but he is most himself, most truly the thwarted idealist, as he addresses a distinctively Shakespearean prayer to the spirit of his new-found gold, asking it to bring mankind to complete ruin so that beasts "may have the world in empire" (IV, iii, 395). When he prays for such confounding of mankind, he himself having retreated to the forest and given up manhood for beasthood, all his company in Athens except his faithful servants are already beastlike. Apemantus, the savage cynic, has not needed to retreat to the forest to embrace beasthood and rejoice in it. The others have exposed their natural beasthood while acting the part of men—the crew of flatterers, the senators, the

whores, even Alcibiades. The most that one can say for
Alcibiades is that his animal quality, which makes bloodshed and promiscuous mating his natural occupations, is
not treacherous and is at times amiable.

In the first scene of the play Apemantus, cursing Timon's
flattering friends, introduces the beast theme:

> The strain of man's bred out
> Into baboon and monkey.
>   (I, i, 260–261)

Toward the end of the play Timon serves notice, when
Alcibiades and the whores visit him in the forest, that he
and his former friends are now beasts together:

> Alcibiades. What art thou there? speak.
> Timon. A beast, as thou art.
>   (IV, iii, 48–49)

Throughout the play, men call each other beasts or themselves beasts, or talk of humanity grown beastly. The commonwealth of Athens is said to have become a "forest of
beasts," the underling of Alcibiades for whom he pleads
before the senate is said to have committed outrages in his
"beastly fury," and the warfare of which Alcibiades makes
an occupation is said to be "contumelious, beastly, mad-
brain'd" (IV, iii, 354; III, v, 72; V, i, 179).

In the climactic mock-banquet scene (III, vi) we find
some of Shakespeare's most effective ringing of changes
upon the beast theme. The author of the academic play on
Timon which is apparently earlier than Shakespeare's tragedy builds a scene around the conception of a mock banquet
of stones offered fittingly to false friends who are "a stony
generation." He brings in no reference to beasts. At the
banquet his Timon serves stones painted like artichokes

and throws them at the guests. Shakespeare has at the center of his corresponding scene the conception of a mock banquet of lukewarm water offered fittingly to lukewarm friends who are to be thought of as fawning beasts with lapping tongues. ("Uncover, dogs, and lap.") The magnificent passage of verse in which Timon denounces his "trencher-friends" as beastlike parasites, calling them "affable wolves" and "meek bears," has the sign manual of Shakespeare.

The beastliness pictured in *Timon* is worse than that of beasts, for it walks in the shape of man and is a constant insult to a sense of decorum. The beastliness of beasts is attractive by comparison. In *Timon* men are condemned as beasts and yet we are given to understand that they would be better if they were actually beasts. Shakespeare puts a strain of animalitarianism into the dialogue, a strain of admiration for the natural and the primitive below the level of civilized human reason. But it is an animalitarianism that does not go very far. The true beast, even the "unkind" beast, is thought of as better than the depraved man of this tragic world, but he is only a beast after all, a subject of admiration *faute de mieux*. There is no turning to unreasoning nature for healing and uplifting of the spirit that has been overwhelmed by the spectacle of man's perversion. Timon flees to the forest not to find his soul in the solitude of nature, but to escape the "wolves" that he has found within the walls of Athens, wolves even worse than those that he will find outside. He cries:

> Timon will to the woods; where he shall find
> The unkindest beast more kinder than mankind.
> (IV, i, 35–36)

His liking for the natural beast is liking at all only because of what he feels for man. As he says to Alcibiades after calling him a beast:

> For thy part, I do wish thou wert a dog,
> That I might love thee something.
> (IV, iii, 54–55)

The implication, of course, is that the dog is a low creature but still better than Alcibiades. Certainly this passage does not show Timon, or Shakespeare, as a dog-lover in any ordinary sense. It has its place beside other passages in *Timon* and in Shakespeare generally which make the dog something less attractive than dog-fanciers find him.[41]

The beastlike men in *Timon* are often ravening devourers of each other. Much is made of this. Early in the play we find that flatterers eat lords, lords similar to Timon:

> TIMON. Wilt dine with me, Apemantus?
> APEMANTUS. No; I eat not lords.
> (I, i, 207–208)

Flatterers sauce their food with Timon's blood:

> APEMANTUS [to Timon]. I scorn thy meat; 'twould choke
>   me, for I should
> Ne'er flatter thee. O you gods! what a number
> Of men eat Timon, and he sees them not.
> It grieves me to see so many dip their meat
> In one man's blood.
> (I, ii, 39–43)

The figure of devouring beastliness in cannibal man spreads to cover others than flatterers. Timon as host guesses that Alcibiades would rather be at a breakfast of enemies than a dinner of friends. And Alcibiades agrees that "so they were bleeding-new, my lord, there's no meat like 'em" (I, ii, 81–82). The thieves who come to Timon in the forest for some of the treasure he has found justify themselves by their want of meat. They say they cannot live like beasts, on grass, berries, and water. No, says Timon, nor on the beasts themselves: "You must eat men" (IV, iii, 431).

Some of this picture of men eating men seems to have been developed from a comparison of Timon's flatterers to birds of prey or beasts of prey that had been made in the Timon legend. As we have seen, such a comparison appears in Lucian and in the academic *Timon*. But also in other places than the Timon legend a reader of the sixteenth century could find the concept of flatterers eating the flattered. Shakespeare doubtless had met with it in one or more of the collections of "sayings of the wise" that were popular in his day. A saying was credited to Alphonsus that "flatterers are not vnlyke Wolues: for euen as Wolues by tickling and clawing are wont to deuour Asses: so flatterers vse their flatterye and lyes, to the destruction of Princes."[42] On the authority of the *Lives of Eminent Philosophers* by Diogenes Laertius a saying was credited to the cynic Antisthenes that "he had rather haue Rauens in house with him, than flatterers: for Rauens ... deuoure but the carkasse being deade, but the flatterer eateth vp the body and soule aliue"; and on the same authority a saying was credited to the cynic Diogenes that the beast "that bitte most greuously" was "emonge beastes, sauage, & furious, he that sclaunderously, and ill reporteth; but emong tame beastes, euermore ye Flatterer."[43] For the Elizabethan the evils of flattery were an attractive subject. He collected much about them from the books that he read, and he wrote much about them.

The beastliness of Apemantus in *Timon* is also backed by more than the Timon legend. Shakespeare's Apemantus is a cynic bearing some relation to the traditional Diogenes, whose reported sayings and doings were current among sixteenth- and seventeenth-century English writers and were often collected. Like Diogenes, Apemantus is called a dog, and like Diogenes he admits that he is a biting dog. And when he is called an "unpeaceable dog" by one of Timon's flatterers, his retort that he would "fly, like a dog, the heels of an ass" (I, i, 283) is in the vein of Diogenes, who supposedly knew always how to discomfit those he disliked by witty reference to his title of dog, as when he said "to two infamous persons stealing away from him: Fear not . . . , doggs eat not thistles."[44] The condemnation of flatterers as devouring beasts which is attributed to Diogenes and which has just been quoted might have served as a model for Apemantus' bitter criticism of Timon's flatterers.

Moreover, the asceticism of the Diogenes of tradition seems to be Apemantus' rule of life. There was thought to be justification for saying that Diogenes "ledde a bestly lyfe," using the good things of the earth "no more than bestes" and drinking water as beasts do.[45] Apemantus at Timon's feast, eating root and drinking "honest water" while "rich men sin," is the same mixture of beastliness and moral fervor that Diogenes had the reputation of being.

One must not yield to a temptation to give Apemantus less than his due, to think that he is a snarling cur no better than Thersites in *Troilus and Cressida*. Like Thersites he is a privileged critic of the life and manners he observes,

and like Thersites he plays a vulgar part very near to that
of an allowed fool, though he is licensed to make himself
even more obnoxious than a fool.[46] But unlike Thersites he
has consistent philosophy in him, in addition to mere scur-
rilousness, and he distinctly does not gloat over the existence
of the evil and folly that he scourges. It was possible in
Shakespeare's age to praise Diogenes as a "heavenly dog."[47]
Probably it was also possible to think that Apemantus in
Timon was a beast for whom something good could be said.

v

It is upon a note of pity for Timon, for Timon with all his
faults, that Shakespeare ends the tragedy. He makes Alcibiades sound the note. Alcibiades, the warrior-politician,
is of much grosser grain than Timon and is much inferior
to him in spiritual worth, but nevertheless he has ability to
meet and overcome hostile forces in the world whereas
Timon can only let himself be crushed by them. The contrast between the success of Alcibiades and the failure of
Timon is somewhat like that between the success of Fortin-
bras and the failure of Hamlet. It contains one of Shakespeare's notable tragic ironies. In the last speech of the play,
Alcibiades makes a comment upon Timon. This comment
has the choral quality often given by Shakespeare to words
of some prominent character in a tragedy which pass judgment upon the hero at the close of the action. After reading
a copy of Timon's misanthropic epitaph, taken from his
tomb on the seashore, the normally insensitive Alcibiades
is moved to say something that we might not think him
capable of saying.

> These well express in thee thy latter spirits:
> Though thou abhorr'dst in us our human griefs,
> Scorn'dst our brain's flow and those our droplets which
> From niggard nature fall, yet rich conceit
> Taught thee to make vast Neptune weep for aye
> On thy low grave, on faults forgiven. Dead
> Is noble Timon; of whose memory
> Hereafter more.
>   (V, iv, 74–81)

Alcibiades does not find in Timon what Antony in a similar choral comment finds in Brutus, a gentle mixture of elements such that

> Nature might stand up
> And say to all the world, 'This was a man!'
>   (*Julius Caesar*, V, v, 74–75)

But though Nature might not offer Timon as another paragon of her gentler workmanship, there was material in his violent being to make it proper that she should weep for and forgive his faults. It is proper that she should shed tears on his grave and forgive even those profound faults that led him finally to have unnatural scorn for the tears of suffering humanity. We are reminded that Timon's good steward, when he pities his fallen master, meditates on the way "noblest minds" can be brought by vile friends to "basest ends" (IV, iii, 464).

The "rich conceit" through which Timon's faults are wept for and forgiven seems to have been contrived by Shakespeare out of conventional matter concerning the burial of Timon. It is prepared for in two passages of the play, in which Timon speaks of wanting a grave on the shore of the sea. He speaks once of lying "where the light foam of the sea may beat" his gravestone daily (IV, iii, 381–382), and again of making his everlasting mansion where once a day "the turbulent surge shall cover" him (V, i, 220–223). The grave on the seashore is in various versions of Timon's legend. Plutarch, it will be remembered, says that Timon was buried on the shore and that the sea chanced to surround his tomb and make it inaccessible. Later tellers of the Timon legend embroidered this matter of burial. According to one account, the unsociable Timon left orders that he should be buried at the brink of the sea and that care should be taken to place his grave where the waves would make approach to it difficult or impossible. This account appears in English in the stories of Alday and Barckley. But Painter, following another account, has it that Timon wished to be buried near the sea because of a desire even more perverse than a desire for privacy in death. Says Painter: "By his last will he ordeined hymself to bee interred vpon the sea shore, that the waues and surges mighte beate, and vexe his dead carcas."[48] Shakespeare is close to Painter when he deals with Timon's burial. His Timon, like Painter's, wishes to have the sea beat upon his body. Yet in Shakespeare's Timon there is not so much a spirit of surliness when he plans to have his grave placed near the sea as there is a spirit of sad weariness. After he has written his epitaph, he can say of himself:

> My long sickness
> Of health and living now begins to mend,
> And nothing brings me all things.
> (V, i, 191–193)

And when we find that the waves shed tears upon his body instead of vexing it, we see fully Shakespeare's intention of leaving in our minds a man-hater worthy of sympathy, instead of one worthy of detestation.

In putting Timon to dramatic use Shakespeare apparently chooses for the first time to present a deeply flawed hero such as we have found to be characteristic of his last tragic world. He chooses for his hero a man who in the Renaissance has generally had a bad reputation as a hater of mankind and has generally been thought unworthy of mankind's sympathy. He lets him have all the faults that have been credited to him by unsympathetic tellers of his story. He tries to make us see these faults in the light of sympathy, but does not try to minimize them. In conclusion he suggests that we should forgive them, as Nature herself seems to forgive them.

The faults of Timon thus offered as forgivable go so deep that he himself is incapable of recognizing their existence. Timon is a remarkable contrast to the conscientious self-critics who are the heroes of Shakespeare's middle tragic world. Unlike Lear, for example, he never achieves by his separation from the vanities of the world a sympathy for the "loop'd and window'd raggedness" of poverty, and if we feel compassion for him after he has turned man-hater we find ourselves in the strange position of having sympathy for a would-be destroyer of sympathy among men. Yet, when he is without pity, he is most capable of winning pity.

In the same way, Timon is most capable of winning admiration when he might seem to be least deserving of it. But his paradoxical nobility of spirit is never that of an effective leader of men. Like Macbeth, Antony, or Coriolanus, he is a rare spirit deeply flawed, but unlike those heroes he does not belong among the rare spirits who "steer humanity."

Chapter III

"MACBETH"

MACBETH is a morality play written in terms of Jacobean tragedy. Its hero is worked upon by forces of evil, yields to temptation in spite of all that his conscience can do to stop him, knows he has given his soul to the common enemy of man, goes deeper into evil-doing as he is further tempted, sees the approach of retribution, falls into despair, and is brought by retribution to his death. The story is reminiscent of those later moralities which end tragically instead of mercifully. But *Macbeth* is unlike the normal morality for the reason that its hero begins his evil-doing with complete understanding of the course he is laying out for himself and with complete willingness to sacrifice his soul in the next world in exchange for the gifts of this world. He is deceived by supernatural agents of evil, but he is not blinded by them morally through the specious argument that vice is not truly vicious or that it is not repulsive, as the hero of the morality is usually blinded. Among the deeply flawed but noble heroes of Shakespeare's last tragic world Macbeth is the only one who deliberately, after a soul struggle, takes evil to be his good. Among them he is the only Satan.

In Shakespeare's tragedy, Macbeth is worse than he is in Holinshed's *Chronicles,* and at the same time better. In Holinshed, Macbeth kills a Duncan who has so much clemency that he is on the whole a weak and unworthy king. We are not told how or where Macbeth kills him.

For the first ten years of his reign Macbeth shows what Holinshed calls "a counterfet zeale of equitie," ruling with exceptional justice and ability, using great liberality toward his nobles, making many good laws, and winning a reputation as a sure punisher of criminals and a sure defender of the innocent. It is only after this that he becomes a cruel tyrant. In Shakespeare, on the other hand, Macbeth murders a completely worthy king who is "clear in his great office," adds to the deep damnation of the king's taking off by doing the deed in base violation of the laws of hospitality, and proceeds to his ruthless acts of tyranny without ever having ruled justly. Yet we find that Shakespeare gives greatness to the spirit of Macbeth and compels us to have fellow feeling for him. With Sir Arthur Quiller-Couch we must recognize the "splendid audacity" with which Shakespeare first makes more difficult the winning of sympathy for a disloyal self-seeking murderer, sympathy without which Macbeth cannot be a truly tragic figure, and then sets out to win that sympathy. As Quiller-Couch says: "Instead of extenuating Macbeth's criminality, Shakespeare doubles it and redoubles it. Deliberately this magnificent artist locks every door on condonation, plunges the guilt deep as hell, and then—tucks up his sleeves."[1]

It will be worth our while to begin an examination of the world of *Macbeth* by looking closely at the three witches and the part given them to play. Before we make up our minds about the guilt of the hero and, finally, the meaning of the tragedy, we must first decide what power these beings wield over the actions and fortunes of the hero.

---

[1] For notes to chapter iii see pages 271–273.

They are witches having the forms of repulsive old women, but they are not mortal witches such as the law might get its hands upon and put to death in the England or Scotland of Shakespeare's day. They are "weird sisters," but the word "weird" as applied to them cannot mean that they have control over Macbeth's destiny and compel him to do all that he does. Macbeth is certainly no mere puppet moving under their manipulation. Nothing is clearer than that Shakespeare writes of Macbeth as of a man who has free will so far, at least, as the choice of good or evil is concerned, and who in choosing evil creates for himself physical misfortune and a spiritual hell on earth. In what they do the witches show themselves to have a power over Macbeth that is limited, however strong it may be. They are supernatural agents of evil, and in working to make fair into foul they reveal both the capacities and the incapacities that the Christian tradition has attributed to devils. They tempt Macbeth to do evil, and tempt him with great subtlety. They cannot force him to do it.

The witches reveal a fate for Macbeth and imply that a part of what will come to him must come, but they reveal no fate of evil-doing for him and never, even by suggestion, bind him to evil-doing. As prophets they are "imperfect speakers." By their imperfect speaking they tempt him to commit crimes for which he is to assume full moral responsibility, a responsibility so complete that it will be not only for doing, but also for forming the thought of doing, each criminal deed. They foretell that Macbeth will be king, and they let that prophecy suggest murder to him. They do not foretell that Macbeth will murder Duncan in order to be king. They foretell that Banquo will not be king but that he will be greater than Macbeth because he will father a line of kings, and they let that prophecy, too, suggest murder to Macbeth. They do not foretell that Macbeth will murder Banquo. With the help of evil powers whom they call their "masters" they let Macbeth know through visions that he is to beware Macduff, that he shall be harmed by none of woman born, that he shall never be vanquished until Birnam Wood shall come to Dunsinane Hill, and that Banquo's issue shall indeed bring forth a line of kings; and they let these visions give Macbeth both fear and rash confidence and stir him again to undertake murder. They do not foretell, and neither do their masters, that he will murder Macduff's wife, children, and servants.

About the witches as they may be seen in the light of the demon lore as well as the witch lore of Shakespeare's age there is much that should be taken into account. Some part of what will now be considered with reference to their demonic quality has not, I think, had the attention it deserves. More particularly this has to do with the reason why as demons they are called witches.

Shakespeare, of course, took the witches from Holinshed's *Chronicles,* where they are not called witches and are not repulsive old women. Holinshed does not pretend to know whether the three women who saluted Macbeth and Banquo, hailing the one as Thane of Glamis, Thane of Cawdor, and King to be, the other as father of a line of kings, were supernatural beings or whether, if they were more than illusions, they were of good or evil character, though he remarks that they were generally thought to be supernatural beings of some sort. He says of them, in thoroughly noncommittal fashion: "It fortuned as Makbeth and Banquho iournied towards Fores, where the king then laie, they went sporting by the way togither without other companie, saue onelie themselues, passing thorough the woods and fields, when suddenlie in the middest of a laund, there met them three women in strange and wild apparell, resembling creatures of an elder world.... This was reputed at the first but some vaine fantasticall illusion by Makbeth and Banquho.... But afterwards the common opinion was, that these women were either the weird sisters, that is (as ye would say) the goddesses of destinie, or else some nymphs or feiries, indued with knowledge of prophecie by their necromanticall science, bicause euerie thing came to passe as they had spoken."[2]

As for later prophecies made to Macbeth, Holinshed reports that after Macbeth had changed from a just king into a tyrant, his cruelties became worse when he was warned to take heed of Macduff by "certeine wizzards, in whose words he put great confidence (for that the prophesie had happened so right, which the three faries or weird sisters had declared vnto him)" and when he was told by "a certeine witch, whom hee had in great trust," that "he should neuer be slaine with man borne of anie woman, nor vanquished till the wood of Bernane came to the castell of Dunsinane."[3] Apparently the wizards were ordinary mortal wizards and the witch was an ordinary mortal witch. In concluding his account of Macbeth, Holinshed makes this comment: "In the beginning of his reigne he accomplished many woorthie acts, verie profitable to the common-wealth (as ye haue heard) but afterward by illusion of the diuell, he defamed the same with most terrible crueltie."[4] The implication is that for Holinshed the wizards and the witch were instruments of the Devil who deluded Macbeth, whatever the three women resembling creatures of an elder world may have been. Shakespeare, like the skillful dramatist he is, makes the three strange women absorb the parts played in the story by the wizards and the witch and makes the devilish delusion of Macbeth begin with the prophecies given to Macbeth and Banquo before Macbeth has become king.

Holinshed bases what he says of Macbeth and what he gives of Scottish history in general upon the *Scotorum Historiae* (1527) of Hector Boece. This was translated by John Bellenden as the *Hystory and Croniklis of Scotland* (*ca.* 1540), and Holinshed uses both the Latin of Boece and the Scottish translation of Bellenden.[5] (A Scottish metrical version of Boece made by William Stewart in 1535 remained in manuscript until 1858.) Behind the work of Boece lies the Latin *Scotichronicon* (*ca.* 1384) of John Fordun and the Scottish *Orygynale Cronykil of Scotland* (*ca.* 1424) of Andrew Wyntown. In Fordun's story of Macbeth there is no Banquo and there are no prophetic women of indeterminate character, no wizards, and no witches. In Wyntown's story there is still no Banquo, but there are three women who appear to Macbeth in a dream, one of whom calls him Thane of Cromarty, another Thane of Moray, and another King. Wyntown says that Macbeth thought it most likely these were "thre werd sisteris," and by the fantasy of his dream was moved to slay Duncan. According to Wyntown, Macbeth met death at the hands of a knight who was not born of woman, and there was a legend, the truth of which cannot be vouched for, that the Devil was the father of Macbeth and had prophesied of him:

> And na man suld be borne of wif
> Off power to reif him his lif.[6]

Boece introduces Banquo and Fleance into the story of Macbeth and tells that story practically as Holinshed tells it, for Holinshed follows Boece fairly closely. In Boece there are the three strange women (presented in terms that will be commented upon later), the wizards ("haruspices"), and the witch ("muliercula futurorum praescia").

There is most to be gained for the understanding of Shakespeare's witches from a consideration of ways in which others than Shakespeare in early seventeenth-century England, including writers later than Shakespeare, retell or interpret the legend of the three prophetic women who encountered Macbeth and Banquo on the way to Fores. There were many Englishmen who acquired an interest in this Scottish legend after James had ascended the English throne. One good reason for their interest was that James found gratification in the fabled prediction that Banquo would father a line of kings. It made him feel that his royal house was established by destiny and that it would long endure. According to tradition, as related by Boece and Holinshed, Banquo's son Fleance fled to Wales after his father's death and had by a daughter of the Welsh king an illegitimate son, who went to Scotland, won honor there as the king's steward, and thus gave the family name of

Stuart to descendants that eventually produced the Stuart line of kings. A sure way to compliment James—and we perceive that Shakespeare thought of this as he wrote *Macbeth*—was to refurbish the tale of the prophecy concerning Banquo's royal descendants.

In August, 1605, King James, with the queen and the prince, paid a visit to Oxford. Before the gates of St. John's College a short dramatic entertainment was staged, for which Matthew Gwinne, a fellow of St. John's, had written Latin verses, but which was given in English for the benefit of the queen and the prince, as well as in Latin. In this entertainment three boys hailed the king by all his titles as a member of a royal house which, as was foretold to Banquo by "prophetic sisters," should never come to an end. The three boys, representing as it were a second appearance of the prophetic sisters, were "quasi Sibyllae," and they came forth out of "a Castle, made all of Iuie, drest like three Nimphes (the conceipt wher of the King did very much applaude)."[7] Though they spoke of Banquo, they said nothing about Macbeth. The fact that they represented nymphs will later be seen to have its importance.

In 1606, which is very probably the year that brought *Macbeth* to the stage, William Warner made capital out of both Banquo and Macbeth in his *Continuance of Albions England*. It is possible that there is some connection between this poem and *Macbeth,* but which work was written first there is no means of telling. Though much of what Warner says of Banquo and Macbeth obviously comes from Holinshed and Boece, he does not make Macbeth a king who rules justly for many years and then turns into a tyrant;

like Shakespeare, he makes a conscience-stricken and self-tormented Macbeth proceed immediately from the traitorous murder of his sovereign to the tyrannous murder of Banquo. Moreover, like Shakespeare and unlike Holinshed and Boece, he does not make Banquo a sharer in the murder of Duncan. Because of the possibility of connection between Warner and Shakespeare it is especially interesting to see what Warner says of the three prophetic women. He has Fleance tell the Welsh princess about them in these lines:

> King *Duncan* when aliue,
> To *Makbeth* and my father did great Dignities deriue,
> As chiefest for their births, their wit, and valour, also thay
> Held friendship long, and luckely in *Scotch* affaires did sway.
> Three *Fairies* in a priuate walke to them appeared, who
> Saluted *Macbeth* King, and gaue him other Titles too:
> To whom my father, laughing, said they dealt vnequall dole,
> Behighting nought thereof to him, but to his Friend the whole.
> When of the *Weird-Elfes* one of them, replying said that he
> Should not be King, but of his Streene a many kings should be.
> So vanish they: and what they said of *Makbeth* now we see.
> But murdred is my father, and of him remaines but me,
> Nor shall what they diuin'd effect, vnlesse sweet Sweet, by thee.[8]

From this account of the apparition Warner goes on to inevitable praise of King James. It is clear, then, that Warner saw the three prophetic women as fairies, more particularly as "weird-elfes," and if it is asked whether beings of this sort have any reality for Warner, he can be allowed to answer for himself. Only a few pages before he gets to the Macbeth-Banquo story he says:

> Of *Fairies, Goblins,* walking Lights, & like chat Grandams much,
> Nor am myself incredulous that haue bin and be such.[9]

It may be thought that Warner's fairies are a far cry from Shakespeare's witches. But Simon Forman, the astrologer, conjurer, and physician, who had a specialist's reason to be interested in both witches and fairies, went to see a performance of Shakespeare's *Macbeth* in 1610 and wrote the following, as part of some brief notes on the play: "Ther was to be obserued firste howe Mackbeth and Bancko 2 noble me*n* of Scotland Ridinge thorowe a wod the[r] stode befor them 3 women feiries or Nimphes And Saluted Mackbeth sayinge: 3 tyms vnto him. Haille mackbeth. king of Codon for thou shalt be a kinge but shalt beget No kinges. &c. then said Bancko What all to mackbeth And nothing to me. Yes said the nimphes Haille to thee Banko thou shalt beget king*es*. yet be no kinge."[10] Forman probably read his Holinshed just before or just after seeing *Macbeth,* as Kittredge suggests,[11] for much that is said in his notes on the play is reminiscent of Holinshed. It seems that he calls the witches "feiries or Nimphes" on the authority of Holinshed, but the point is that he does call them so, on whatever authority.[12] In other words, he found the terms applicable to the "secret, black, and midnight hags" that he saw on the stage when he witnessed the acting of *Macbeth.* By "feiries or Nimphes" he undoubtedly means beings known as fairies in his own age and as nymphs in the classic age. Nymphs were often taken to have been fairies by Elizabethan and Jacobean writers.

Forman does not use the word "witches." Does he mean to imply that Shakespeare's supernatural hags are properly to be called fairies, but not witches—that they cannot be called both? Probably he does not. For when we come to

Peter Heylyn, we find a teller of the Macbeth story who makes the three prophetic women into "fairies," "witches," or "weirds"—that is, into beings who may be given one or all of these designations.

Heylyn had his troubles with royalty, and his telling of the Macbeth story is one of his peace offerings to King James. Thus it has a special value as an indication of what James himself, interested as he was in the folklore of witches and fairies, would accept as an interpretation of the three prophetic women. Heylyn probably took the greatest pains to find out what he had better say and what not say in writing about Macbeth and Banquo.

In 1621, when he was only twenty-one years old, Heylyn published his *Microcosmus, or a Little Description of the Great World,* with a dedication to the Prince of Wales. The book was highly successful and found a wide variety of readers, but its youthful author had been guilty of grave indiscretions in what he had written about Scotland, and when he revised the work for its second edition, which was published in 1625, he sought to make amends for these. We can see that as he did his revising he was greatly concerned to please the king. In the edition of 1621 he says that the Scots "haue one barbarous custome yet continuing" and goes on to speak of their feuds in which they disregard law and take justice into their own hands.[13] In the edition of 1625 he says instead that the Scots "had not long since one barbarous custome," that of carrying on feuds, but His Majesty was able to control these feuds and has thus won a great victory.[14] Heylyn made several changes of this sort. One of them, which is certainly not the least amusing revelation of his desire to placate the king, brought the story of Macbeth into the edition of 1625.

In the edition of 1621 Heylyn remarks with an air of scholarly superiority that he leaves out of his history of Scotland a "rabble of kings mentioned by Hector Boetius."[15] These are the very early kings of legend. Among the Scottish kings whom he does take into account he includes Macbeth, but he merely mentions him in a list. In the edition of 1625 Heylyn softens the blow of his remark about the "rabble of kings" by saying, "Neither shall I herein I hope offend the more iudicious sort of the *Scottish* nation, especially since I deal no more vnkindly with their *Scota,* and her successours than I haue done already with our own *Brutus,* & his."[16] Then he proceeds to give some little information about this rabble of kings, though, as he says, they are fabulous. And then, while he is talking about legends, he says with transparent guile that before he settles down to Scottish history he will relate the story of Macbeth, "then which for variety of action, or strangenesse of euent, I neuer met with any more pleasing." One is bound to ask whether this devotee of pure history, who suddenly finds that fabulous matter he has previously scorned contains something extremely "pleasing," may not here be echoing judicious words of royalty. Certainly the story of Macbeth was more pleasing to James than to Heylyn himself. Heylyn begins the story as follows:

> *Duncan* King of Scotland, had two principall men whom he employed in all matters of importance; *Machbed* and *Banquho.* These two travelling together through a forrest were mette by three Fairies, or Witches (*Weirds* the *Scots* call them) whereof the first making

obeisance vnto *Machbed,* saluted him *Thane* (a title vnto which that of Earle afterward succeeded) of *Glammis,* the second, *Thane* of *Cawder,* and the third, King of *Scotland.* This is vnequall dealing said *Banquho,* to giue my friend all the honors and none vnto me: to whom one of the *Weirds* made answere, that he indeed should not be King, but out of his loynes should come a race of kings that should for euer rule *Scotland.* And hauing thus said they all suddenly vanished. Vpon their arriuall to the Court, *Machbed* was immediately created *Thane* of *Glammis;* and not long after, some new service of his requiring new recompence, he was honoured with the title of *Thane* of *Cawder.* Seeing then how happily the prediction of the three Weirds fell out in the two former; hee resolued not to be wanting to himselfe in fulfilling the third; and therefore first hee killed the King, and after by reason of his command among the Souldiers and common people, he succeeded in his throne. Being scarce warme in his seat he called to minde the prediction giuen to his companion *Banquho,* whom herevpon suspecting as his supplanter he caused to be killed, together with his whole kindred, *Fleance,* his son onely with much difficulty escaping into *Wales.*[17]

As Heylyn proceeds, he tells of the prophecies concerning Birnam Wood and Macbeth's lack of need to fear any man born of woman, which he says were given by "certeine wizards." He concludes with Macbeth's death at the hands of Macduff and the establishment of the Stuart royal line by descendants of Fleance.

There can be no doubt that in using the words "Fairies, or Witches (*Weirds* the *Scots* call them)" Heylyn means to say that the three prophetic women were fairy witches, i.e., weirds, and does not mean to say that they were either fairies or human witches, and weirds if they were human witches. In the fourth edition of the *Microcosmus,* that of 1629, which shows the author still polishing his text, the description is changed to make the meaning quite clear. It becomes "Fairies, Witches (*Weirds* the *Scots* call them)."[18] Heylyn presented to the Prince of Wales the edition of 1625, with its carefully revised account of Scotland. It came to the king's hands. So far as we know, James found nothing wrong with the author's version of the Macbeth story or with anything else in the new treatment of Scotland. But poor Heylyn had been so assiduous in changing his account of Scotland that he had neglected other parts of his book, and royal displeasure now fell upon him because he had called France a "larger and more famous kingdome" than England.[19] He explained that he had meant to say it was *at one time* larger and more famous. He was forgiven.[20]

Robert Burton and Thomas Heywood show that according to lore inherited by the early seventeenth century the three prophetic women of the Macbeth story could be classed as devils and at the same time be thought of as fairies or nymphs. Both Burton and Heywood class them as water devils. Burton says, in his *Anatomy of Melancholy* (1621):

Water diuels, are those *Naiades* or water *Nymphes,* which haue beene heretofore conuersant about Waters and Riuers. The water, as *Paracelsus* thinks, is their Chaos, wherein they liue, some call them *Feries,* and say that *Habundia* is their Queene, these cause inundations, many times shipwracks, & deceaue men seuerall waies, as *Succubæ* or otherwise. *Paracelsus* hath seuerall stories of them, that haue liued and bin married to mortall men, and so continued for certaine yeares with them, and after vpon some dislike haue forsaken them. Such a one was *Ægeria* with whom *Numa* was so familiar, *Diana, Ceres,* &c. *Olaus Magnus,* hath a long narration of one *Hotherus* a King of *Sueden,* that hauing lost his company, as hee was hunting one day, mette with these water Nymphes or Fayries, and was feasted by them. And *Hector Boethius,* of *Mackbeth* and *Banco,* two Scottish Lords, that as they were wandering in the Woods, were told their fortunes by three strange women.[21]

Burton does not go on to give more of the Macbeth story. Heywood in his *Hierarchie of the Blessed Angells* (1635) tells the story at some length and introduces it as follows (I omit references to Egeria and other classic "nymphs"):

> Spirits that haue o're Water gouernment,
> Are to Mankinde alike maleuolent:
> They trouble Seas, Flouds, Riuers, Brookes, and Wels,
> Meeres, Lakes, and loue t'enhabit watry Cels;
> Thence noisome and pestiferous vapors raise.
> Besides, they Man encounter diuers ways;
> At wrackes some present are; another sort
> Ready to crampe their joints that swim for sport.
> One kind of these th'Italians *Fatæ* name;
> Fée the French; We, Sibils; and the same
> Others, White Nymphs; and those that haue them seen,
> Night-Ladies, some, of which *Habundia* Queene.
> . . . . And of this sort
> (Namely White Nymphs) *Boëthius* makes report,
> In his Scotch Historie: Two Noblemen,
> *Mackbeth* and *Banco-Stuart,* passing then
> Vnto the Pallace where King *Duncan* lay;
> Riding alone, encountred on the way
> (In a darke Groue) three Virgins wondrous faire,
> As well in habit as in feature rare.[22]

What Heywood has to say further about Macbeth and Banquo need not be considered.

II

The witches in Shakespeare's *Macbeth* are loathsome old crones, but according to contemporary fairy-lore they are just as truly fairies as the "virgins wondrous fair" found in Heywood's story of Macbeth and Banquo. Also, they are just as truly devils. When Forman saw them as fairies, he saw them with the eyes of a man of his day.

The Gothic mythology of fairies, as Dr. Johnson called it, contained a great deal that has not been passed on into our later tradition of fairies.[23] Our later tradition finds its most authentic picture of the fairy world in Shakespeare's *Midsummer Night's Dream* and takes imaginative delight in a part of the old mythology that was never very provocative of awe or terror. Even when the modern mind appreciates that the fairy world was sometimes profoundly fearsome to our forefathers, it does not easily understand how this could be. Shakespeare knew a lore of malignant evil fairies who had power to harm men greatly, and doubtless he knew it as well as he knew the lore of relatively amiable or merely mischievous fairies, the little people who were often appealing in their jollity or delicate beauty. Like Chaucer, Shakespeare knew not only of

> The elf-queen with hir joly companye

but also of the elves and "wightes" from which men prayed to be spared and against which men said charms to avert evil.[24] In *Cymbeline* he could make Imogen pray:

> To your protection I commend me, gods!
> From fairies and the tempters of the night
> Guard me, beseech ye!   (II, ii, 8–10)

When Christianity attempted seriously to put fairies into its scheme of things, it tended to class them as devils. Many writers of Shakespeare's time classed them so, as Burton and Heywood did. It was commonly held, of course, that the supernatural beings recognized by pagan mythology were in reality devils, and many of these seemed to be fairies.

Some of them, some which "the fantasticall world of Greece ycleaped *Fawnes, Satyres, Dryades, & Hamadryades,*" were credited with "merry prankes" and were obviously the not very harmful "Robbin-good-fellowes, Elfes, Fairies, Hobgoblins of our latter age,"[25] but others, especially certain nymphs and certain beings like the furies, were just as obviously fairies with evil propensities. When fairies were regarded as devils, the worst among them were always woman devils, and these woman devils were frequently given designations out of the classical past.

As early as 1483 "an Elfe" is defined in the English-Latin wordbook *Catholicon Anglicum* as "lamia, eumenis."[26] It may be gathered that the definer of the word thought of elves or fairies in their most evil guise,[27] as female demons who could either be deceptively fair in appearance, as lamiae sometimes were, or fittingly repulsive, as furies always were; and it may be guessed, from what many others write later, that one evil action which he thought they performed was the harming of children, by sucking their blood, by devouring them, by bewitching them so that they would be transformed into ill-favored elf children, or by stealing them. The demon lamia received her name from the mortal Lamia beloved of Zeus, whose children were destroyed by jealous Hera and who, after she had died of grief, preyed upon the children of others in revenge. Both the lamia and the fury of the fairy mythology harmed children, but the lamia, by assuming an aspect of beauty, might also "allure young men to company carnally" with her and then devour them.[28] Female demons who harmed children were also called "striges" (*strix* being the Latin word for a screech owl which according to ancient belief sucked the blood of young children).

But the most common name in Shakespeare's age for the worst sort of female demon to be found in fairy mythology was "hag." The word is of Anglo-Saxon origin, but did not come into frequent use until the sixteenth century. It became an inclusive term for female fiend, sometimes applied to the fury, lamia, or strix that harmed children, sometimes to a demon that was the nightmare,[29] sometimes to one of some other special character, and sometimes to one that was devoted to evildoing in general.

The word "hag" was of course also applied to the human witch, as was the word "strix." At this point we must recognize that the lore of fairies frequently merges with the lore of witches, and that the fairies and those human beings who practiced witchcraft seem to have had an affinity for each other. Sometimes human witches visited the fairies to gain powers of enchantment or second sight, or for other reasons. King James says in his *Daemonologie* (1597): "Sundrie Witches haue gone to death with that confession, that they haue ben transported with the *Phairie* to such a hill, which opening, they went in, and there saw a faire Queen, who being now lighter, gaue them a stone that had sundrie vertues which at sundrie times hath bene produced in judgement."[30] Sometimes fairies and human witches rode through the air together by night, had the same mother witch (who was variously known by such names as Diana, Hecate, Habundia, Nic Neven, and Herodias), and had the same power to sail over bodies of water in sieves, make charms, work enchantments, cause nightmares, harm chil-

dren, and foretell the future.[31] Therefore the word "hag"
was the more easily taken to mean either a fairy or a human
being.

The word "witch" had a similar double meaning. It
could mean to the Elizabethan a demon of the fairy order
as well as a human being who had made a compact with
the Devil. Richard Huloet in his early English dictionary,
the *Abcedarium Anglico Latinum* (1552), gives two definitions which show the two kinds of witches. The first
definition has to do with the human witch: "Witche,
Fatiloqua, æ, malefica, saga, æ, triuenifica."[32] The second
has to do with the demon witch: "Wytches, or nighte furies
that do transforme, or alter nature, called hegges. *Striges.*"[33]
If we turn to what Huloet has to say about "hegges," or
hags, we find: "Hegges or nyght furyes, or wytches like
vnto olde women, as Lucan and Sere do suppose, which do
sucke the bloude of children in the nyght. *Striges.*"[34]
Huloet's hags are witches, and it is certain that they are not
witches who *are* old women, but witches who are *like* old
women. They are furies, or demons. The evil work they are
credited with doing is that which folk known to Huloet
feared most they would do: the harming of children by
altering their nature or by sucking their blood.

That such hags, or demons, were known as witches is
confirmed by John Baret in his *Alvearie or Triple Diction-
arie, in English, Latin, and French* (1573). He makes it
clear that they were fairies. This is his definition for "hag":
"An *Heg* or fayrie, a witch that chaūgeth yᵉ fauour of
children. Strix, strigis, f.g. Plin."[35]

When John Florio defines *strega,* the Italian word for

"witch," in his *Queen Annas New World of Words, or Dictionary of the Italian and English Tongues* (1611, a revision of his *World of Wordes*, 1598), he makes it mean both the human witch and the fairy hag: "Stréga, a witch, a sorceresse. Also a hag or fairie, such as our fore-elders thought to change the fauour of children."[36] In the same dictionary he defines the Italian *fata* as "a Fairy, an Elfe, a Hag, a witch."[37] It is to be noted that Florio takes a superior attitude toward the belief that hags harmed children. When Florio wrote, this belief was certainly not dead, but non-human hags were probably coming more and more to be thought of, at least by Florio's acquaintances, as demons of a general character. The anonymous author of *Englands Wedding Garment, or a Preparation to King Iames his Royall Coronation* (1603) is rejoiced that James has escaped from "traitor plots" and thus from

> Black poyson and the murdering knife,
> Contriu'd by Hagges of darkest hell.[38]

In 1659, William Somner published his Anglo-Saxon dictionary called *Dictionarium Saxonico-Latino-Anglicum.* One of Somner's definitions is this: "Hægesse. Larva, lamia, furia, Hecate. a hagg, a witch, a furie or fiend, a woman-Divell."[39] Another is this: "Hægtesse. *i.e.* hægesse. *item,* Erynnis, Eumenis. Furies of Hell."[40] Somner seems to use the word "fury" in a broad sense as meaning a woman fiend or hag and in a narrow, classical, sense as meaning one of the avenging Eumenides. We have found Huloet calling hags that are certainly not eumenides by the name of "nyght furies." Huloet, like Somner, gives recognition to classical furies in a special definition.[41] The "larva" mentioned by Somner was sometimes called a hag. Sir Thomas Eliot in his *Bibliotheca Eliotae* (1548) offers the following definition: "Larua, æ. f.g. and Laruę arum, plur. a spirite, whiche appereth in the nyght tyme. some call it a hegge, some a goblyn. some a goste or an elfe."[42]

III

Thus the witches in Shakespeare's *Macbeth* are demons of the fairy order such as the Elizabethans also called hags or furies. They are fiends in the shape of old women who do evil wherever and however they can, but for the time being they are particularly concerned with the contriving of murder through the use of a susceptible man, Macbeth, and with the destruction of that man. By Macbeth himself, when he comes to know them well, they are called what they are: "secret, black, and midnight hags" (IV, i, 48), "filthy hags" (IV, i, 115), and "juggling fiends" (V, vii, 48). They do things which at times make them seem human and they are thereby the more effectively bodied forth dramatically, but their witchcraft in general is that which Elizabethans thought of as practiced by fairies as well as by human beings. They are called witches not because they resemble human witches, but because to the Elizabethan mind they *are* witches. It is to be remembered that Heylyn writes of the three prophetic women of the Macbeth story as being "fairies, witches," and says that the Scots know such beings as "weirds."

In three passages of *Macbeth* which are generally thought to have been written by another hand than Shakespeare's

(III, v; IV, i, 39–43, 125–132), Shakespeare's superhuman witches are changed into human witches, who work for "gains" and under Hecate's leadership dance about the cauldron

> Like elves and fairies in a ring.
>
> (IV, i, 42)

Their art of witchcraft brings it about that they are compared to fairies when they cease to be fairies. It must be said in favor of D'Avenant that when, in his "improvement" of *Macbeth,* he makes Macduff and Lady Macduff meet the witches on the heath, he has the understanding to make Macduff take them for "foul spirits."[43]

Shakespeare's witches call themselves weird sisters, and both Macbeth and Banquo call them that also. What does Shakespeare mean by the term? He took it from Holinshed, who in turn took it from Bellenden's Scottish translation of Boece. As to what Holinshed means by it, there cannot be any doubt. He means the Fates. Boece says that the people thought the three strange women to be "Parcas aut nymphas aliquas fatidicas diabolico astu praeditas,"[44] and Holinshed, translating more fully and closely than Bellenden, renders these words as "either the weird sisters, that is (as ye would say) the goddesses of destinie, or else some nymphs or feiries, indued with knowledge of prophecie by their necromanticall science."[45] In other words, Holinshed says that the people thought the three women to be the weird sisters known to Scottish folklore (who might be interpreted for his English readers as goddesses of destiny) or else to be something different, namely, fairies (or nymphs, meaning fairies) able to foretell the future by means of necromantical science, i.e., witchcraft. Shakespeare made his weird sisters fairy demons and he gave them necromantical science. It appears that in doing so he was guided by Holinshed's second interpretation of the three women. Nevertheless he took for them the name "weird sisters" from Holinshed's first interpretation. A natural result of his use of that name has been a belief on the part of some scholars that he thereby made them "goddesses of destiny," at least in the sense that the Norns of Scandinavian mythology, with whom the weird sisters of Scottish mythology sometimes show relationship, were such goddesses.[46] Both the Norns and the Scottish fates called weird sisters could be malignant beings. They were both of the fairy world.

It is a question whether Shakespeare knew the lore of the Scottish weird sisters in their Nornlike character, but a more important question is whether he actually makes his weird sisters shapers of destiny, whether he gives them the power not merely to prophesy but to determine the future. They have "masters." If they themselves are directors of fate, why do they call such beings up before Macbeth? Moreover, they never imply that they are directors of fate, nor does anyone else in the play ever make the claim that they are, unless use of the term "weird sisters" is to be taken for such a claim. In fact, any argument that they are directors of fate really rests on the fact that Shakespeare brought the term "weird sisters" into the play.

It was quite possible, as Warner demonstrates by his use of the word "weird," for Shakespeare to take the term "weird sisters" from Holinshed and yet make it mean something other than Holinshed had made it mean. And what

Shakespeare did make it mean we should gather not from what Holinshed had made it mean, but from what the witches in Shakespeare's play show themselves to be by their actions—sisters who are able to foretell destiny because they are able to foresee future events by necromancy.[47] When Warner told the story of Macbeth and Banquo in his *Continuance of Albions England* (1606), "weirds" was a well-established synonym for "weird sisters," and like "weird sisters" it had been used to mean the classical Fates.[48] Warner, as we have seen, calls the three women who prophesied to Macbeth and Banquo "weird-elfes." Yet he certainly does not think of them as fates. He thinks of them as fairies with the power of divination, power to foresee future events and not to control them, for he speaks of "that euent diuin'd by them" and again of "what they diuin'd."[49] Just as Warner's weird-elves are not fates, so Shakespeare's weird sisters are not fates. Nor did Warner alone among Shakespeare's contemporaries think of the three sisters of the Macbeth story as soothsayers instead of fates. In the short dramatic entertainment devised by Matthew Gwinne which was staged before the gates of St. John's College when King James made a visit to Oxford in August, 1605, the boys who were dressed like nymphs and who represented the prophetic sisters ("fatidicas sorores") were supposed to be sibyls ("sibyllae"), not the Parcae.[50]

As soothsayers, demons were always thought by the Renaissance, just as by earlier Christian ages, to be "imperfect speakers."[51] In *The Treasurie of Ancient and Moderne Times* (1613), which Thomas Milles drew from various

Continental authors, the question is raised "Whether euill
Dæmons and Spirits, can foretell things to come, they hauing no certaine knowledge." The answer is:

Neither do the Good Angelles, or the euill Spirits, know or appre-
hend things futurely to happen, as of themselues, for that is in the
power and Science of the liuing God onely. True it is, that the good
Angelles haue an intelligence of future occasions, yet not in their
owne Nature, but according as God giues it to them by reuelatiō.
The Deuils also do sometimes foresee what is to ensue, yea a long
time before it hapneth, by disposition of the celestiall and inferiour
bodies; like as men do sometimes foretell by knowledge in Astrology,
bad and sterile seasons, from fruitfull and plenteous. As *Thales
Nilesius* (by meanes of the Stars) foretolde the abundance of Oliues
which should be the yeare following. Sometimes likewise, the euill
Dæmons or Spirits, doe presage future matters, by coniecture only,
and then their predictions do euer fall out to the contrary. For it is
their habit and custome, to mingle lyes with trueth, to the end, that
they may the more easily perswade the falshoode. Euen in like
manner, as they vse to do, that are preparing a poyson, they mingle
it with Wine, Hony, or some sweet thing, that the deadly venome
may bee couered & hidden vnder the sweet shaddow: & it doth not
a little delight those peruerse spirits, when they can anyway abuse
the credulity of men, by lying, in their Mystical prædictions of things
to happen.[52]

Shakespeare makes Banquo suspect that the witches may
have hidden some such "deadly venome" under a "sweet
shaddow" when Macbeth finds himself to be Thane of
Cawdor immediately after they have hailed him by that
title. Banquo says:

> And oftentimes, to win us to our harm,
> The instruments of darkness tell us truths,
> Win us with honest trifles, to betray's
> In deepest consequence.
>
> (I, iii, 123–126)

The demons, or evil angels, were thought to have a strictly limited power to foresee the future, because all angels, including those who had fallen, were creatures of God. It was not to be expected that God's creatures would know all that God knew. Evil angels could delude man by pretending to know all about the future, but like good angels they could not interfere with human free will. Heywood puts orthodoxy into rhyme when he writes:

> For, as Angels Creatures bee,
> Th' are limited in their capacitie;
> In all such things as on Gods Pow'r depend,
> Or Mans Free-Will, their skill is at an end,
> And vnderstand no further than reueal'd
> By the Creator: else 'tis shut and seal'd.
>   Hence comes it that the euill Angels are
> So oft deceiv'd, when as they proudly dare
> To pry into Gods Counsels, and make show
> By strange predictions future things to know.
> This makes their words so full of craft and guile,
> Either in doubts they cannot reconcile,
> Or else for certainties, false things obtruding,
> So in their Oracles the World deluding.[53]

For Shakespeare's Macbeth there is a destiny, and the witches know enough of that destiny to let us feel the weight of it. But as demons they cannot know all of it. They look upon the seeds of time that are allotted to Macbeth. Some they are sure will grow. Others they hope will grow. They do their best to get Macbeth to make these others grow, and they succeed.

IV

Macbeth is a tragedy of criminal ambition and thus reminds us of *Richard III.* Like *Richard III,* it shows a pyramid of rising and falling fortune for a murderous hero. Both Macbeth and Richard proceed through blood to attain kingship, and then, when they have attained that height, are driven by a sense of insecurity to proceed further in blood. Richard resolves to kill the princes in the Tower and declares:

> I am in
> So far in blood, that sin will pluck on sin.
>
> (IV, ii, 63–64)

Immediately after the murder of Banquo, Macbeth resolves to continue upon his course of bloodshed, and echoes Richard in these lines:

> I am in blood
> Stepp'd in so far, that, should I wade no more,
> Returning were as tedious as go o'er.
>
> (III, iv, 136–138)

Neither Macbeth nor Richard finds security in crimes committed after the attainment of kingship; each begins his fall almost as soon as he sets out to win security, and for each the shedding of blood finally becomes disordered cruelty. But Macbeth is not, as Richard is, a melodramatic villain-hero, though he is a villain-hero.[54] He makes a demand upon our sympathy that Richard cannot make, chiefly because as a devotee of evil he is always self-tortured. Macbeth has a dearest partner in villainy who is not always self-tortured, but she is almost his equal in claiming sympathy.

In order to win sympathy for Macbeth and Lady Macbeth, Shakespeare might have made them greatly but honestly ambitious at the opening of the play and then have brought them gradually, under stress of temptation, to a point where they would have entertained evil suggestion. He did not choose to do so. He refused to take the easier way of giving Macbeth and Lady Macbeth a tragic hold upon us, because, even more daringly than in *Timon,* he was creating heroic imperfect humanity for his last tragic world, instead of the imperfect heroic humanity that he had created for his middle tragic world.

When the witches prophesy to Macbeth that he will be king, and thereby suggest to him the murder of Duncan, he clearly does not have an innocent mind. Banquo's question, why he starts at and seems to fear the words which sound so fair, can only mean that Macbeth has already entertained the thought of murder and because of it has already known the soul-shaking fear he later shows to his wife. The words of prophecy instantly place before Macbeth an image which they could not so soon have brought to an utterly innocent man, a horrid image which, as he says a few lines later, makes his seated heart knock at his ribs. Thus the witches offer their suggestion of murder to a man who has already prepared himself to receive it, who has, we may say, summoned them by his thoughts, and who has shown that there is a mysterious affinity between him and them by his unconscious echoing of their

> Fair is foul, and foul is fair

in the first words that we hear him speak:

> So foul and fair a day I have not seen.
> (I, iii, 38)

Macbeth is never allowed to forget that the evil to which he allies himself and devotes himself is evil that arouses horror and loathing. Neither are we. Never for a moment does Shakespeare palliate that evil; he challenges us to perceive it in its darkest color—and yet to perceive the human worth of Macbeth and of the woman who arms him for his villainy. He goes far in risking alienation of sympathy for both his hero and his heroine when, at the very end of the play, he allows us to see them through the eyes of Malcolm as "this dead butcher and his fiend-like queen." He goes equally far in risking alienation of sympathy for his hero when, as he brings him to catastrophe, he allows us to see him through the eyes of Angus as a dwarfish and even ridiculous figure:

> Now does he feel his title
> Hang loose about him, like a giant's robe
> Upon a dwarfish thief. (V, ii, 20–22)

Miss Spurgeon draws attention to "this imaginative picture of a small ignoble man encumbered and degraded by garments unsuited to him," and remarks upon two aspects of Macbeth, one in which he is "magnificently great" and another in which he is "but a poor, vain, cruel, treacherous creature, snatching ruthlessly over the dead bodies of kinsman and friends at place and power he is utterly unfitted to possess."[55] More successfully than the Jacobean Chapman, the Jacobean Shakespeare can subject a tragic hero to belittling scorn and even to sharp ridicule and nevertheless give him indubitable nobility of spirit.

Shakespeare's Macbeth has a constantly active and insistent conscience, whereas his Richard III has nothing of the sort. Richard's conscience is shown only when retribution is about to overtake him, and then only momentarily, as a quickly conquered aberration, but Macbeth's conscience is one of the most impressive things about him. Over and over again it draws us to him and asks us to pity him. It asks us to see him as a man who knows the demands of goodness and decency, however much he refuses to meet those demands.

This does not mean that Macbeth's conscience is all that a human conscience should be, for even in the process of giving Macbeth a conscience Shakespeare has contributed to making him a deeply flawed character. The conscience given him is itself deeply flawed. It has great power but is distinctly one-sided and therefore of limited scope, and furthermore, it shows its strength in the least admirable of possible ways. It works by arousing fear. Macbeth learns from it to be terrified at the thought of evil-doing and its consequences but not to love goodness and all its works. In short, Macbeth's conscience is merely negative, not both negative and positive, in the counsel it gives him. The terror it inspires in him shakes his "single state of man" through-out the play and is the psychological core of a tragedy that is filled with motions of fear.[56] Macbeth's conscience has been condemned as no conscience at all "in the strict sense,"[57] but this is saying more against it than is warranted.

As we see it in operation, Macbeth's conscience reveals clearly its defectiveness. Yet there is a well-known passage in which Lady Macbeth says that she fears her husband is "too full o' the milk of human kindness" to catch the nearest way to kingship. What are we to make of this? Moulton, who believes that Macbeth is always merely a practical man in his moral judgments and not a tenderhearted man, takes "human kindness" to mean "humankindness" and explains it as not an inclination toward good as good but only "that shrinking from what is not natural, which is a marked feature of the practical nature."[58] One may dispose of the passage less ingeniously by saying that because Lady Macbeth has no sympathy with her husband for hesitating to win the crown by murder, she calls him tenderhearted in scornful irony, and that when she calls him tenderhearted she does not literally mean what she says any more than when she declares that what he would "highly," that he would "holily." After she has spoken of his milk of human kindness and his desire to act holily, she finally characterizes him in terms that fit the conception of him that we draw from his own words. "Thou'ldst have," says she,

> that which rather thou dost fear to do
> Than wishest should be undone.
>
> (I, v, 25–26)

With all her hardness Lady Macbeth is able to show humanity toward Duncan, and to show it in such a way as to reveal her husband's inhumanity by a flash of contrast. The occasion comes soon after Macbeth has soliloquized upon the considerations that for him are strong against the murder of Duncan. Let us look first at these considerations, marshaled by Macbeth, which are presented to him by his conscience but are nevertheless a sign of his inhumanity. One of them is the justice of the life to come, a retribution he can "jump" because his values are worldly rather than otherworldly; another is the justice of this life, a retribution more to be feared; still another is the violation of the code of honor involved in his killing of a kinsman to whom he owes loyalty, a king to whom he owes fealty, and a guest to whom he owes protection; and the final consideration is the turning of public opinion against him by his killing of an eminently virtuous man to satisfy his vaulting ambition. In his soliloquy Macbeth shows that he knows what pity is, for he speaks of a general pity among the people of Scotland that would "blow the horrid deed in every eye" and bring him into disfavor; but he shows no capacity for pity in himself. So far as we can see, he never gets away from fearful self-centered weighing of consequences. He holds a violation of the code of honor to be a wrong action, but there is no sign that he does so with any thought except that it could contribute to the turning of public opinion against him. He does not manifest any affection for Duncan that could work to prevent the murder, and he does not even think of the good and kindly King Duncan as a human being for whom he might or should have affection. In a few words that Lady Macbeth speaks as she waits for her husband to commit the murder we have the contrast between her humanity and his lack of humanity. These words prove that, despite her praying to be unsexed and to be filled with direst cruelty, she is capable of feeling natural compassion. They show that in her there is something which can arouse pity for Duncan by making her compare him to her father. For she says of him:

> Had he not resembled
> My father as he slept I had done 't.
> (II, ii, 14–15)

Lady Macbeth breaks under the strain of evil-doing whereas Macbeth does not. Are we to understand that in the long run her strength proves less than his? Or are we to understand that her conscience is of a higher order than his and that therefore violation of conscience finally puts a greater burden upon her than upon him? Certainly her conscience is not a fear-conscience. Before the murder of Duncan, she is able to nerve her husband against fear not only because she strongly wills to do so but also because she does not have his susceptibility to fear. Later, in the sleep-walking scene, she is ridden not by fear of consequences but by horror rising from a sense of her uncleanness, as she lets us see clearly in these lines from her inner drama: "What need we fear who knows it, when none can call our power to account? Yet who would have thought the old man to have so much blood in him? ... The Thane of Fife had a wife: where is she now? What! will these hands ne'er be clean?" (V, i, 40–48). The stain which a little water will not remove is profound. It penetrates a part of her being which is capable of pity not only for Duncan but also for Lady Macduff.

On his last battlefield Macbeth says to Macduff:

> But get thee back, my soul is too much charg'd
> With blood of thine already.
>
> (V, vii, 34–35)

All that Macbeth has shown us of himself before this is against our acceptance of these words as a final expression of pity, and thus they seem rather to be an expression of belated concern over that retribution in the next world which he has recognized as possible but has been willing to risk.

In giving Macbeth a conscience that works by arousing fear Shakespeare takes his lead from Holinshed. He proceeds not only from what Holinshed says about Macbeth's fear of being served as Duncan had been served, but also from what Holinshed says about the Scottish king Kenneth's fear of divine punishment for the murder of his nephew Malcolm.[59] Holinshed, following Boece,[60] makes Macbeth show the conscience of a murderous tyrant: "Shortlie after, he began to show what he was, instead of equitie practicing crueltie. For the pricke of conscience (as it chanceth euer in tyrants, and such as atteine to anie estate by vnrighteous means) caused him euer to feare, least he should be serued of the same cup, as he had ministred to his predecessor."[61]

Elizabethans usually, but not always, held that fear was one of the passions stirred by conscience. Richard Barnfield in *The Combat, betweene Conscience and Couetousnesse, in the Minde of Man* (1598) thinks of fear as a passion too ignoble to be stirred by conscience and reserves the term "conscience" for a motion of the mind toward good unforced by fear:

> Fond wretch, it was not *Conscience,* but feare,
> That made the first man (Adam) to forbeare
> To taste the fruit of the forbidden Tree,
> Lest, it offending hee were found to bee,
> According as Iehouah saide on hye,
> For his so great Transgression, he should dye.
> Feare curbd his minde, it was not *Conscience* then,
> (For *Conscience* freely, rules the harts of men)
> And is a godly motion of the mynde,
> To euerie vertuous action inclynde,
> And not enforc'd, through feare of Punishment,
> But is to vertue, voluntary bent.[62]

But to most Elizabethans it seemed that fear not only could be stirred by conscience but could demonstrate the power of conscience in a fashion highly instructive, and many Elizabethan moralists had something to say about guilty fear in conscience-stricken malefactors. Such fear is well described by William Perkins in *A Discourse of Conscience* (1596), when he speaks of five "passions and motions in the heart" as the chief of those stirred by conscience, and thinks of fear as being certainly not the least of them. The five passions are shame, sadness, fear, desperation, and a general perturbation "wherby all the powers & faculties of the whole man are forth of order." Of fear Perkins says:

The third is *feare:* in causing whereof conscience is very forcible. If a man had all the delightes and pleasures that heart can wish, they can not doe him any good, if conscience be guiltie.... Yea the guiltie conscience will make a man afraid, if hee see but a worme peepe out of the ground, or a silly creature to goe crosse his way, or if hee see but his own shadowe on a suddaine, or if he do but forecast an euill with himselfe....[63]

Tyrants were well known to be notable sufferers from guilty fear. In 1605 a translation of a French work by Pierre Le Loyer was published under the title *A Treatise of Specters or straunge Sights, Visions and Apparitions appearing sensibly vnto men.* One of its sections is labeled "Of the feares of notorious malefactours, terrified by the guiltinesse of their owne consciences," and another, immediately following, "Of the feares and terrours of tyrants and vsurpers of estates." Some of the illustrations of fears and terrors offered in the latter section show in the tyrant a conscience such as Shakespeare gives to Macbeth. Among them we find phantasms and imaginations tormenting the tyrant asleep and awake, and we even find the phantasm of the murdered victim appearing at the feast.[64]

In still another section of the *Treatise of Specters* sleep-walking is mentioned as one of the manifestations of a guilty conscience, and a case is cited of a man who had murdered a child and was drawn to the place of the murder as he walked in his sleep.[65] Not only the sleepwalking of Lady Macbeth, but also her conviction that there is an ineffaceable stain of blood upon her hands, has a background of traditional material.[66]

Two markedly conscience-stricken tyrants who appeared on the English stage about ten years before the close of the sixteenth century, in an age much less sophisticated than the Jacobean, may be regarded as the dramatic precursors of Shakespeare's Macbeth. These two are Richard III and King John, but not the Richard and John of Shakespeare. They are the hero of the anonymous *True Tragedie of Richard the Third* and the hero of the anonymous *Troublesome Raigne of King John*. When Shakespeare wrote his own *Richard III* and *King John*, the psychological interest in conscience that he was to show in writing *Macbeth* was apparently little developed. There is much less of conscience in his Richard than in the Richard of the *True Tragedie*, and much less in his John than in the John of the *Troublesome Raigne*. Yet it is certain that he knew the *Troublesome Raigne* and used it in writing *King John*.

In the *True Tragedie* Richard begins to suffer from his conscience immediately after the murder of the princes in the Tower. He finds that his goal is got and his golden crown won, but that a fearful shadow follows him and has summoned him "before the seuere judge." His conscience is witness of the blood he has spilt, and his crown is turned into "a fatall wreathe of fiery flames." He is terrified at the thought of fiends with ugly shapes in attendance upon him. Then comes the thought that he can repent:

> Nay what canst thou do to purge thee of thy guilt?
> Euen repent, craue mercie for thy damned fact,
> Appeale for mercy to thy righteous God.[67]

But he forces the thought away from him and vows that he will let those that list crave mercy of God. Still the fears raised by conscience will not down. Later his page describes his "great discomfort" of mind, his ghastly looks, his sighs and fearful cries, his starting up with his hand upon his dagger at the sound of anyone stirring in his chamber. All this fear is a just revenge sent from heaven:

> Those Peeres which he vnkindly murthered,
> Doth crie for iustice at the hands of God,
> And he in iustice sends continuall feare,
> For to afright him both at bed and boord.[68]

Just before his downfall, Richard muses upon "the hell of life" that hangs upon his crown, a hell made up of daily cares, nightly dreams, and horror at the thought of his bloody practice. This, says he,

> Strikes such a terror to my wounded conscience
> That sleepe I, wake I, or whatsoeuer I do,
> Meethinkes their ghoasts come gaping for reuenge,
> Whom I haue slaine in reaching for a Crowne.[69]

He names his victims and thinks that everyone cries, "Let the tyrant die." As he faces death he decides that he will at least die a king, though for keeping to his tyrant's course he must "make report among the damned soules." It is a question whether in Shakespeare's *Richard III* the ghosts who subject the protagonist to his one long-delayed attack of "coward conscience" on the eve of Bosworth Field are developed from those imagined in the *True Tragedie* as crying for revenge.

In much the same way that Richard in the *True Tragedie* begins to suffer from fear after he has had the princes murdered in the Tower, John in the *Troublesome Raigne* begins to suffer from fear after he has commanded that the young Prince Arthur, a threat to the security of his throne, should be blinded, and after he has been told that the prince has died under torture. At first John thinks that his cares have died with Arthur. But certain of his nobles let him know the strength of public opinion against him, and John, in fear that Arthur's death is something by which he may be pulled down, curses his crown and his making of the crown his care. He sees himself shunned as "a tragick Tyrant," a pitiless butcher:

> Art thou there villaine, Furies haunt thee still
> For killing him whom all the world laments.[70]

He is the more susceptible to such fear because the Prophet of Pomfret has foretold, not long before, that he will lose his crown. There is no change in John's tragic course when the news that Arthur is blinded and murdered turns out false. Arthur is soon dead in truth, having killed himself in leaping from the prison in which the king has placed him. John foolishly thinks that he has rid himself of the prince without incurring blame and hangs the prophet who has helped to terrify him. But suspicious nobles hold the king responsible for Arthur's death—as he is, indirectly. They rise against him and ally themselves with France. The power of the Church, which he has defied, is also brought against him. He loses his crown. He gets the crown back by yielding to the Church, but he falls into illness and despair as he continues to struggle against foes, and he meets his death by poison at the hands of a monk who still counts him an enemy of the Church. As John sickens and despairs, he cries that the world has wearied him and he it, but that "Death scorns so vilde a pray."[71] As he dies he goes over the catalogue of his sins:

> Me thinks the Deuill whispers in mine eares
> And tells me tis in vayne to hope for grace,
> I must be damnd for *Arthurs* sodaine death,
> I see I see a thousand thousand men
> Come to accuse me for my wrong on earth,
> And there is none so mercifull a God
> That will forgiue the number of my sinnes.
> How haue I liud, but by anothers losse?
> What haue I loud but wrack of others weale?[72]

Yet though his conscience paints his sins so blackly, he has hope enough to call upon God for mercy.

Thus we may see in Shakespeare's Macbeth a conscience-stricken tyrant of a kind well known not only in Renaissance books but also on the English stage. Macbeth comes to live in fear that he has given bloody instructions to his subjects and that these instructions will return to plague the inventor; he finds that he has murdered sleep; he learns that the murdered man can come back to terrify his murderer; he knows the loneliness of being without honor, love, obedience, troops of friends; and at last he falls into a despair in which life seems but a tale told by an idiot, signifying nothing. In all this he is a counterpart of the Richard of the *True Tragedie* and the John of the *Troublesome Raigne,* though he is given a greatness of spirit they do not have.

But between the conscience of Macbeth and the consciences of these two there is a difference that must not be overlooked. Because Richard and John both know well what religious repentance means, they are both driven by fear to review sins committed and to think of begging for the mercy of God. Richard puts the thought away from him, but John brings himself to act upon it. As for Macbeth, no religious thought of humbling his soul by repentance and finding forgiveness for his sins ever crosses his mind, and thus a recalcitrance in evil-doing is added to his ruthlessness. We know that the mature Shakespeare was capable of seeing a man who could commit murder to win a crown as one who could also bow stubborn knees to ask forgiveness, for he was capable of seeing the king in *Hamlet* as a limed soul struggling in prayer to be free. But he saw Macbeth as quite another sort of man.

It is not that the fear felt by Macbeth fails to compel repentance because it is in any way less powerful than the fear of Richard and John. Macbeth's fear is in all ways more powerful than theirs, and it has particular power in its imaginative reach. Shakespeare has even made it operate before the commission of crime as well as afterward. There is nothing in the *True Tragedie* and the *Troublesome Raigne* to correspond with the "horrid image" which comes to Macbeth's mind as the prophecy is spoken that he will be king, or with the vision of the air-drawn dagger dripping with blood which appears to him as he goes to murder Duncan.

By his conscience, as much as by anything else in his make-up, Macbeth arouses in us a mixture of feelings such as the heroes of Shakespeare's last tragic world are wont to arouse. His conscience is little if anything more than a self-centered fear and therefore it is a grossly imperfect sense of right and wrong. It has no power to make him see why his crimes are horrible, however much it shakes his single state of man, and no power to conquer his pride. Moreover, the terrors that afflict him as he goes from crime to crime have an aspect of being a villain's just retribution, and if we are not perverse they confirm in us an antipathy to the villain we see in him. Yet this conscience of Macbeth's is after all a peculiarly vivid, though limited, realization that evil is evil. We cannot fail to see that its imaginative power and the gift of expression seemingly given to him by that power lift the man into the rank of poets and seers.

v

Upon more than one occasion Macbeth is completely un-nerved by fear, and when we see him thus unnerved we may wonder whether there is not an element of cowardice in him and whether this does not make it impossible to think of him as a noble spirit. Before and after the murder of Duncan, Lady Macbeth chastises her husband with her tongue for what she believes to be his lack of courage. But Macbeth has true courage, despite the fact that it is a vulnerable courage, and in desperation he can always screw it to the sticking place, even when he no longer draws support from his wife. His courage, as well as his conscience, gives him a paradoxical nobility. It can fail ignominiously, but thereby it has opportunity to prove its essential strength.

At the beginning of the play, Macbeth is introduced as valor's minion and Bellona's bridegroom, and on the field of battle fighting for Duncan he well deserves the name of brave. After he has told Lady Macbeth that he will not murder Duncan, she charges him with cowardice, with letting "I dare not" wait upon "I would." He defends himself by stating a truth: fear is dishonorable except when it is a fear of being dishonorable, for who dares do more than may become a man is no man. But after being urged by his wife, he dares do more than may become a man, and from that time onward he must be judged according to the quality of his new daring. Thereafter, his shrinking from a criminal course of action which he never truly wishes to abandon has an aspect of cowardly irresolution and therefore of baseness, no matter how much it is a shrinking from evil and dishonor. Nevertheless, when we see him continue his criminal course despite his failures of nerve, we are bound to remember the soldier's daring which Shakespeare has made part of his nature, and thus we come to understand that there is a reservoir of strength upon which Macbeth calls in order to restore his criminal resolution.

Macbeth's most degrading failure in resolution comes immediately after the murder of Duncan. Lady Macbeth persuades him to catch the nearest way to kingship, and he bends up each corporal agent to perform the murderous act. It says much about his character that the argument of Lady

Macbeth which finally does persuade him has nothing to do with what might become a man, but is concerned with feasibility. In answer to his question, "If we should fail?" she tosses aside the possibility of failure and shows him how to commit the murder and make innocent men suffer the blame for it. He thoroughly understands the need she presents for making Duncan's two chamberlains seem guilty. Because he so thoroughly understands this need, it must be granted that he shows an infirmity of purpose entirely worthy of her scorn when he not only fails to leave the daggers of the grooms by the dead king, but, completely mastered by fear, refuses to go back to the murder chamber and complete his work:

> I'll go no more:
> I am afraid to think what I have done;
> Look on't again I dare not.
>
> (II, ii, 51–53)

To do Macbeth justice, he has no means of knowing, before the murder, how far his conscience will surround that deed with horror. He misjudges the power of his conscience and that of his resolution. By constitution he is peculiarly unfitted to be a self-possessed murderer. But the hard fact remains that he is ignominious as he leaves it to his wife to take the daggers back into the murder chamber. On the other hand, to do Lady Macbeth justice, though she scorns her husband for having a mind and soul disordered by fear when he comes from the chamber, she gives him full credit for being no ordinary coward by saying, "You do unbend your noble strength." She reminds us that a noble strength is in him though for the moment it is like an unstrung bow and ignobly useless.

The quality of Macbeth's recovery from the breakdown after the murder of Duncan is indicated by his ability to form a plot for the assassination of Banquo and Fleance without the spiritual support of Lady Macbeth. He does not even tell her the details of the plot, but only says to her that she will applaud what it will achieve. He gets underlings to set about the actual bloodshed. Though he makes a trial of Machiavellian subtlety when he persuades them that Banquo has wronged them, he is not at all by nature a Machiavellian villain. He has committed his first murder by direct action. This putting of his own hands into blood has produced for him more horror than he could stand, and it remains for him to see whether murder can be done through the agency of others without the production of horror.

The murder of Banquo brings Macbeth a new experience of fear: it brings the ghost of Banquo to haunt him. This visitation comes not only because Macbeth is guilty of Banquo's death, but also because in the rashness of his renewed confidence he actually challenges Banquo to appear and prove him guilty. Each time that Banquo comes as a ghost to sit at Macbeth's banquet table, he does so just as Macbeth is about to express a hypocritical desire for his presence; it is as though a thought summons Banquo as it is on its way to become words. Macbeth, of course, does not intend the challenge, but nevertheless gives it by his hypocritical effrontery. The challenge to Banquo is also a challenge to the divine power, which, as Shakespeare's age firmly believed, could work justice upon murderers by supernatural means.[73]

Some have believed that the ghost of Banquo, seen as it is by no one on the stage but Macbeth, is a figment of Macbeth's imagination like the air-drawn dagger. But ghost lore has always allowed that ghosts might appear to one person and not to others in a company. That Shakespeare's audience when it saw the ghost of Banquo represented by an actor took it to be a real ghost, and that Shakespeare intended his audience to do so, seems certain. Before and after his first murder, Macbeth is subjected to fear by forces within himself. After his second murder, he is subjected to fear by forces both within himself and without. After this murder, his conscience obtains supernatural support for the work which it does through his imagination.

As Macbeth is put to the test by the ghost of Banquo, we realize that between his first and second crimes he has grown greatly in criminal fortitude and that now, having recovered from one severe breakdown in courage, he meets another by drawing upon his underlying strength much more quickly than before. We have seen him, after the murder of Duncan, ignominiously mastered by fear and remaining so to the end of a scene. We now see him ignominiously mastered by fear at first, then able to outface fear, and finally restored in resolution, all in one scene.

When Macbeth first sees Banquo's ghost, he is so much overcome that he seems like a guilty schoolboy cringing before an accuser and twisting the truth to escape punishment. For a moment he is so completely unmanned that he can plead with the specter:

> Thou canst not say I did it: never shake
> Thy gory locks at me.
>
> (III, v, 50–51)

He has only procured the murder; he has not done it! This is one of the points at which Shakespeare risks complete destruction of sympathy for his hero. We can easily forgive Macbeth for being terrified at a supernatural visitation of punishment upon him, but we cannot easily forgive him for writhing under it despicably.

Even while the ghost is making its first appearance, Macbeth begins to show a desperate courage, and just before it leaves he reaches the point of saying, "Why, what care I?" and of daring it to speak, since it can nod. At its reëntrance he cries, "Avaunt, and quit my sight!" and begins at once to exorcise it by outfacing it. He throws at it the accusation that it does not have reality because it does not have marrow-filled bones, warm blood, and intelligently seeing eyes. He challenges it to be alive again and let him prove with the sword that he has daring proper to a man. He completes the exorcism by commanding this "horrible shadow," this "unreal mockery," to go hence—and the ghost leaves.

Though Lady Macbeth tries to convince Macbeth that the ghost is created by his imagination, he is obviously not persuaded that he has merely looked upon an empty stool at the banquet table, and because he is not so persuaded we must give him all the greater credit for recovery of courage. In his exorcism he makes much of the ghost's lack of flesh-and-blood reality, but the specter is to him a "shadow" and a "mockery" only in the sense that it is the shade of Banquo and is thus unable to take arms and meet an opponent in combat, not in the sense that it has no reality whatever. Soon after the ghost has made its final exit, he speaks of it to Lady Macbeth in a way which shows his assumption that it has supernatural reality. He says, "It will have blood, they say," and goes on to mention the supernatural hounding of murderers by such other means as stones that move and trees that speak. He accepts the ghost as a conclusive sign that forces more terrible than any found in nature are arrayed against him. Yet he comes immediately to a decision that he will not retreat but will press onward through blood.

The ghost scene is crucial for an actor who takes the part of Macbeth. It is said that Garrick at first conceived Macbeth in this scene as "utterly oppressed, and overcome by the sense of his guilt," and that then, because a critic argued convincingly that Macbeth was not a coward, he changed his conception. Later, in answer to another critic, who apparently thought that Macbeth *was* a coward, Garrick wrote that, in his view, to let Macbeth "sink into pusillanimity" in the ghost scene "would hurt the character and be contrary to the intentions of Shakespeare," for in truth Macbeth shows rising strength as the scene proceeds. "The first appearance of the spirit overpowers him more than the second; but even before it vanishes at first, Macbeth gains strength—'If thou canst nod, speak too,' must be spoke with horror but with a recovering mind; and in the next speech with him he cannot pronounce 'Avaunt and quit my sight!' without a *stronger exertion* of his powers."[74] The difficulty for the actor is that much of the paradox of Macbeth's character is in this scene packed within the compass of a few lines. As those lines are spoken, sympathy should first be taken away from Macbeth and then restored. The restoration should even raise him in the esteem of the audience to a position higher than that held before the taking away, and yet, when all is said and done, he must remain Macbeth the villain.

His next murderous act Macbeth performs not only without needing support from Lady Macbeth in the planning of it, but also without being haunted by it afterward. Neither images and voices created by his imagination nor the ghosts of the newly slain subject him to a test after he has given the wife, children, and servants of Macduff to the sword. He has put his fear to the hard use that was wanting when he was a novice in murder and has almost quelled his conscience, though at the cost of making life seem to him a tale told by an idiot. The supreme effort he has made to outface fear in the ghost scene has brought him to a point where his senses no longer cool to hear a night-shriek and his fell of hair no longer rouses and stirs at a dismal treatise.

Once more before the end, however, he is ignominiously unnerved by fear. He, Bellona's bridegroom, is forced to suffer the peculiar degradation of being unnerved on the field of battle. As he prepares to meet Malcolm's army he vows to fight until the flesh is hacked from his bones and promises himself that he will not taint with fear till Birnam Wood comes to Dunsinane. When he is told that Birnam Wood is indeed coming to Dunsinane, he begins to know that this battle is to be like no other he has ever fought. But though he then pulls in resolution, he does not yet allow it to fail him; at least he will die with harness on his back. Finally comes the encounter with Macduff. The revelation that Macduff is not of woman born strips him of manhood. "I'll not fight with thee!" he cries, and draws down on himself for the last time the accusation of cowardice. His shedding of blood has at last raised a nemesis who can do what he has challenged the shade of Banquo to do, a nemesis who can dare him to the desert with a sword, and as he stands trembling before it he must be protested the baby of a girl, despite his former confidence that if he should ever encounter such a nemesis he could never be thus disgraced. It is only for a moment that we see him so. His next words are, "I will not yield." He defies destiny and goes to his death in a burst of valiant fury.

Lady Macbeth has profound love for her husband, but it is never capable of leading her to a true understanding of his character. She, whose conscience works by other means than the excitation of fear, when it is finally aroused, never knows what her husband has to face in order to pursue his murderous course, and thus she never knows the depth of his strength.

Macbeth has profound love for his wife, and it is a truly understanding love. It leads him to praise in her that which should make her bring forth men children only, keeps him from feeling resentment when she calls him coward, and makes him regard her as his "dearest partner in greatness." Does it help him to perceive a temporary breaking of her spirit when she faints as he describes the murdered Duncan, and does it therefore lead him to keep her ignorant of the plot for the assassination of Banquo and Fleance ("Be innocent of the knowledge, dearest chuck") in order to spare her? We may think so if we think that her fainting is not pretended. The way he greets the news of her death is certainly not to be taken as coming from any shallowness, but from absolute weariness of soul.

VI

Macbeth is darkly oppressive in its display of evil. For the hero himself life comes to seem meaningless, a procession of fools marching toward dusty death. His "tomorrow and tomorrow" speech gives emphasis to the oppressive quality of the tragedy and leaves a heavy mark upon us, no matter how firmly we force ourselves to realize that in this rejection of life Macbeth is not Shakespeare, but a character of Shakespeare's, made to talk for himself with complete dramatic appropriateness.

Yet *Macbeth* is not the darkest of Shakespeare's tragedies. If the chronology of *Timon, Macbeth, Antony and Cleopatra,* and *Coriolanus* is as I have taken it to be, then as Shakespeare settled into the presentation of his last tragic world his tragic mood lightened. It lightened in some degree between the writing of *Timon* and the writing of *Macbeth,* and in a much greater degree between the writing of *Macbeth* and the writing of *Antony and Cleopatra* and *Coriolanus.* It was most somber during the writing of *Lear* and *Timon.* If *Timon* is the "still-born twin of *Lear,*"[75] as it seems to be, and if *Lear* and *Timon* were written before *Macbeth,* as they seem to have been, then *Macbeth* is the last of those plays which provide any acceptable basis for a theory that Shakespeare passed through a time of severe emotional strain in the opening years of the seventeenth century. By some who hold this theory *Macbeth* is interpreted as showing a relaxation of strain for Shakespeare and a promise of recovered equanimity.

When Dowden characterizes by the phrase "Out of the depths" the period of Shakespeare's career extending from about 1600 to about 1608, the period of the bitter comedies and the great tragedies, he sees it as one in which Shakespeare knew sorrow and reflected his sorrow in his plays. It seems to him that in this period Shakespeare "needed to sound, with his imagination, the depths of the human heart; to inquire into the darkest and saddest parts of human life; to study the great mystery of evil." The next and last period, the period of the dramatic romances, Dowden calls "On the heights," and thinks of as one in which Shakespeare looked "down upon life, its joys, its griefs, its errors" with grave, almost pitiful, tenderness because, having "learned the secret of life," he had "ascended out of the turmoil and trouble of action, out of the darkness and tragic mystery, the places haunted by terror and crime, and by love contending with these, to a pure and serene elevation."[76]

Since Dowden's time much has been written about a surmised "unhappy period" in Shakespeare's life, but *Macbeth* has not tended to be one of the tragedies offered as showing Shakespeare at his unhappiest. Bradley does not put *Macbeth* among those tragedies which, as he thinks, "show the pressure of painful feelings."[77] Placing *Macbeth, Antony and Cleopatra,* and *Coriolanus* after *Timon,* he finds that signs of this pressure end with *Timon* and notices particularly that from *Hamlet* to *Timon* the subject of lechery and corruption, with an undercurrent of disgust, is constantly put before us in one shape or another, whereas this is not so after *Timon*.[78] Professor J. Dover Wilson also finds that *Macbeth* shows Shakespeare as having passed his crisis of spiritual perturbation. He agrees with Sir Edmund Chambers in thinking that the crisis came with *Timon* and that it was extremely serious, but disagrees with him in placing *Timon* just before *Macbeth* instead of last among Shakespeare's tragedies. He says: "Shakespeare came very near to madness in *Lear*. How near may be seen in *Timon of Athens,* which Sir Edmund Chambers, while striving to prove himself the most objective and cautious of critics, has suggested must have been written 'under conditions of mental and perhaps physical stress, which led to a break-down.' Yet he pushed forward, for in *Macbeth,* the next play, we feel somehow, terrible as the atmosphere still is, that Shakespeare is himself not so deeply involved."[79]

That there was a time when Shakespeare was preoccupied with dramatic presentation of the darker aspects of life, and that this preoccupation reached its height in certain of his tragedies, is plain enough. There was indeed a time when he drew material out of the depths of human experience. He may or may not have been impelled to do so by sorrows of his own. Men do not have to suffer sorrow to see life as tragedy, and when they do see it as tragedy, they do not have to suffer extreme sorrow to see it as dark tragedy. This is especially true of men who have the genius to embrace with sympathy and understanding, and to absorb as reality, a large body of human experience that is not their own. Genius of that kind we know Shakespeare to have had in the highest degree.

Taking *Hamlet, Othello, King Lear, Timon,* and *Macbeth* as Shakespeare's dark tragedies, we may see most clearly the relation of *Macbeth* to the other four if we consider how each one of the group presents certain aspects of mortal life dwelt upon by medieval contempt of the world. The Middle Ages said much about the imperfection of the world. They tended to contemplate that imperfection with disgust, but not to be shocked by it. In the main they saw lack of justice, lack of order in general, transitoriness, corruption, the final indignity of death, and the human suffering caused by all these as quite natural in this life. Faith that there was justice in a spiritual life to come tended to keep them from brooding over the world's shortcomings, no matter how much they might dwell upon its horrors. They found that to dwell upon the horrors was a means of making them innocuous because it was a means of breaking the hold of the world upon man's heart and turning his desire toward heaven's perfection. Shakespeare's dark tragedies say much that is reminiscent of medieval contempt of the world, but they often say it in a spirit that is not medieval.

As the Renaissance proceeded with its discovery of intrinsic worth in mundane life, it fostered in many men the thought that the world should be more perfect and the hope that it could be more perfect. In having this thought and this hope, men laid themselves open to the danger of disillusionment, and when disillusionment came, it frequently found expression—especially in the late Renaissance—in terms of medieval contempt of the world altered to suit a new spirit. At such times the grave and all things leading to the grave wore an aspect they had not possessed when faith had fixed man's hope and desire upon the next world. "Do we affect fashion in the grave?" asks the Duchess in Webster's *Duchess of Malfi*. "Most ambitiously," answers Bosola; for, as he goes on to say with wistful bitterness, the medieval fashion of showing hopeful desire for heaven is now no longer followed, and in accordance with a new fashion of funerary sculpture,

> Princes images on their tombes
> Do not lie, as they were wont, seeming to pray
> Up to heaven: but with their hands under their cheekes,
> (As if they died of the tooth-ache)—they are not carved
> With their eies fix'd upon the starres; but as
> Their mindes were wholy bent upon the world,
> The selfe-same way they seeme to turne their faces.[80]

The dark tragedies of Shakespeare may not show him as a man disillusioned by his experiences, but they certainly show him as one deeply concerned with questions that would never have been raised if the Renaissance had never been disillusioned by the world, in other words, if the Renaissance had not upon occasion lost its guiding faith in the world and turned to despair of the world.

In *Hamlet* the world seems to its hero a prison where he is locked up behind the walls of mortality and faced with the necessity of solving problems to which mortality provides no answers. He cannot be a Stoic and commit suicide, however attractive suicide may seem to him, because he recognizes "God's canon 'gainst self-slaughter" and feels that it must be respected. He cannot be a medieval Christian and leap the boundaries of the world by taking into consideration an eternal destiny for man, because he has too much of the modern skepticism toward what will happen after death. A part of the medieval faith he has, but another part he lacks.

All the problems of mortal life tend, for Hamlet, to merge into one great problem of justice. He is faced with the duty of taking vengeance and thus obtaining justice for a father murdered; but he is peculiarly ill suited to do what is demanded of him, and thus there is injustice in the very fate that assigns him the duty of obtaining justice. The medieval thinker rose above the lack of justice found in the world, but Hamlet, the Renaissance thinker, is shocked by it and broods over it. Early in the play he goes to the heart of a problem that is particularly his. Human beings should not be held responsible for the faults they are born with, and yet certain men suffer general censure "for some vicious mole of nature in them." Even though their virtues may be pure as grace, the stamp of one defect which is merely nature's livery or fortune's star can ruin them.

This is a clear statement of a question often implied in Shakespeare's presentation of his middle tragic world—a world which shows the imperfect heroic in man rather than the heroic imperfect, a world in which the flaw of the hero tends to be out of keeping with his nobility rather than paradoxically a part of his nobility. The question, in its simplest terms, is why the powers over us should be so disorderly and unjust as to mingle in a man some little but powerful part of bad with many parts of the greatest good and allow the bad to outweigh all else and bring him to catastrophe.

Among the whips and scorns of time in an unjust world Hamlet finds:

> The oppressor's wrong, the proud man's contumely,
> The pangs of dispriz'd love, the law's delay,
> The insolence of office, and the spurns
> That patient merit of the unworthy takes.
>
> (III, i, 71–74)

By example his mother teaches him that vows may be "as false as dicers' oaths," and his uncle that a man "may smile, and smile, and be a villain." To cap all, he finds the injustice of death. Contemplation of death in the manner of medieval contempt of the world cannot for him remove its sting, for he regards death as an offensive negation of man's aspiration in this world, if not an insult to it. Man, the paragon of animals, noble in reason, infinite in faculty, in action like an angel, in apprehension like a god, is after all nothing but "quintessence of dust," and the "fine revolution" of man's greatness that produces loam to stop a beer barrel, or bones to be knocked about by a sexton's spade, makes Hamlet's bones "ache to think on 't." Hamlet is like Webster and Donne in his knowledge of what Mr. T. S. Eliot calls "the anguish of the marrow" and "the ague of the skeleton."

In *Othello* the problem of the world's injustice becomes even more urgent, and the manifestations of that injustice even more painful. But the hero does not ponder on the imperfections of the world as his tragedy develops, for until the action of the play is almost finished he is completely deceived by Iago and all that Iago represents. Hamlet knows early that a man "may smile, and smile, and be a villain," whereas Othello knows late that a man may seem "of exceeding honesty," or indeed "full of love and honesty," and be a villain. One of the ironies of Othello's tragedy is that he does injustice while thinking that he is doing justice. He kills Desdemona because, like Hamlet, he believes that to be honorable he must take private vengeance for a wrong done. While he still is convinced that Desdemona has been guilty, he says of his act:

> O! I were damn'd beneath all depth in hell
> But that I did proceed upon just grounds
> To this extremity.
> (V, ii, 135–137)

And after he knows that Desdemona has been innocent, he calls himself in bitter desperation "an honourable murderer":

> For nought I did in hate, but all in honour.
> (V, ii, 294)

In the death of the innocent Desdemona we witness a miscarriage of justice much more painful to contemplate than the death of the innocent Ophelia, and it is partly because of this miscarriage of justice that *Othello* has been found by many to be a peculiarly intolerable tragedy.

But in *Lear* the world produces still greater refinements of injustice than those in *Othello,* and becomes so much more evil than Hamlet's prison that it can be called a torture chamber. Lear finally comes to think that a prison in which he could have Cordelia beside him, and in which they together could take upon them "the mystery of things," would be a blessed relief from the world he has known. Says Kent as Lear dies:

> O! let him pass; he hates him
> That would upon the rack of this tough world
> Stretch him out longer.
> (V, iii, 315–317)

Both Lear and Gloucester are stretched upon the mundane rack and subjected to a cruelty more terrible than that to which Othello is subjected by Iago, for this cruelty springs from a filial ingratitude leading the child that justly should love and protect its father to hate and torment him. The death of the innocent Cordelia is painful to contemplate, not only because it violates justice, but also because it happens after valid hope has been aroused that it might be averted. In *Lear* the world is not merely imperfect; it is becoming more and more imperfect. A virus of corruption it at work upon it, turning human beings into animals and devils. Hamlet broods over the world's imperfection, but Lear curses its depravity.

We have already found that when we turn to *Timon* and enter Shakespeare's last tragic world, we once more encounter, in this companion piece to *Lear,* gross ingratitude that degrades man and general depravity that brings forth curses from the hero. But the depravity here is less dynamically evil than that shown in *Lear,* though it is thoroughly repulsive, and in Timon's Athens there is no Desdemona or Cordelia to suffer from injustice. *Lear* and *Timon* are Shakespeare's darkest tragedies, but between the writing of *Lear* and the writing of *Timon* the problem of mundane injustice loses some of its importance for Shakespeare. Timon is as wrongfully treated as Lear by ungrateful associates, and yet, because he is a deeply flawed hero like other heroes in Shakespeare's last tragic world and does so much to help in the bringing about of his catastrophe, his tragedy has an aspect of justice more pronounced than that of Lear's. There is never any doubt that Lear's tragedy offers a dominant aspect of injustice. Timon's tragedy shows its aspects of justice and injustice so confusingly that one may find it hard to tell which is meant to be dominant.

In the writing of *Macbeth,* Shakespeare reaches a point where interest in a deeply flawed hero who fully deserves a tragic fall pushes the problem of mundane injustice well into the background. This is the chief reason why *Macbeth* is not one of his darkest tragedies, despite the pall of evil that hangs over its scenes. In *Macbeth* injustice is suffered by virtue in the person of Duncan, whom Macduff calls "a most sainted king," and by innocence in more than one person, but the fall of the hero is brought about so largely by retribution that so far as he is concerned the action is a demonstration of the manner in which the mills of justice can grind exceeding small. It is essential to realize that Macbeth is far from being a mere plaything of fate, suffering injustice because he is compelled by decree to do evil and suffer the consequences. The witches, as we have found, are demons who have some power to read the future and use that power to tempt a susceptible man, but who never even imply that Macbeth will by necessity do evil.

There is no spreading corruption in Macbeth's Scotland like that in Lear's Britain and Timon's Athens, though there are cankers growing in Macbeth and Lady Macbeth. To Scotland in general the tyrannical rule of Macbeth brings sickness, but this is something forced upon the realm by the cramping and suffocating power of Macbeth, not something due to intrinsic lack of soundness in the realm. Malcolm, as the conqueror of Macbeth and the restorer of just government, is the "medicine of the sickly weal."

Chapter IV

"ANTONY AND CLEOPATRA"

Technically the protagonist of *Antony and Cleopatra* is Antony, but one finds it difficult to think of Cleopatra as the less important tragic figure of the play, and one finds it impossible, even if one is proof against her spell, to give less attention to her than to her "man of men." Both Antony and Cleopatra are finished studies in paradoxical nobility, and the title of their tragedy, pairing their names as it does, is appropriate. Lady Macbeth, by attraction and repulsion exerted together, arouses in us a mixture of emotions somewhat comparable to that which her husband arouses, but her tragic paradox is definitely subsidiary to his. For a time she shares the center of the stage with him. Later she is withdrawn from this position, and her death has representation only in a cry of women offstage. Cleopatra, on the other hand, is given so much of the stage that as long as Antony is alive she shares the center of it with him, and then, when he is dead, makes the center all her own. It may be said that the last act of *Antony and Cleopatra* belongs to Cleopatra, and that in this last act she does not neglect any of her opportunities to improve her position in the drama.

As he wrote *Antony and Cleopatra,* Shakespeare kept Plutarch's *Lives* open before him. The paradox of Antony he found there in a well-developed form that he was willing to accept with minor changes, and the paradox of Cleopatra in a limited form that he felt called upon to expand and make over. Other literary characterizations of Antony and Cleopatra besides Plutarch's were easily available to him. That he paid Samuel Daniel the compliment of putting to use his *Cleopatra* is pretty clear, though it has been doubted, and I will later take account of the indications that as Shakespeare built his play upon Plutarch he had in the back of his mind not only this Senecan tragedy of Daniel's but also Daniel's *Letter from Octavia to Marcus Antonius*. Some of these indications, I believe, have been overlooked. It may be that Shakespeare also knew the Countess of Pembroke's *Antonius,* the translation of Robert Garnier's Senecan tragedy *Marc Antoine* which had inspired Daniel to write his *Cleopatra.*

Because Plutarch is a thoroughgoing moralist, he sees much in Antony and Cleopatra to condemn, and yet in his analysis of their characters he strives honestly to be balanced and fair according to his lights. That analysis needs to be extracted from its narrative context to be fully appreciated. As it came to Shakespeare in North's translation of the life of Antony it was essentially as follows.[1]

Antony as a young man fell under an influence which "trayned him on into great follies, and vaine expences vpon women, in rioting & banketing." In Greece he came to use a manner of speech called Asiatic, which "was much like to his manners and life: for it was full of ostentation, foolishe brauerie, and vaine ambition." But as a military leader he proved to have many real virtues. He could show magnanimity and he had a desire to win honor. After the capture of Pelusium, Ptolemy, because of the malice he bore

---

[1] For notes to chapter iv see pages 274–276.

the city, wanted to put all the Egyptians in it to the sword, but Antony "withstoode him, & by no meanes would suffer him to doe it." In battles and skirmishes Antony "did many noble actes of a valliant and wise Captain." He "had a noble presence, and shewed a countenaunce of one of a noble house." He won much love among his soldiers by "things that seeme intollerable in other men, as to boast commonly, to ieast with one or other, to drinke like a good-fellow with euerybody, to sit with the souldiers when they dine, and to eate and drinke with them souldierlike." More-over, "being giuen to loue: that made him the more desired, and by that meanes he brought many to loue him." Because he had great liberality, he "gaue all to the souldiers, and kept nothing for him selfe."

And so, "when he was growen to great credit, then was his authoritie and power also very great, the which notwith-standing him selfe did ouerthrowe, by a thousand other faults he had." Even while he won the love of his soldiers, "he purchased diuers other mens euill willes, bicause that through negligence he would not doe them iustice that were iniuried, & delt very churlishly with them that had any sute vnto him: and besides all this, he had an ill name to intise mens wiues." He was gross in his drinking and in his association with common harlots. He was, in every sense of the word, "dissolute." He could show "himselfe (to his great shame and infamie) a cruell man." He was "a plaine man, without suttletie," and thus, though he desired to punish offenders and reward well-doers, his officers often committed robberies by his authority because "he ouer-simply trusted his men in all things." The love of Cleopatra was for him "the last and extreamest mischiefe of all other," for she "did waken and stirre vp many vices yet hidden in him." In short, "if any sparke of goodnesse or hope of rising were left in him, *Cleopatra* quenched it straight, and made it worse than before."

Cleopatra had beauty and "excellent grace and sweetnesse" of tongue. She met Antony and captured his heart "at the age when a womans beawtie is at the prime," and at an age when she was "of best iudgement." As an experienced charmer and enchanter of men she was confident of winning Antony because of "the former accesse and credit she had with *Iulius Cæsar,* and *Cneus Pompey* (the sonne of *Pompey* the great) only for her beawtie." Yet her beauty was not her chief weapon, for it was not so passing great as to be "vnmatchable of other women." Of more power than her beauty were her company and conversation; these were "so sweete . . . that a man could not possiblie but be taken." She was a fluent speaker of many languages, and her tongue was "an instrument of musicke." She was able to please and flatter Antony in an infinity of ways, and she even diced, drank, hunted, and jested with him, but she could make him admire her magnificence and fineness of taste in worldly display as well as captivate him by joining in his lowest pleasures. Thus she completely overcame him "with the sweete poyson of her loue" and reduced him to such a state that he came to have an "effeminate mind."

When Antony was preparing for the decisive battle with Octavius, she had made him so subject to her will "that though he was a greate deale the stronger by land, yet for *Cleopatraes* sake, he would needes haue this battell tryed by sea." She was utterly selfish in forcing him to this plan of battle, "considering with her selfe how she might flie, & prouide for her safetie, not to helpe him winne the victory, but to flie more easily after the battel lost." When Antony deserted his forces and followed her ship as she fled from the Battle of Actium, he "shewed plainely, that he had not only lost the corage and hart of an Emperor, but also of a valliant man." After Actium, Cleopatra made experiments to find "poysons which made men dye with least paine." When she and Antony begged clemency from Octavius, Octavius was deaf to Antony but tempted Cleopatra by telling her "that he woulde deny her nothing reasonable, so that she would either put *Antonius* to death, or driue him out of her contrie." Antony had doubts of her loyalty to him: first when she received Octavius' messenger Thyreus and "did him great honor," so much honor, in fact, that in jealousy Antony had him whipped and sent back to Octavius; again when the city of Pelusium was rumored to have been surrendered to Octavius by Cleopatra's consent; and yet again when the ships still left to Antony rowed out toward the enemy ships and instead of offering battle joined with them, apparently by prearrangement, at the same time that his forces on land failed him. (Plutarch does not pretend to know whether Cleopatra ever did entertain thoughts of betraying Antony. Much as he disapproves of her, he seems to give her on this point the benefit of the doubt.)

Antony killed himself because Cleopatra, "affraied of his fury" after his ships had yielded to those of Octavius, ordered that he be told she was dead. He thought that she had killed herself and he wanted to show no less of "corage and noble minde" than he thought she had shown. Also, he wanted to join her in death. After he had given himself a mortal wound and had been carried to the monument in which Cleopatra had taken refuge, she showed great grief "and called him her Lord, her husband, and Emperour, forgetting her owne miserie and calamity, for the pitie and compassion she tooke of him." He died thinking unselfishly of her future, for "he earnestly prayed her, and perswaded her, that she would seeke to saue her life, if she could possible, without reproache and dishonor."

Cleopatra killed herself for reasons that are much less clear. Octavius had a great desire "to get *Cleopatra* aliue, fearing least otherwise all the treasure would be lost: and furthermore, he thought that if he could take *Cleopatra,* and bring her aliue to ROME, she would maruelously beawtifie and sette out his triumphe." He sought to make her think that he would treat her with kind consideration. But she would not yield herself. She was taken after entrance to her monument had been gained by trickery. As she was taken she offered to kill herself with a dagger and had to be disarmed. She buried Antony sumptuously, was "altogether ouercome with sorow & passion of minde," tore her flesh and "martired" it, fell into a fever, and made up her mind "to absteine from meate" and die. Octavius, guessing her intent, "threatned to put her children to shameful death," and "Cleopatra for feare yelded straight, as she would haue yelded vnto strokes: and afterwards suffred her selfe to be cured and dieted as they listed." At an interview with Octavius during which it appeared that she was trying to hide from him some of her money and treasure she acted "as though she were affrayed to dye & desirous to liue."

What finally determined her to die was apparently the news given her by Dolabella that Octavius was to leave Alexandria "& that within three days he would send her away before with her children." She offered last oblations at the tomb of Antony, addressing him as "my deare Lord Antonius" and speaking, in her farewell to him, of those who guarded and kept her alive "onely to triumphe of thee." (From this speech, and from some of her actions as reported by Plutarch, it is possible to gain the impression that Cleopatra brooded over the possibility of being shamefully led in triumph through the streets of Rome. She did not resolve to kill herself until she was sure that she was to be taken away from Alexandria. Was a desire to avoid personal disgrace at Rome the primary reason, perhaps even the whole reason, for her decision to die, despite whatever she said and did that indicated profound grief for the loss of Antony? If so, why does Plutarch not say something definite about such a desire? He dwells upon her expressions of grief.) Cleopatra wrote to Octavius, requesting "that he would let her be buried with *Antonius*," and soon thereafter she died suddenly by self-administered poison; some said it was by the bite of an asp which she applied to her arm. Octavius gave her credit for showing admirable qualities by her suicide, for "though he was maruelous sorie for the death of *Cleopatra*, yet he wondred at her noble minde and corage, and therefore commaunded she should be nobly buried, and layed by Antonius."

Thus the paradox of Antony is much more complete than that of Cleopatra, as Plutarch reads their characters. Plutarch presents Antony as having exhibited a baffling conglomeration of good and bad qualities all through his career, and in his analysis of him he obviously takes care to show that the good qualities at times even made one with the bad. He demonstrates that Antony constantly showed nobility but that his nobility frequently had curiously ignoble aspects, as when his noble presence became a foolishly ostentatious presence, his liberality became negligence of justice, and his loving nature became a grossly sensual nature. It was typical of Antony therefore that he should win the love and respect of his soldiers by undignified acts that seemed intolerable in other men. It was also typical of him that his suicide should be both praiseworthy and unpraiseworthy. In the comparison of Demetrius and Antony following the life of Antony, Plutarch grants that Antony is to be given credit for bringing himself to the point of ending his life in time to keep his enemy from having power over his person, but he says that the manner of his death was cowardly, pitiful, and ignoble. Doubtless Plutarch is thinking of the fact that Antony did not steel himself to end his life until he thought that Cleopatra had ended hers, and of the fact that he used his sword so clumsily when he did turn it against himself that he died a lingering death.

Plutarch presents Cleopatra, on the other hand, as having shown a character basically composed of bad qualities until some time after the Battle of Actium. Beauty she certainly had when she cast a spell over Antony, and charm even more certainly, but the moral Plutarch is not the man to lose his head over beauty and charm. He never lets one think that before Antony lost the world Cleopatra was anything other than a calculating queenly strumpet, vitally alluring though she might be and completely able to subjugate lovers. Apparently she had gained "accesse and credit" with Julius Caesar and Cneus Pompey without the embarrassment of having to mix anything that could be called love for them with her selfish emotions. She won Antony and sailed with him into battle at Actium without, so far as Plutarch lets us know, entangling herself in any feeling of love for him, even the smallest. Indeed, Plutarch says in downright fashion that in a selfish spirit only, with every thought for her own safety and none for Antony's success, she planned the battle and forced Antony to accept her plan. It was ironic, then, though Plutarch does not underline the irony, that this designing queen who had traded herself to one Roman after another, apparently with thoughts only for her position in the world that Rome ruled, should have developed what appeared to be love for Antony after Antony had lost all power in that world.

Did Cleopatra really rise to a true love for Antony when she drew toward the end of her life? Plutarch leaves it to the reader to answer that question, though he encourages him to answer that she did. The reader must remember that she could make Antony think of her as basely disloyal even on the day of his death and could at least give the appearance of bringing about her own death for fear of a Roman triumph, rather than for love of Antony. The reader must balance these considerations against her moving expressions of grief for the loss of Antony.

After Actium, Plutarch's Cleopatra is found to have a certain ill-defined amount of paradoxical nobility. Before Actium her character is subtle but has nothing in it of baffling inconsistency. It is subtly bad, not subtly good and bad. After Actium it is plainly not incapable of being good and bad both at once—of being both unselfish and selfish, both courageous and cowardly,—but Plutarch refuses to analyze the later character of Cleopatra into good and bad qualities and thus treat her paradox as he treats the paradox of Antony. When we consider the way Plutarch handles Cleopatra's death, we may justifiably think that he should have allowed himself to comment upon a change in her character. He goes so far as to declare that after her death Octavius "wondred at her noble minde and corage," but he does not declare that he himself wonders at them. Yet he manages to make it clear that he, a censorious moralist, has fallen somewhat under the spell of Cleopatra before he finishes her story and that he is much more kindly disposed toward her at the end than at the beginning.

As we shall see, Shakespeare departs from Plutarch by making Cleopatra thoroughly paradoxical. He makes her paradoxical both before and after Actium. He is more kind than Plutarch to the earlier Cleopatra and less kind to the later. But he makes her rise to grandeur in death even more surely than Plutarch does.

II

In 1592 the Countess of Pembroke, lending her very considerable influence to the support of religious, moral, and literary standards that had been upheld by her brother Sir

Philip Sidney, published a volume containing two translations: the *Discourse of Life and Death Written in French
by Ph. Mornay* and *Antonius, A Tragedie written also in
French by Ro. Garnier.* Her *Antonius* is a competent rendering of Garnier's *Marc Antoine* (1578), one of the better
Senecan tragedies of the sixteenth century, but it is in no
way an inspired rendering. It did not, by its example,
change the character of popular tragedy being written for
the Elizabethan public stage, as the countess and her coterie
no doubt hoped it might. Nevertheless, it brought Antony
and Cleopatra into English drama and has its importance
in the dramatic history that led to Shakespeare's writing of
Antony and Cleopatra.

Antonius keeps faithfully the spirit of Garnier's work.
That spirit is one born of the Renaissance at a time when
new and old ideas of the world were often brought together
by learning and artistry into complex combinations filled
with simple inconsistencies. The comments made by the
choruses, taken with some of the comments made by the
characters, show that the basis of the tragedy is a tangle of
ancient ideas of fate, Christian ideas of punishment for
sin, ancient and medieval ideas of the power of Fortune
over man, and Renaissance ideas of the power of man to
shape his own fortune. As Cleopatra prepares to join
Antony in the world of the dead she crowds the worst of
the tangle into a few exclamatory lines:

> O cruell Fortune! ô accursed lott!
> O plaguy loue! ô most detested brand!
> O wretched ioyes! ô beauties miserable!
> O deadlie state! ô deadly roialtie!

O hatefull life! ô Queene most lamentable!
O *Antonie* by my fault buriable!
O hellish worke of heau'n! alas! the wrath
Of all the Gods at once on vs is falne.[2]

These inconsistencies, sometimes struggling to be paradoxes (as in "wretched ioyes," "beauties miserable," and "hellish worke of heau'n"), are far removed from the paradoxes of *Antony and Cleopatra* and help to make one realize how quickly the Renaissance was able to reach full ripeness in the years that brought Shakespeare to maturity.

But though the tragedy seems by such passages of comment to be based upon a much-clouded philosophy of man and his sufferings, yet the hero and heroine contrive to be uncomplicated souls, clear and unequivocal in their tragic characters, and this in spite of the fact that, like Shakespeare's Antony and Cleopatra, they come out of Plutarch. Everything is done to make us sympathize with them and admire them. They have been faulty and they have sinned, but they show commendable desire to do right and to make up for past shortcomings before they die. Both engage in agonized soul-searching. Both confess and repent. They are, to a degree, object lessons made to show the wages of sin, but what is noble in them stands free in the face of death. As they draw sympathy to themselves there is never any question of their drawing sympathy to their imperfections except when we come to one rather doubtful matter: Antony has been grossly sinful in loving Cleopatra, and yet at the end he does not renounce her, but as he dies loves her more than anything else in the world. This matter seems to be taken care of by the very great purity of motive that Cleopatra has developed as she has been faced with catastrophe, a purity that somehow cancels out the sin of Antony's continuing to love her. The tragedy leaves the final impression of being highly moral in the most orthodox sense.

The action begins with Antony in despair, convinced that Cleopatra has betrayed him by yielding to Octavius the city of Pelusium and the last of their forces. He thinks of himself as having foregone his country, wronged his wife Octavia and her "tender babes," lost his soldierly valor and honor, and lost a great empire, all for wanton love of a cruel traitress. He finds himself

A slave become unto her feeble face.[3]

Yet, however inconstant she may be to him, he will remain constant to her. Later, Antony calls himself a fool for loving Cleopatra, but he still has such constancy that though he is sure she is utterly false he is willing that Caesar should take away everything but her. His lamentation is:

So foolish I, I cannot her forget.[4]

It was not Fortune that brought him low; he brought himself low. He says of his fall:

Nay, as the fatted swine in filthy mire
With glutted heart I wallow'd in delights,
All thoughts of honor troden under foote.
So I me lost.[5]

One thing only remains for him to do, and that is to kill himself. He must by "a noble death" wipe out an ignoble record. He states his duty in the following terms.

I must deface the shame of time abus'd,
I must adorne the wanton loues I us'de
With some couragiouse act; that my last daie
By mine owne hand my spotts may wash away.[6]

He thus settles upon suicide in a kind of sacrificial spirit, and does so before he hears the false news that Cleopatra is dead. By dying he not only will prove himself a noble Roman, who will not allow himself to be captured and made to follow Caesar's chariot in a triumphal procession, but, more important, will give himself as a burnt offering to what is right.

While Antony is facing death thus nobly, Cleopatra is facing it no less nobly. She is not by any means what he believes she is. She has never for a moment thought of betraying him to Octavius, and apparently, though she has "snared" him, and though because of her faults she has ruined him, her love for him has always been true. He is her life, her soul, her sun; and his love is to her

More deare than Scepter, children, freedome, light.[7]

She fled in fear from Actium, and his love drove him to follow her. She alone was to blame for his crucial defeat. He, well knowing the strain that the war would put upon a "fearfull woman," had urged her to stay at home, but her consuming love had made her jealous and she had insisted on going with him, for she had been afraid that without her by his side he would go back to Octavia. (Plutarch says Cleopatra was afraid that Antony would go back to Octavius and be reconciled to him through the agency of Octavia, and thus he makes out that she desired to go with

Antony because of political considerations, not because of love for him.)

Charmion, who considers herself well equipped to solve the problem of fate and free will, argues with Cleopatra that ruin comes to men and to kingdoms according to ordinances of high heaven, but that we must always hope and act for the best, even to the very last, in order that the mischief may not grow from ourselves. She urges Cleopatra to consider that Antony's ruin has been accomplished, and has obviously been accomplished according to fate, but that for her, Cleopatra, there is still hope. The Queen of Egypt must retire from "Antonies wracke" lest it bring about her own, and she must regain from Caesar her royal diadem. Never will she do this, vows Cleopatra. "Liue for your sonnes," says Charmion. "Nay, for their father die," answers Cleopatra. "Hard-hearted mother," says Charmion. "Wife kind-hearted I," answers Cleopatra. She has a duty to die, argues Cleopatra high-mindedly, and her duty is grounded on virtue, the only good. But she must procure that Antony be no more incensed against her. She sends Diomed to tell Antony that she has already died for love of him.

News that Antony has turned his sword against himself after receiving false news of Cleopatra's death is brought to Octavius while he and Agrippa are discussing the fall of Antony. Agrippa has argued that Antony's ruin is entirely just, brought to pass by two tragic flaws, "presumptuouse pride" and "voluptuose care of fonde and foolish loue," and Octavius has agreed. Dircetus appears, bringing Antony's bloody sword. In telling of Antony's end Dircetus reveals that Cleopatra has locked herself in her monument because she has made up her mind not to be part of a Roman triumph:

> We bare him to the Tombe but entred not.
> For she, who feared captiue to be made,
> And that she should to Rome in triumph goe,
> Kept close the gate.[8]

He tells of Antony's being drawn up into the monument and says he assumes that Antony is now dead. Octavius shows pity for his fallen rival, but at the suggestion of Agrippa turns quickly to practical matters. He sends Proculeius to make sure that Cleopatra shall not burn her jewels and other treasure and not destroy herself, and he declares that the thing he most desires is to keep her safe so that she may beautify his triumph at Rome.

But though it is later shown again that Cleopatra has fear of being made a part of Caesar's triumph, this fear is not what finally makes her resolve to die. There is no Dolabella to sharpen the fear by telling her that she is to be taken away from Alexandria, and she resolves to die, as she shows quite plainly in her final words, not only because she owes it to Antony to end her life after forcing him to lose empire, honor, and life, but also because her love draws her to join him in the world of shades. She is again urged to live for her children. They are brought before her, and she is reminded that they too many be intended as victims for the triumph. "Rather a thousand deaths," she says. But she leaves them to their fate, though she faints under stress of emotion as she says farewell to them; the father means more to her than the children. And so, calling upon Antony in

the name of their "true loues," their "holy marriage," and
their "deare babes," she cries:

> My dolefull voice thy eare let entertaine,
> And take me with thee to the hellish plaine,
> Thy wife, thy frend.[9]

She does not die before the end of the play; in the last scene
she is briefly delaying her death in order to give due funeral
rites to Antony.

If Shakespeare read *Antonius,* he found in it an idealized
and sentimentalized pair of lovers that he was not disposed
to use for his own dramatic purposes. Moreover, he found
no very remarkable poetry. Hence if he did read *Antonius,*
the reading produced no telltale effects upon *Antony and
Cleopatra. Antonius* has a fifth act concerned with the actions of Cleopatra which follow the death of Antony, and
at the end of Shakespeare's play the space given to those
actions is large. But Shakespeare did not need to learn from
Antonius that in a tragedy having to do with Cleopatra's
ruination of Antony the death of Cleopatra could take over
the stage after the death of Antony and yet be something
better than an anticlimax. *Antonius* shows a dramatic appreciation of the destiny which brought the great Roman
empire under the rule of one man and thereby brought the
Pax Romana into a war-torn world—an appreciation not so
profound, certainly, as that shown in *Antony and Cleopatra,* but genuine. It has a chorus of Roman soldiers, weary
of killing and being killed, who envisage peace and chant:

> Our banks shall cherish now
> The branchie pale-hewed bow
> Of *Oliue.*[10]

These lines remind the reader of the following spoken by Shakespeare's Octavius:

> The time of universal peace is near:
> Prove this a prosp'rous day, the three-nook'd world
> Shall bear the olive freely.   (IV, vi, 5–7)

But neither did Shakespeare need to learn from *Antonius* about the Pax Romana, or the olive as an emblem of peace.

III

Samuel Daniel gives the Countess of Pembroke all due credit for stimulating him to rise above the level of his Delia and achieve his Cleopatra. His *Tragedie of Cleopatra,* which first appeared in 1594 in a collection of his works entitled *Delia and Rosamund augmented. Cleopatra,* is dedicated to the countess. Daniel says of her in the dedication that she called up his spirits from low repose to sing of state, to frame tragic notes, to give her *Antonius* company in a *Cleopatra,* and to take part with whatever poor strength he had in the war begun by her valiant brother against "Grosse Barbarisme," that foul foe grown strong enough to become the "tyrant of the North." With Senecan weapons, then, Daniel was to fight Gothic barbarism, particularly, one may suppose, its domination of drama written for the English public stage. With his *Cleopatra* he was to fight a power which would soon produce Shakespeare's *Antony and Cleopatra.*

Daniel did so little to change the prevailing character of popular tragedy that *Antony and Cleopatra* is outstanding as a flagrant but successful violation of Renaissance classical rules; and yet Daniel apparently had his effect upon *Antony*

and Cleopatra, chiefly because he had spontaneous poetry
in him, despite his allegiance to cut-and-dried Senecanism,
and because Shakespeare was therefore not averse to reading him and not unappreciative of some of his best images
and turns of phrase. Daniel had the imaginative power to
take a long step beyond Garnier and the Countess of Pembroke in what he did with the character of Cleopatra. He
gave his Cleopatra a certain complexity and thus made her
more subtly tragic than the heroine of *Antonius.*

Daniel was not easily satisfied with any primary inspiration granted by his muse, for he was capable of revising a
work and then piling revision upon revision, until he sometimes no longer improved his poetry by polishing but only
wore it thin. *Cleopatra* went through many editions in the
author's lifetime and acquired much revision.[11] Major
changes appeared in the editions of 1599 and 1607, the
changes of 1599 amounting to an extensive revision of lines
and those of 1607 to a recasting of the play. After the death
of the author, his brother John, ignoring the version of 1607,
published in 1623 a text that is practically that of 1599.[12]

It seems that Shakespeare read *Cleopatra* in its earlier
form, that is, in the form it had before it was recast in 1607.
There are several passages in the earlier *Cleopatra* for which
there are notable counterparts in *Antony and Cleopatra.*
All these passages appear in the first edition of Daniel's play
and remain in the play substantially unchanged through
all editions published before 1607. Some do not appear in
the edition of 1607. What is to be said of the earlier *Cleopatra* in this chapter will be based upon the first edition,
that of 1594.

It is possible that the recast *Cleopatra* of 1607 owes something to *Antony and Cleopatra*. Similarities in phrases and ideas that cannot be accounted for by reference to Plutarch have been found between *Antony and Cleopatra* and the matter that is new in the *Cleopatra* of 1607, but they are not so close as such similarities between *Antony and Cleopatra* and the earlier *Cleopatra*. The question rests mainly on the fact that Daniel did three things as he recast his play: he frequently brought dialogue into the place of soliloquy or narrative; he introduced new characters, who are in Plutarch, it is true, but who are also in *Antony and Cleopatra;* and, more particularly, he introduced a scene in which Dircetus brings Antony's sword to Octavius and relates the events preceding Antony's death very nearly as Shakespeare represents them.[13] The possibility that Daniel did his 1607 recasting of *Cleopatra* under the influence of *Antony and Cleopatra,* after seeing it on the stage, is good enough to be one of the reasons why 1607 is taken as an acceptable date for Shakespeare's play.[14] It may be that Daniel provides the instructive spectacle of a scorner of "Grosse Barbarisme" unwittingly lending a modicum of aid to it and then being corrupted by what he has helped it to achieve.

In the *Cleopatra* of 1594 the heroine offers much self-analysis in long passages of soliloquy that follow the right Senecan pattern. At the opening of the play, Antony is dead, and Cleopatra, soliloquizing, wonders that she remains alive, since it is not because she still loves life that she still lives. As she looks back upon her life she finds that it has been "foule." Her lusts have brought Antony and herself to ruin and have destroyed her kingdom. She has been cast down from a lofty place of glory, honor, and delight, to be

> Leuell'd with low disgrac'd calamitie.[15]

Thus her "loathsome soule" finds her body only a "hatefull prison." This is a repentant Cleopatra but not an abject one, for she vows never to forget that she was born a queen and never to let anything that comes to her take away her royal spirit.

Hence, as she considers what she is to do, her first thought is of Octavius and his desire to take her to Rome as an adornment of his triumph. That Octavius has this desire she does not doubt. She assumes that because he plans to lead her captive in the streets of Rome, he "seekes to entertaine" her life "with wiles," with promises, flatteries, and threats, but she is confident that he cannot keep her alive to enslave her. The royal courage with which she was born will not desert her, and as a queen she will kill herself. She declares:

> I must not be, vnlesse I be mine owne.
> Tis sweet to die when we are forst to liue.[16]

Cleopatra's second thought is of her children. She says that she would not have remained alive thus long had she not feared that Octavius would offer injury to them after her death. She decides that she still lives, still feigns content, and still soothes Octavius because calamity has made her crafty, and that she temporizes with Octavius out of a desire to procure her children's safety. But she promises that it will not be for long. Honor calls.

> My soule yeelds honour vp the victory,
> And I must be a Queene, forget a mother:
> Yet mother would I be, were I not I.[17]

Perhaps the heavens have decreed, and her sins have de-
served, that the line of the Ptolemies should fail. If so:

> Yet let a glorious end conclude my dayes,
> Though life were bad, my death may yet be prais'd.[18]

Cleopatra's third and last thought is of Antony. According to her interpretation of their tragedy, she and Antony
have been equally faulty, though faulty in different ways,
and they have grappled in an ocean of pride

> To sinke each others greatnes both together.[19]

Her basic fault has been ambition, and his has been folly.
She was enamoured of his greatness, and he was bewitched
by her vanity. He came to her "lasciuious Courte" inured
to wars but unlearned in woman's wiles, and he fell "to
love in earnest," even became her "doting Louer," while
she feigned love for him because her ambition sought to use
his greatness. At that time she was incapable of love. Her
greatness and her beauty made her think that all men must
love her duty-bound and that she must love none in particular. She had "vagabond desires" and, moreover, "to thinke
on loue had neuer leysure." But now that Antony is dead
she has come to love him. She makes this avowal:

> Our like distresse I feele doth sympathize
> And euen affliction makes me truly loue thee.
> Which *Anthony*, (I must confesse my fault,)
> I neuer did sincerely vntill now;
> Now I protest I doe, now am I taught,
> In death to loue, in life that knew not how.[20]

She is determined not to survive their "common faulte," since, for one thing, the world would hate her if she did (she has already shown regard for the world's opinion in wanting to make a "glorious end"), and, for another thing, she owes a debt to the sincere lover Antony, who deserves much more than she has given him. In dying she will pay that debt to him faithfully at the same time that she proves herself a courageous queen able to deceive and elude Caesar:

> My death, my loue and courage shall reueale,
> The which is all the world hath left t' vnstaine me.[21]

Octavius knows that he has captured but not yet conquered a woman of royal spirit. He wants to vanquish her utterly and lead her in triumph, but fears he may not be able to do so. For, as he says to Proculeius, who to capture Cleopatra has entered her monument by trickery and who has had to keep her from stabbing herself at the moment of capture:

> Princes (like Lyons) neuer will be tam'd.
> A priuate man may yeeld, and care not how,
> But greater harts will breake before they bow.
> And sure I thinke sh' will neuer condiscend
> To lyue to grace our spoyles with her disgrace.[22]

Octavius goes to talk with Cleopatra, hoping against hope to get her to live and allow herself to be made "the greatest Trophey" of his travels. He reproaches her for wrongs she has done to Rome and to himself, and she excuses herself by saying that she did all she did because she was dominated by the greatness of Antony. When her treasurer exposes her concealment of a large amount of treasure, and when she beats the informer, Octavius forgives her, as in Plutarch, and promises that she will have generous treatment. He is deceived into thinking that she is now content to live.

Dolabella, who accompanies Octavius when this interview takes place, admires Cleopatra and is smitten with love for her. Octavius tells him that he plans to send her and her children to Rome immediately, and Dolabella informs Cleopatra in a letter that Octavius means to do this and that he intends to place both her and her children in his triumph. In the letter Dolabella makes known his love. Cleopatra gets satisfaction from the knowledge that her face can still win a lover, and she is grateful to Dolabella for his message, but she does not have any thought of making capital once more of her power to charm. She replies to Dolabella by messenger:

> As for my loue, say *Anthony* hath all,
> Say that my hart is gone into the graue
> With him, in whom it rests and euer shall.[23]

Dolabella's message makes Cleopatra determine to die without more delay. She will shun disgrace, fly to her love, escape her foe, free her soul, and act the last of life with glory by dying like a queen. A *nuntius* tells the Chorus of her death. He was sent by her to procure two aspics and he brought them to her in a basket of figs. She bared an arm to receive the poisoned sting, saying:

> And heere I sacrifize these armes to Death,
> That Lust late dedicated to Delights.[24]

For a moment she hesitated while Life and Honor struggled within her for victory. Honor won. She received the sting and died. Her face retained a grace that graced death,

And in that cheere, th'impression of a smile
Did seeme to shew shee scorned Death and *Cæsar*,
As glorying that she could them both beguile.[25]

Messengers from Caesar found Charmion dying, while she rearranged Cleopatra's crown with her last strength, and Eras dead at Cleopatra's feet. Cleopatra they found stretched on a bed of gold in her richest royal attire. One of them asked Charmion whether this was well done, and received the memorable reply that it was well done indeed and that it was a proper act for one descended from a race of great kings.

What Daniel does, then, is to make Cleopatra into a heroine with mixed motives, instead of letting her remain one with a single motive, as he has found her in the Countess of Pembroke's *Antonius*. Furthermore, though in *Antonius* Cleopatra has a love for Antony important enough to be her single motive, Daniel gives her a love for Antony that is not even her dominant motive. Before all else his Cleopatra is a queen. Since Antony's death she has come to have true love for him, and the proof lies in her ability to forego a pleasure that would once have been irresistible, that of making a conquest of the doting Dolabella. But she has always had royal pride, even when vagabond desires made her most vain as a light-o'-love. The roots of her royal pride have grown through all the years of her life, and those of her sincere love for Antony through only a few days at the end of her life. In making this plain, Daniel shows himself to be a very respectable artist, as he does also in complicating and to some extent mingling the two motives of royal pride and love for Antony. In dealing with a third motive, Cleopatra's love for her children, he is not so successful, but is not without skill and understanding.

To show Cleopatra's royal pride as her dominant motive, Daniel seizes upon the theme of Caesar's coming triumphal progress through the streets of Rome—a theme only slightly developed by Garnier from Plutarch—and makes much of it. At the opening of the play, as we have seen, he has Cleopatra think of the triumph first of all as she considers suicide and has her decide that she, a queen, will never be exhibited as Caesar's slave. Then he has Caesar express doubt that her royal spirit can be so tamed that she will grace a triumph with her disgrace. Then he has Dolabella, with his news of Caesar's decision to send her to Rome, give her the effective impulse toward suicide. In a sense Daniel builds his drama on the theme of Caesar's triumph.

But aside from Daniel's employment of this theme there is much to let the reader know that his tragedy is primarily that of a royal Cleopatra. His heroine is guided by a truly aristocratic conception of honor, even when she takes account of her new-born love for Antony. By dying she will "fly to her love," but she will also pay an honorable debt owed by a queen to an emperor, will show courage and scorn of death, without which aristocracy has no honor, and will keep herself from being hated by the world as dishonorable—indeed, will gain glory. Her last inner struggle is between life and honor, not between life and love, though it is true that after honor has gained the victory she feels that her soul "parts free to *Anthony.*" As for what she feels for her children, that is so much less than her regard for honor that, in order to be a queen, she is entirely willing to forget that she is a mother.

The choruses of *Cleopatra* are not filled with conventional complaints against Fortune, but consistently interpret the tragedy as showing a train of suffering caused by the faults of Antony and Cleopatra. The last chorus puts the question whether man's pride is not limited by a tendency in greatness to destroy itself:

> Is greatnes of this sort,
> That greatnes greatnes marres,
> And wracks it selfe, selfe driuen
> On Rocks of her owne might?
> Doth Order order so
> Disorders ouer-thro?[26]

Though the choruses bring moral fervor to the condemnation of Cleopatra's sins, they are not at odds with the body of the play. They hold up for the reader's sympathy and admiration a true queen, who, whatever her faults, can win glory by dying honorably.

IV

The signs that Shakespeare knew Daniel's *Cleopatra* in its earlier form are of a kind to indicate that he read it just before writing *Antony and Cleopatra,* retained in his memory certain details, and put them to his own uses casually, perhaps with occasional refreshment of his memory as he wrote. Plutarch was Shakespeare's standby; but Daniel seems to have been helpful.

It looks as though Shakespeare supplemented a passage from Plutarch with a corresponding passage from Daniel when he wrote his version of the interview between Proculeius and Cleopatra at the monument. At the beginning of the interview as Shakespeare gives it, Cleopatra says that

she will beg nothing from Caesar but the kingdom of
Egypt for her son; and Proculeius, standing outside the
monument, answers:

> Be of good cheer;
> You're fall'n into a princely hand, fear nothing.
> Make your full reference freely to my lord,
> Who is so full of grace, that it flows over
> On all that need; let me report to him
> Your sweet dependancy, and you shall find
> A conqueror that will pray in aid for kindness
> Where he for grace is kneel'd to.
>
> (V, ii, 21–28)

Proculeius enters the monument by surprise and thwarts a
resultant attempt made by Cleopatra to stab herself. When
he reproaches her for trying to wrong both herself and
Caesar, Cleopatra asserts that she will not have death
wrongfully denied her, do Caesar what he can. Finally
Proculeius says that he will say to Caesar what Cleopatra
pleases, and she sends him away curtly with the injunction:
"Say, I would die" (V, ii, 70).

Plutarch says in his account of the interview that those
who were outside the monument with Proculeius "vn-
derstoode, that *Cleopatra* demaunded the kingdome of
Ægypt for her sonnes: and that Proculeius aunswered her,
that she should be of good cheere, and not be affrayed to
referre all vnto Cæsar."[27] As for Cleopatra's desire to die,
he merely tells of her attempt to stab herself when she
found that Proculeius had entered the monument and of
the way in which Proculeius reproached her for offering
wrong to herself and Caesar. He says nothing about the
"grace" of Caesar or any feeling on the part of Cleopatra
that to die was her sacred privilege.

Daniel brings in reference to Caesar's "grace." He makes Proculeius begin a report of the interview to Caesar as follows:

> But through a Grate at th'entry of the place,
> Standing to treat, I labour'd to aduise her,
> To come to *Cæsar,* and to sue for grace.
> Shee saide, shee crau'd not life, but leaue to die,
> Yet for her children, prayd they might inherite.[28]

And Daniel makes Proculeius go on to say that after he had entered the monument and wrested the dagger from Cleopatra, he reproached her for attempting injury to herself and Caesar and she lamented that Caesar, stretching forth his ambitious hand unto the very right of death, should violate her privilege of dying.

Thus, like both Plutarch and Daniel, Shakespeare has the plea of Cleopatra that her kingdom may continue to be ruled by her royal line and the reproaches of Proculeius for the wrong offered to herself and Caesar by her effort to stab herself; like Plutarch alone, he has the advice of Proculeius to "be of good cheer" and to "refer" all to Caesar; and, like Daniel alone, he has the advice of Proculeius to sue for Caesar's "grace," the reference made by Cleopatra to the violation of her privilege of dying (even dogs, says Shakespeare's Cleopatra, are granted death to rid them "of languish"), and the message of Cleopatra to Caesar declaring that she wishes to die (which Shakespeare makes specially emphatic by converting it into Cleopatra's final word). Caesar's "grace," which in Daniel is to be sued for, and in Shakespeare, more concretely, to be kneeled for, is a prominent topic of discourse in Daniel. Daniel is so fond of the subject that it comes up three several times in what he makes Proculeius report of his interview with Cleopatra.

There are two touches in Shakespeare's version of this interview which correspond with matter in Daniel's *Cleopatra* though not with matter in Daniel's version of the interview, and which do not correspond with anything in Plutarch. The first touch is Cleopatra's cry when she draws her dagger to stab herself:

> Quick, quick, good hands.   (V, ii, 39)

This is an echo of a speech of Cleopatra's in an earlier scene of Shakespeare's in which, after the dying Antony has told her that she must trust none about Caesar but Proculeius, she declares:

> My resolution and my hands I'll trust:
> None about Cæsar.   (IV, xiii, 49–50)

The idea common to these passages is to be compared with the content of a line in the soliloquy that opens Daniel's tragedy, a line spoken by Cleopatra in defiance of Caesar's promises, flatteries, and threats:

> I haue both hands, and will, and I can die.[29]

The second touch is Cleopatra's warning that she will not suffer as a pinioned captive in Rome, where she would come under the eye of her rival Octavia:

>   Know, sir, that I
> Will not wait pinion'd at your master's court,
> Nor once be chastis'd with the sober eye
> Of dull Octavia.   (V, ii, 52–55)

This is to be compared with an expression of determination which Daniel gives his Cleopatra, likewise in her opening soliloquy, never to let Rome in general and Octavia in particular see her as a captive with bound hands:

> And neuer thinke I can be so low brought,
> That Rome should see my scepter-bearing hands,
> Behinde mee bounde, and glory in my teares.
> That I should passe, whereas Octavia stands
> To view my misery, that purchast hers.[30]

Shakespeare, following a sure psychological instinct, goes farther than Daniel with the idea of making Cleopatra experience horror at the thought of letting Octavia see her degraded in a Roman triumph and twice shows the effect upon her of such horror before her interview with Proculeius (IV, x, 50–52; IV, xiii, 27–29).

When he deals with Cleopatra's death, Shakespeare has the same conception that Daniel has of a necessity for the readjustment of her crown. He implies that at the moment of death Cleopatra forces her crown awry, for he makes Charmian say, after she has closed Cleopatra's eyes:

> Your crown's awry.
> I'll mend it, and then play.   (V, ii, 320–321)

Plutarch remarks only that, after the death of Cleopatra, Charmion was found "trimming the Diademe which *Cleopatra* ware vpon her head";[31] he offers nothing in the way of explanation. Daniel, in the report of Cleopatra's death which he assigns to a messenger, has the "wrying" of the crown by Cleopatra as she sinks down at her death and the righting of it immediately by Charmion.

> And sencelesse, in her sinking downe shee wryes
> The Diadem which on her head shee wore,
> Which *Charmion* (poore weake feeble mayd) espyes
> And hastes to right it as it was before.[32]

There are other details upon which there is agreement between Shakespeare's tragedy and Daniel's and which have no basis in Plutarch. Shakespeare makes Cleopatra call Antony "the demi-Atlas of this earth" (I, v, 23). Daniel makes her call him

> The *Atlas* and the Champion of my pride,
> That did the world of my whole fortune sway.[33]

Shakespeare makes her describe herself as "wrinkled deep in time" (I, v, 29) and no longer the possessor of such beauty as had won former lovers. Daniel makes her soliloquize upon her wrinkles and her waning beauty, bought so dearly by Antony:

> And yet thou cam'st but in my beauties waine,
> When new-appearing wrinkles of declining,
> Wrought with the hand of yeeres, seem'd to detaine
> My graces light, as now but dimly shining.[34]

Shakespeare has the success of a master with the lines in which Cleopatra, after ordering her best attire in preparation for death, announces:

> I am again for Cydnus,
> To meet Mark Antony.
> (V, ii, 227–228)

Daniel, even though incapable of achieving so much with such fine economy of effort, has no mean success with lines about Cleopatra's death given to his messenger in which he

develops the same conception of Cleopatra as going again
to Cydnus in all her royal array:

> Euen as shee was when on thy cristall streames,
> O Cydnos shee did shew what earth could shew.
> When *Asia* all amaz'd in wonder, deemes
> Venus from heauen was come on earth below.
> Euen as shee went at first to meete her Loue,
> So goes shee now at last againe to find him.[35]

Shakespeare also shows his mastership in the lines spoken
by Cleopatra beginning:

> Give me my robe, put on my crown; I have
> Immortal longings in me.

They rise to the climax:

> I am fire and air; my other elements
> I give to baser life.
> $\qquad$ (V, ii, 282–292)

Daniel does only passably well with comparable lines which
do not have exactly the same imaginative kernel as that in
these lines of Shakespeare's but which do make Cleopatra
think of a contrast between immortality and base life as
she decides to die. He allows his messenger to report:

> But Honor scorning Life, loe forth leades he
> Bright Immortalitie in shyning armour:
> Thorow the rayes of whose cleere glory, shee
> Might see Lifes basenes, how much it might harm her.[36]

The words "Base life" appear in what Daniel's messenger
has to say further about Cleopatra's rejection of life and dishonor and her acceptance of immortality and honor.

Some of these correspondences between Shakespeare's
Antony and Cleopatra and Daniel's earlier version of *Cleo-*

patra may of course be accidental. But it is most unlikely that all of them are.[37]

It appears that not long before Shakespeare wrote *Antony and Cleopatra* he read another work of Daniel's, the *Letter from Octavia to Marcus Antonius*. That he read at least the "Argument" prefixed to that poem there is very good reason to believe. The *Letter* was first published in 1599 in Daniel's *Poeticall Essayes*. It represents Octavia as writing to Antony after she has tried to take provisions and men to him for his intended war against Parthia and has been stopped at Athens. It shows her as a noble, long-suffering, modest, sweet-tempered, and ever-faithful wife begging Antony to leave Cleopatra and come back to her.

Two separate passages in *Antony and Cleopatra* indicate that Shakespeare knew the "Argument" attached to Daniel's *Letter*. At the beginning of the play, Antony, aroused by disturbing news demanding his departure from Egypt, resolves to free himself from the fetters with which Cleopatra has held him:

> These strong Egyptian fetters I must break,
> Or lose myself in dotage.   (I, ii, 125–126)

Immediately after his marriage with Octavia has been arranged, he declares in a soliloquy that he makes the marriage for reasons of policy and that he intends to find his pleasure again in the East: I will to Egypt;

> And though I make this marriage for my peace,
> I' the east my pleasure lies.   (II, iii, 38–40)

Thus Shakespeare presents Antony as unable to forget Cleopatra at the time of his marriage to Octavia and as even

then unfaithful to Octavia in thought. Plutarch does not
speak of a breaking of Egyptian fetters when he tells of
Antony's being impelled to leave Cleopatra by the disturbing news. He uses a different figure of speech. He says:
"Then began *Antonius* with much a doe, a litle to rouse
himselfe as if he had bene wakened out of a deepe sleepe,
and as a man may say, comming out of a great dronken-
nes."[38] Nor does Plutarch make Antony incapable of forgetting Cleopatra at the time of his marriage to Octavia.
According to his account, Antony seemed to have put Cleopatra completely out of his mind until after he had lived
with Octavia for some years: "Then beganne this pestilent
plague and mischiefe of *Cleopatraes* loue (which had slept
a longe tyme, and seemed to haue bene vtterlie forgotten,
and that *Antonius* had geuen place to better counsell)
againe to kindle, and to be in force, so soone as *Antonius*
came neere vnto SYRIA."[39] But the Antony bound by Egyptian fetters is in Daniel's "Argument," and so is the Antony
whose heart is in the East even as he marries Octavia.
Daniel writes: "For *Antonie* hauing yet vpon him the
fetters of Ægypt, layde on by the power of a most incomparable beautie, could admit no new lawes into the state
of his affections, or dispose of himselfe being not himselfe,
but as hauing his heart turned Eastwarde whither the point
of his desires were directed, touchte with the strongest
allurements that ambition, and a licencious soueraintie
could draw a man vnto: could not trulie descend to the
priuate loue of a ciuill nurtred Matrone...."[40]

We know that Shakespeare had not been above taking
poetic concepts from Daniel before he wrote *Antony and*

Cleopatra. A close reading of Daniel, especially of his *Rosamond,* had left its mark upon Shakespeare's earlier work, both dramatic and nondramatic.[41]

V

Shakespeare gives regal greatness of spirit to both Antony and Cleopatra, and in doing so he is very different from Garnier and Daniel. Shakespeare's Antony is born to lead men and to make crowns and crownets wear his livery. It is part of his tragedy that, though he has a luxuriant personal force which seems irresistible, he is not equal to the task of crushing a less opulent great spirit like Octavius and winning the rulership of the entire world. Shakespeare's Cleopatra is born to assume queenly position and to make the world accept her as royally magnificent. Though she is not gifted with anything like Antony's force, she has woman's subtlety to the fullest degree. It is part of her tragedy that with her subtlety she wins control of his force and by winning this control ruins him and herself. Garnier is not really concerned to make Antony and Cleopatra into regal characters, but to make them into repentant wrongdoers who feel that duty drives them to wipe out their disgrace by ending their lives. Daniel, unlike Garnier, seizes upon and develops the suggestion of Plutarch that Cleopatra had a proud queenly spirit which would not allow her to be led in a Roman triumph. Daniel lets Cleopatra feel repentance for wrong she has done to Antony and lets her have true love for Antony, but he suspends all this within her aristocratic sense of honor. He succeeds in giving his heroine royal stature, but sometimes loses Cleopatra the woman in Cleopatra the queen, as Shakespeare never does. As for Antony, Daniel does not make him a character in his play, and neglects in what he allows to be said of him to give him qualities of true greatness. Indeed, he lets Cleopatra, when she speaks of the way she has sub-jugated Antony, make him into a figure much more pitiable than admirable.

Largely because Shakespeare takes care to give his hero and heroine regal natures that demand expression, *Antony and Cleopatra* is not a drama in which the world is well lost for love. That is, it does not show the world to be, to the losers, as nothing when compared to their love. We certainly do not find Shakespeare implying that the world which is finally lost to Octavius weighs little in the balance against what Antony and Cleopatra find in each other. He lets us know that it weighs very much indeed.

Shakespeare does not organize his tragedy as a drama of the love of Antony and Cleopatra, but as a drama of the rise and fall of Antony in the struggle for world rulership that takes place after he has met Cleopatra. Shakespeare does not open the tragedy with the colorful meeting of the lovers at the river Cydnus, as he might well have done if he had wanted to construct it upon the frame of their love. He opens with Antony's freeing of himself from the fetters put upon him by Cleopatra in Egypt and his launching of himself back into the world of affairs that he has neglected because of Cleopatra. At this point Antony looks upon his love as "dotage," and is able to say of Cleopatra, "Would I had never seen her!" When she resorts to cunning to keep him in Egypt, he matches cunning with strength of will.

Antony frees himself and goes to Rome. His meeting with Octavius and Lepidus shows him at his best as a contender for position in the world. With Octavius he takes exactly the right course, for he stands on his dignity, gives the impression of having complete confidence in the power at his command, and, though he shows defiance, makes his case in statesmanlike fashion and never lets the argument turn into a downright quarrel. He is appreciably in the wrong. He does not pretend to be wholly in the right, but he gives himself advantage in the argument. Out of the meeting comes his marriage with Octavia. This marriage implies a recognition by Octavius that Antony is his equal, and a willingness on the part of Octavius to let him hold sway in the East so long as the terms of an alliance are duly kept. Thus Antony rises to undisputed control of half the world. Lepidus has already shown himself a nonentity who must step down from his place in the triumvirate, and he quickly does step down.

But Antony returns to his "Egyptian dish." Thus he slights Octavia, angers her brother, and precipitates a war for the leadership of the world as a whole. This time he does not throw off Cleopatra's fetters and free himself for action in the arena of the world. He takes Cleopatra into the Battle of Actium, and she loses it for him. This is the turning point in his fortunes at which he begins his fall. In his fall he is gradually stripped of his leadership, and when Enobarbus leaves him we know how catastrophic that fall is to be. But to the end of his life he shows something of the great spirit that has made him Antony, and even after his death the power of his spirit is manifested.

The memory of what he was when his reared arm crested the world helps to nerve Cleopatra in her planning of a noble death—noble by his standards and by hers.

Yet though Shakespeare organizes his tragedy as Antony's struggle for world rulership and gives it a pyramidal form showing a rise and fall in the hero's fortunes, he develops within it a psychological drama of love with a course of its own. The action of this drama is in general a rising action to the end. It has its falls, but they are minor, even though sometimes sharp. It takes Antony and Cleopatra from a low point in their relationship to the height reached at their death. Beginning with Antony in revulsion from the dotage produced by the meeting at the Cydnus, and with Cleopatra showing all the light-mindedness of which she is possessed, it rises to a point at which the Cleopatra who has scorned Octavia as "the married woman" exclaims in all simplicity as she dies, "Husband, I come!" But the love of Antony and Cleopatra, like themselves, never ceases to be deeply flawed, however much it becomes capable of arousing admiration. It is like them in having a paradoxical nobility.

We cannot fail to see that Shakespeare has sympathy for Antony and Cleopatra, and especially for Cleopatra. Anyone who does not fall in some degree under the spell of Shakespeare's Cleopatra is resolute in resistance to her and to Shakespeare himself. The danger is that one may fall too far under her spell and give her a sympathy that Shakespeare does not justify. It has been said that of the critics who have written on the play "there is hardly one who has not been left in love with Cleopatra," and that "grave and

reverend signiors declare her to be the flower of womanhood, the *ewige weibliche*,... a strange conception, due,
perhaps, to that very English desire, the other side of the
Puritan medal, to find a woman to whom they could phys-
ically and morally abandon themselves, though in reality
they might flee from her arms to those of the mother of the
Gracchi."[42] But there is criticism of the play in which the
Puritan medal has been turned face up. Mr. Bernard Shaw,
in the preface to his *Three Plays for Puritans,* a volume
which includes his *Caesar and Cleopatra,* says with Shavian
seriousness: "Shakespear's Antony and Cleopatra must
needs be as intolerable to the true Puritan as it is vaguely
distressing to the ordinary healthy citizen, because, after
giving a faithful picture of the soldier broken down by
debauchery, and the typical wanton in whose arms such
men perish, Shakespear finally strains all his huge command of rhetoric and stage pathos to give a theatrical sublimity to the wretched end of the business, and to persuade
foolish spectators that the world was well lost by the
twain."[43] Mr. John Bailey, about whose entire seriousness
there can be no question, agrees with Shaw. He finds Cleopatra "a vain, selfish, treacherous woman," despite her
"magic and fascination," and thinks that "of what we mean
by worth she has nothing." "Indeed," he remarks, "we may
say that this is of all the plays in the world the one in which
'the expense of spirit in a waste of shame' is shown most
nakedly as almost a glorious and entirely a splendid business."[44]

It was not the tendency of the age in which Shakespeare
wrote to wash out the faults of Antony and Cleopatra in

romantic sentiment. Garnier sentimentally lightens the
faults of Cleopatra, it is true, but he has moral condemnation both for her faults and for Antony's, and the Countess
of Pembroke obviously finds it a labor of love to preserve
this morality of Garnier's. Daniel has even more moral
condemnation for the faults of the lovers, and though he
gives Cleopatra a reformed character as he brings her to her
death, he presents her as having shown gross failings in the
past. Samuel Brandon in his closet drama *The Tragi-
comoedi of the Vertuous Octauia* (1598) makes one of the
characters offer with some eloquence a romantic justification of the love of Antony for Cleopatra as something
dictated by nature, too strong to be resisted, a force such as
that which makes the steel cleave to the lodestone. But
Brandon does this only to make another character overwhelm the justification with an argument that no matter
how powerful the nature which forms our bodies may be,
God has given us power to control it when it leads us to
do ill:

> Tis true, that nature did these buildings frame.
> And true, that they to natures power are thrall.
> And true, that imperfections foyle the same.
> And true, that we by natures weaknesse fall.
> And this is true, that God vnnatured all,
> And gaue vs wisdome to suppresse our will:
> He gaue vs perfect reason to recall,
> Affections scoutes from following what is ill.[45]

Elizabethan writers who found cause to mention Antony
and Cleopatra in passing were apt to deal harshly with
them: Antony was "besotted" upon Cleopatra and lost
fame, power, and life through "blind loue" of her;[46] Cleo-

patra, "Antonius harlotte," was a woman who worked mis-
chiefs "by subtill meanes," and it was known that there
were "horrible murthers she had done of manye Princes
and noble men of all coūtreyes where she came";[47] Antony
and Cleopatra got "that punishment which they both deserued," a punishment that was one of "Gods heauy iudgements."[48]

Nor can it be said with truth that the final effect of Shakespeare's play is a romantic washing out of the faults of his
hero and heroine. Certainly the spirit in which he deals
with their faults is not that of the preaching moralist; but
neither is it that of the preaching romanticist who, because
of sympathy for Antony and Cleopatra, would free them
from the judgment of the moralist. Samuel Johnson's remark, in the preface to his edition of Shakespeare, that
Shakespeare "seems to write without any moral purpose,"
but that from what he writes "a system of social duty may
be selected, for he that thinks reasonably must think
morally," is peculiarly true of the Shakespeare we find in
Antony and Cleopatra. Despite the appeal that the matter
of the play has to Shakespeare's sympathy and imagination
and despite the warmth and "happy valiancy of style"
resulting from this appeal, Shakespeare can, and often does,
turn upon his subject a cold white light. In doing so he
seems ruthless; but he never seems bitter. As Bradley says:
"The subject no more embitters or seduces him than the
ambition of Macbeth. So that here too we feel the angelic
strength of which Coleridge speaks. If we quarreled with
the phrase at all, it would be because we fancied we could
trace in Shakespeare's attitude something of the irony of

superiority; and this may not altogether suit our conception of an angel."[49]

Shakespeare is challenged by the faults of Antony and Cleopatra just as he is by those of Timon and Macbeth. He is challenged to take them more or less as they have been pictured by those who have condemned them and to make them not admirable in themselves but ineradicable parts of admirable characters. He accepts the faults of Antony substantially as they are in Plutarch. He leaves out Antony's Parthian fiasco, of which Plutarch gives a long description, and he does not show so much of Antony's cruelty as Plutarch does, but all this may be mainly because of a desire to compress Antony's story for dramatic purposes.[50] If his Cleopatra is somewhat better than Plutarch's before the Battle of Actium, she is, as I have said, somewhat worse afterward.

In all fairness it must be admitted that there is something to go upon for critics of *Antony and Cleopatra* like Shaw and Bailey. Perhaps they can find most to support their argument in the unforgettable laudation of Cleopatra for her infinite variety which is addressed by Enobarbus to Maecenas and Agrippa and which concludes with these words:

> For vilest things
> Become themselves in her, that the holy priests
> Bless her when she is riggish.   (II, ii, 246–248)

Undeniably Shakespeare has given Enobarbus splendid poetry with which to make "vilest things" seem splendid when they are part of Cleopatra.

It is to be remembered, though, that to this same Enobarbus, who here speaks a language utterly different from that of the moralist, Shakespeare gives the standard language of the moralist when Cleopatra asks him whether she or Antony is at fault for the defeat at Actium. This is the way Enobarbus answers:

> Antony only, that would make his will
> Lord of his reason . . . .
> The itch of his affection should not then
> Have nick'd his captainship; at such a point,
> When half to half the world oppos'd, he being
> The mered question.   (III, xi, 3–10)

Any Elizabethan moralist might have condemned Antony for not making his spiritual reason the lord of his physical desire, but Enobarbus, of course, is not an ordinary Elizabethan moralist. He has a soldier's morality of a sort which distinguishes sharply between finding a riggish Cleopatra splendid and irresistible when there is no work to do and finding her so when there is a battle to fight, especially a battle for the rulership of the world. In short, Enobarbus thinks that Cleopatra is "a wonderful piece of work" for the soldier to bless himself withal on his travels, but only if the soldier does not find her too wonderful. Surely Enobarbus shows something of the irony of superiority in his attitude toward Cleopatra, and surely Shakespeare did not create Enobarbus without wanting that irony in the play.

As for the ending of the play, if it is to be called merely theatrical, it must be called so because of Cleopatra. As Antony dies, he achieves a quiet dignity and rises to an unselfish consideration of Cleopatra's future that shows deepened love for her. He is not theatrical in his farewell to her, however theatrical she may be in her farewell to him. Theatricality is so deeply ingrained in Cleopatra that when she herself dies she does her theatrical best with the occasion. The question whether there is more than self-centered theatricality in the magnificence of her exit from the world is one that must be taken up later.

VI

Let us look more closely at Antony and Cleopatra as dwellers in Shakespeare's last tragic world. The opening scene of the play is one that we should not expect from an author who can get himself accused of treating the love story of Antony and Cleopatra so perversely as to make an "expense of spirit in a waste of shame" into "almost a glorious and entirely a splendid business." A scene less calculated to predispose anyone to sympathy for the lovers or to admiration for them and for what they feel toward each other can hardly be imagined. Its first lines are a condemnation of Antony by one of his friends for having fallen into a dotage, for having turned his captain's heart into the bellows and the fan to cool a gypsy's lust, for having transformed himself from one of the three pillars of the world into a strumpet's fool. The condemnation of Antony is contemptuous enough, but it involves a condemnation of Cleopatra even more contemptuous. What immediately follows in this first scene is seeming justification for all that has been said there in denigration of the lovers. Antony daffs the world aside in the person of a messenger from Rome and is willing to let the arch of empire fall while he finds the nobleness of life in embracing a Cleopatra who apparently accepts his love only to taunt him, to make a blushing fool of him, and in general to prove her power over him.

In *Macbeth* it is by enveloping his hero in praise that Shakespeare begins his work of creating tragic humanity that shall be deeply flawed and yet worthy of sympathy, but in *Antony and Cleopatra* he begins work of this sort by enveloping both his hero and his heroine in scorn. In *Macbeth* he handicaps himself for his work of creating sympathy for his hero, but only after he has first taken some pains to begin that work. In *Antony and Cleopatra* he handicaps himself for his work of creating sympathy for his hero and heroine before he does anything else. It seems that when Shakespeare thus imposes a severe handicap upon himself at the very opening of *Antony and Cleopatra,* he does so in a spirit of happy valiancy like that which characterizes the poetic style of the play.

But Shakespeare loses little time in beginning to overcome this handicap. Almost at once after the opening scene we know that we are asked to make no such simple judgment concerning the characters of Antony and Cleopatra as that scene seems to demand. Antony breaks the spell cast upon him by Cleopatra—and does so in a masterful manner—when he decides that the world needs him in Rome. Cleopatra, when she finds that her artifice will not serve to keep Antony from leaving her, says farewell to him in a way that makes us wonder whether she may not after all be capable of more than light-mindedness. We cannot be certain that there is depth of feeling in the speech of Cleopatra ending:

> O! my oblivion is a very Antony,
> And I am all forgotten.   (I, iii, 90–91)

But if this speech shows only artifice taking a new course, it is artifice that is successful in speaking like sincerity.

As the play proceeds, we find that to understand Antony and Cleopatra we must understand that they are voluptuaries,[51] but to understand them thus is to understand much that is admirable in them as well as much that is not admirable. In large part their paradox is that by being voluptuaries, for which they may be scorned, they are led to have certain qualities for which they may be respected. Since they do not offer a bid for sympathy by reforming or by undergoing purgation, they have a very different tragic quality from that given by Garnier to his Antony and Cleopatra or that given by Daniel to his Cleopatra. At the end of the tragedy they are essentially the same voluptuaries that they are in the opening scene.[52] Cleopatra still has the instincts of a strumpet and Antony is still capable of being a fool in her hands because of his desire for her. But as the drama unfolds it shows them to be much more than an ordinary strumpet's fool and an ordinary strumpet, much more than the typical "soldier broken down by debauchery" and the typical "wanton in whose arms such men perish." It also shows them as apparently incapable of being their greater selves except through being their lesser selves.

Antony is a man who fights for high place in the world because he has an unlimited desire to gratify his senses. He can waste time with Cleopatra in the most inane amusements, but his sensualism drives him to high endeavor as well as to such wasting of time. He has love for the strongest colors the world can show and the most pompous grandeur it can yield. To win commanding position in the world and the delight that for him goes with it he is capable at times of denying himself and even of undergoing rigorous hardship. He is a great leader because he is a fearless and able general and because, though he can now and then be cruel, as the selfish sensualist tends to be cruel, his love of the world includes love of the human scene. He understands people, craves boon companionship, and wins affection from followers. His love for the human scene can even, at rare intervals, produce the truest humanity in him, as it does when he hears of Fulvia's death.

Before he brings Antony to Rome, Shakespeare writes two scenes in which he subjects him to character analysis at the hands of rivals. In the first of these scenes Octavius makes a case against Antony, and Lepidus makes one for him. Octavius disavows hate for his "great competitor," but he obviously despises him for his failings. He sees him as a man who once showed a true soldier's capacity to overcome hardship but who is now fallen into the worst depths of lascivious effeminacy and is completely given over to "his voluptuousness." He thinks of him as

> the abstract of all faults
> That all men follow.   (I, iv, 9–10)

But Lepidus will not have it that Antony shows faults enough to "darken all his goodness." Moreover, he argues that the faults of Antony are of a kind he cannot be expected to correct. They are ingrained and must be accepted along with his goodness. They are

> hereditary
> Rather than purchas'd; what he cannot change
> Than what he chooses.   (I, iv, 13–15)

Lepidus is called "too indulgent" by the coldly self-controlled Octavius, and perhaps rightly. He is of an easygoing nature and would naturally plead that heredity might excuse a man from trying to conquer his failings. But his comment that Antony's faults are ineradicable serves to remind us that Antony is one of the deeply flawed heroes of Shakespeare's last tragic world. In the second scene of such character analysis it is Pompey who, as he weighs his chances against the triumvirate, has his say about Antony. He rates him as a "libertine," an "amorous surfeiter," and a "ne'er-lust-wearied" dallier with "salt Cleopatra," but does not make the mistake of underrating his soldiership:

> His soldiership
> Is twice the other twain.
>
> (II, i, 34–35)

Antony, as I have already said, is at his best as a statesman-like contender for world power when he deals with Octavius in Rome. He says to Octavius that he will play the penitent to him as nearly as he may, but will not let his honesty make poor his greatness. He does play the penitent, and at no cost to his greatness. That he is honest when he speaks penitently to Octavius of "poisoned hours" spent in Alexandria we may doubt. It is very soon after this that to Octavia he confesses an ill-regulated past life and promises reformation, only to declare to himself, when she has left him and he has had an opportunity to talk with the sooth-sayer, that he will return to Egypt and its pleasures. The Antony of *Antony and Cleopatra,* like the Antony of *Julius Caesar,* can cloak dishonesty with plausibility.

The scene of the banquet on Pompey's galley is one of

Shakespeare's masterstrokes in the combination of appeal
to the groundlings and appeal to the more discerning members of his audience. It puts the competitors for world power
into antic disguise and has the aspect of being an interlude
of low comedy, but it is actually one of the crucial scenes of
the tragedy because of its character revelation. As the wine
flows, during the competition of the drinking bout, the
principals expose themselves in a way that foreshadows the
outcome of the larger struggle. *In vino veritas* would be
the right motto for the scene. Antony is thoroughly in his
element, all too willing to put the cares of the world out of
his mind and exercise his genius for revelry. Poor Lepidus
goes down and out, no more able to succeed in a drinking
bout than in a bout for world rulership. Pompey shows himself incapable of winning the world by ruthlessness, which
is the only way he can possibly win it. At the end of the
scene it is plain that Antony has nothing to fear from
Lepidus and Pompey and everything to fear from Octavius.
In the course of the scene Octavius reveals an ominous ability to remain master of himself and keep "graver business"
in mind. Antony dominates the revelry, but Octavius dominates the gathering.

From what we see of Cleopatra before Antony returns
to her, we know surely that there are depths in her character which the opening scene of the play does not lead us
to suspect. We are not surprised when she beats the messenger who brings news that Antony has married Octavia,
or when she hales him up and down by the hair, or even
when she threatens to take his life with her dagger. These
demonstrations of passionate folly amuse us and do not in

any way shock us. We are prepared for them. But we are
not prepared for the demonstration of something other
than folly that is made by Cleopatra when she herself finally
is shocked by her mistreatment of the innocent bearer of
ill tidings and declares that she has acted ignobly. Even her
royal spirit is paradoxical. It can produce both the pettiness
shown by her assault upon the messenger and the high-
mindedness shown by the following condemnation of that
assault:

> These hands do lack nobility, that they strike
> A meaner than myself; since I myself
> Have given myself the cause. (II, v, 82–84)

While Antony is in Rome, Cleopatra is willing to un-
people Egypt in sending messengers to him. Her thoughts
are with him constantly, and she has no zest for her usual
round of frivolities. All this does not prove that what she
feels for Antony has great depth, but it does prove that what
she feels has some depth. At the very least it proves that she
is captivated by her demi-Atlas and has for the time being
made him the supporter of her world of sensuous pleasure.
Shakespeare brings her to this state of captivation on his
own authority. From what Plutarch says, one might guess
that when Antony left Alexandria for Rome, Cleopatra was
heartless enough to go on with her normal life of pleasure,
whatever wound her pride may have suffered. Thus we
begin to see that Shakespeare is more charitable than Plutarch toward the Cleopatra of that part of the story which
precedes the Battle of Actium.

We continue to see this greater charitableness on the
part of Shakespeare when he shows Antony and Cleopatra

reunited and moving toward the battle. In the period of preparation for the battle there is no devious action by Cleopatra against Antony—no bribing, as there is in Plutarch, of Canidius by Cleopatra in order that she may take care of her own interests at the expense of Antony's. There is nothing to indicate that Cleopatra wants to fight the battle by sea in order to have an easy way to save herself should the action be lost, despite the very plain statement by Plutarch which would justify the giving of that selfish motive to her. Nor does Cleopatra, with a jest, irresponsibly make light of danger when the advance of Octavius becomes known, as she does in Plutarch; instead of suggesting that the advance of Octavius to Toryne means little, she says sharply that it shows a celerity in Octavius which Antony has lacked. As she takes part in the preparations, Cleopatra is a dignified queen, asserting her responsibility as the "president" of a kingdom and declaring firmly that she will appear in the battle "for a man."

Cleopatra flees from the battle because she is unqueened by fear. In Antony a natural physical courage exists in combination with sensualism. In Cleopatra it does not. This is not merely to say that Antony is a man used to the danger of battle, and Cleopatra a woman unused to it. Sensualism, with its appetite for the worldly pleasures to be obtained through rulership, helps to make Cleopatra a queen, as it helps to make Antony a shaper of empire, but it works upon her, as it does not work upon him, to make flight from pain instinctive. When she finally takes her own life, with what she conceives to be queenly courage, it is only after she has made a search for "easy ways to die."

After Antony has followed Cleopatra away from Actium "like a doting mallard" and then with a kiss has forgiven her "fearful sails," there is never any real question that he is firmly bound to her by love. His judgment of men and affairs decays as he gives himself more and more completely to her, and Enobarbus draws attention to the decay. As a leader Antony becomes a pitiful figure. Yet he retains nobility. He still shows largeness of heart toward his followers, and still shows bravery. Enobarbus, dying as a conscience-stricken renegade, assesses him finally in these terms:

> O Antony!
> Nobler than my revolt is infamous.
> (IV, ix, 18–19)

But after the defeat at Actium we soon find ourselves confronted with a very real question about Cleopatra's feelings toward Antony: we are forced to wonder whether she is bound to him as he is to her. The question rises when Octavius, hoping that Cleopatra will betray Antony, sends Thyreus to talk with her. At this point Shakespeare deals less charitably with Cleopatra than Plutarch, who, without giving us any very definite cause to doubt Cleopatra's faithfulness, says briefly and noncommittally that she did such honor to Thyreus and talked so long with him that Antony in jealous anger had him whipped and sent back to Octavius. Shakespeare gives us much more definite cause to suspect Cleopatra as he presents her interview with Thyreus. When Thyreus says that Caesar knows she embraced Antony not as she did love but as she feared him, Cleopatra exclaims, "O!" This interesting "O!" certainly does not mean that Cleopatra is shocked to hear the suggestion that she never loved Antony but was merely forced into an alliance with him. What follows makes it quite clear that, as Kittredge says: "Cleopatra's exclamation is meant to convey to Thyreus not only eager acceptance of Caesar's theory of her union with Antony, but also gratified surprise that Caesar should have shown so sympathetic an understanding of the case."[53] It is possible, of course, that Cleopatra eagerly accepts the suggestion of Thyreus because she plans to beguile Caesar in the interests of both Antony and herself. But Enobarbus, without hesitation, interprets Cleopatra's reply to Thyreus in the worst possible way. "Thy dearest quit thee" is what he thinks Antony must be told. Shakespeare has made Enobarbus a shrewd judge of character, and by making him now suspect the worst of Cleopatra he seems to be leading us to suspect the worst.

It must be added that Cleopatra appears to be dallying with the thought of using her charm to make one more conquest when she says archly, as she allows Thyreus to kiss her hand:

> Your Cæsar's father oft,
> When he hath mus'd of taking kingdoms in,
> Bestow'd his lips on that unworthy place,
> As it rain'd kisses.
> (III, xi, 82–85)

To say the least, the reminiscence is in bad taste. It is one that a Cleopatra faithful to Antony and bound to him by common disaster might well have foregone. Antony's ordering that the hand-kissing Thyreus be whipped and sent back to Octavius is like an action recorded in Plutarch, but his ensuing excoriation of Cleopatra for having been "a boggler ever," incapable of faithfulness in love, is like nothing in Plutarch. How much or how little are we meant to discount the furious lines in which Antony implies that he has given himself wholly to a woman who cannot give herself wholly to any man, and implies further that his eyes have been seeled by the gods so that he will adore his errors as he goes to his confusion? His instant forgiveness of Cleopatra after he has disposed of Thyreus and after she has sworn with a few working words that her love for him is not cold seems to confirm what he has said about adoration of errors. It rounds out the picture he has given of his subjection to her and does nothing at all to make her words and actions in the interview with Thyreus less suspicious.

This scene shows, as much as any, whatever irony of superiority Shakespeare brings to his handling of Antony and Cleopatra. Here he lays himself out to prove that though he presents these two as worthy of sympathy he is no special pleader for them. The marvel is that his detachment can be so great and yet leave room not merely for some sympathy, but for much sympathy. Shakespeare shows detachment in all the plays that make up his last tragic world, but in no one of the others, perhaps, is his combination of detachment with sympathy so remarkable as in *Antony and Cleopatra.*

Shakespeare gives no reason why Cleopatra should be suspected of playing false when the ships and land troops remaining to Antony refuse to fight, and when Antony, thinking that she has betrayed him, turns once more against her in fury. It adds to the poignancy of Antony's tragedy that at the end he needs little cause to distrust Cleopatra and can all too easily revive the thought of her being a "triple-turn'd whore," but nevertheless is completely hers. When he hears the false news of her death, he falls on his sword with intent to overtake her in the next world and weep for pardon. When he finds that he is dying because she has practiced one of her artifices and that she is alive and free to deal with Octavius if she will, he is beyond being able to feel resentment. With true unselfishness he even urges her to deal with Octavius and gain safety if she can.

Antony's death brings from Cleopatra an expression of grief that may seem either superbly histrionic or superbly genuine. The question raised at this point is whether Cleopatra has developed a love for Antony that makes it impossible for her to live without him. Will love for him be the actual cause of her suicide and will she, then, die in the odor of sanctity as one of Cupid's saints? In the manner of her suicide will it be plain that, to use Chaucer's words, there "was nevere unto hire love a trewer quene"?

An assumption that Cleopatra took her life for no other reason than that she wanted to avoid being led in triumph by Octavius was made often enough in Elizabethan England. Writers who made that assumption saw no reason to think that a woman of her character was capable of being true in love and of dying for love. They were allowed, though certainly not compelled, by what they found in Plutarch, to think that Cleopatra would not have killed herself if Octavius had not taken steps to have her sent to Rome. Richard Reynoldes, in *A Chronicle of All the Noble Emperours of the Romans* (1571), says that she killed herself to save her honor as a queen—to keep herself from being degraded and made a laughing stock in Caesar's triumph. Reynoldes thinks so little of her that he has her capable of trying the poison of an asp upon her two faithful waiting women, who, he says, were unsuspecting objects of experiment. This is the way he tells the story of her death:

When *Octauius* the Emperour ouercame *Antony,* hee was purposed to take *Cleopatra* aliue, and to bringe so royall a person to Rome in triumphe, when *Cleopatra* vnderstode the minde of *Octauius* the *Emperour,* she thought it more honour and renowne to her to dye a queene thoughe she killed her selfe, then to goe to Rome in triumph at the will of other, a captiue, a spectacle, a laughinge stock to all ye world, wherevpon she sought the way to murder herselfe, she called to her the ii faythfull maydes she had, *Naera* and *Carmion* was theyr names, who alwayes serued to the adorninge and deckinge of her bodye, the one of them foulded her heares, the other to pare her nayles: she commaunded that they should bringe vnto her a certaine serpente called *Plyas* couered with figge leaues and vyne leaues whereby she thoughte to deceiue the keepers and watche men, and she made a proufe of poyson of her two gentle women *Naera* and *Carmion* they not knowing of the poison as sone as she sawe the poyson to take effecte sodenlye vpon them, she applyed ye same vnto her selfe, some write that she applyed ii Serpētes vnto her brestes and so dyed of them, somme write that shee made a longe and deepe wounde vppon her arme first with her teethe, and then the poyson taken of ye Serpent, she put it in a cuppe, and so the poyson with his infected qualitye, destroyed her sodainly: *Cleopatra* was found with her righte hand to holde vppon her heade a princelye Crowne, that in her death shee mighte appeare a Queene to all that behelde her.[54]

Without such elaboration, Thomas Beard, in *The Theatre of Gods Iudgements* (1597), says that "to the intent she might not be carried in triumph to Rome" Cleopatra "caused an aspe to bite her to death,"[55] and William Fulbeck, in *An Historicall Collection of the Continuall Factions, Tumults, and Massacres of the Romans and Italians*

(1601), says with equal brevity that "because she would not grace Octauius so much as to be led in triumph by him, she put Aspes to her breasts, and was by them done to death."[56]

We have seen that though Garnier makes Cleopatra die mainly for love, Daniel makes her die mainly for honor. Whereas Garnier makes little of her fear that Octavius would lead her in triumph, Daniel makes much, and has that fear drive her to shun disgrace, escape her foe, free her soul, and act the last of life with glory as a queen. Daniel's Cleopatra flees to her love when she dies, but the thought of that from which she flees has determined her to die. Both Garnier and Daniel present Cleopatra sympathetically as a mother who loves her children and tears herself away from them. Garnier makes her decide that her children have less call upon her than Antony has, Daniel that they have less than her honor has. Daniel, of course, shows general sympathy for Cleopatra, no less than Garnier. If he makes her reveal selfishness in dying for honor rather than love, it is at least a kind of selfishness that is an infirmity of noble minds.

In writing the closing scenes of *Antony and Cleopatra* Shakespeare pays his compliments in two directions with marked evenhandedness, now to the tradition that Cleopatra was really moved to end her life by concern for herself and her honor, and now to the tradition that she was really moved to do so by love for Antony. His evenhandedness can be exasperating to anyone bent upon determining whether his Cleopatra does or does not die as one of Cupid's saints; he takes and uses effectively almost everything to be found in either tradition.

The result is that as Shakespeare's Cleopatra builds up a conviction that she must kill herself, she is swayed alternately by the thought of Caesar's triumph and the thought of Antony. The thought of the triumph is the first to take hold upon her. While Antony is still alive she comes to a decision that if she can avoid being led in triumph only by dying, then she will die. Antony, it would seem, puts the thought of the triumph in her mind. When he thinks she has arranged to let their remaining fleet desert to Octavius, he tells her in his anger that she is marked to follow Caesar's chariot, to become a spectacle for the Roman mob, and to suffer attack upon her visage by the "prepared nails" of Octavia. This word picture apparently has a profound effect upon her. When Antony is brought dying to the monument in which she has taken refuge, she refuses to open its gate because she dares not risk being captured and put to the degradation which he has described. She vows, as she asks his pardon for not opening the gate, that if knife, drugs, or serpents can kill, she will not let Octavius and Octavia acquire honor by looking upon her as a dishonored captive in Rome. But after Antony has been lifted into the monument and has died in her arms, the thought of him seems to drive away the thought of the triumph. Immediately after his death, she makes up her mind that she cannot abide in a dull world from which he is absent and that because of her loss of him she will end her life in the "high Roman fashion."

When next we see Cleopatra, just before her interview with Proculeius, her mind has reverted to the triumph and to the escape from Caesar's power that suicide will provide;

she thinks now only of outwitting an antagonist whom she scorns as "Fortune's knave." After Proculeius has entered the monument, she promises to take her life, whatever Caesar can do, and to cheat Caesar, Octavia, and the Roman varletry of their triumph. But as Proculeius leaves and she begins to talk with Dolabella, her mind turns again to the incomparable Antony whom she has lost.

Then, as she comes to the end of her interview with Dolabella, she asks what is apparently a most significant question:

> Know you what Cæsar means to do with me?
>
> (V, ii, 106)

Why, we may ask, should she be worried about what Caesar means to do with her if she has fully made up her mind to leave the dull world that no longer contains Antony? To her question about Caesar's intention Cleopatra obtains from Dolabella a definite answer, for he assures her that Caesar will lead her in triumph. He leaves her no room for doubt when he says:

> Madam, he will; I know't.
>
> (V, ii, 110)

The entry of Caesar is announced as soon as Dolabella has spoken these words, and there is no immediate indication of Cleopatra's reaction to them, but it cannot be thought that she takes them lightly or forgets them during her interview with Caesar. Caesar labors to play the merciful conqueror in what he says to her, though he does make a threat that he will take the lives of her children if she takes her own life. He encourages her to think that if she allows herself to live she will be in every way well treated. He even forgives her for making an incomplete list of her treasure, a list which her treasurer Seleucus exposes as showing no more than half of what she possesses, and he says that she may keep all her treasure. Shakespeare is very careful not to let us know whether Cleopatra has made this incomplete list because she has thought, before talking with Dolabella, that possibly she would decide to remain in the dull world and would thus perhaps have use for some of her treasure, or because, having arranged with Seleucus for the exposure, she has undertaken to mask a full-formed intention to die by giving the appearance of wanting to live.

Immediately after Caesar and his train have departed, Cleopatra turns to her women with these words:

> He words me, girls, he words me, that I should not
> Be noble to myself.   (V, ii, 190–191)

Then she whispers to Charmian and sends for the asps. Apparently the assurance given by Dolabella that Caesar will lead her in triumph remains fixed in Cleopatra's mind while Caesar "words" her, and as Caesar departs it becomes the cause of her first effective step toward suicide. Her desire to "be noble" to herself appears to be a desire to save herself from the ignoble fate that Caesar plans for her. Thus it seems to be about herself and about her honor that Cleopatra is thinking when she sends Charmian for the asps. There is no sign that she is thinking about Antony. Neither, we must take notice, is there any sign that she is thinking about her children. Caesar's threat that he will put her children to death if she kills herself has seemingly passed her by. It has produced in her no visible struggle to decide whether her children bind her to life. Unlike Garnier and Daniel, Shakespeare gives Cleopatra no love for her children that has dramatic meaning.

When Dolabella hastily returns and tells Cleopatra in a brief second interview that Caesar has decided to leave Alexandria and within three days to send her and her children before him, she is confirmed in her purpose to die. She will not be shown as a spectacle to the mechanic slaves of Rome. She will not see her greatness belittled by the quick comedians of the Roman stage.

Now Antony comes back into her mind. He remains there and is dominant during the few moments of life that are left to her. She will not see her own greatness belittled on the Roman stage, and neither will she see Antony's. She will go to Antony. She will go in her best attire, as though going once more to meet him on the Cydnus. It is the call of Antony that she hears as she proceeds to the fulfillment of her "immortal longings." She makes answer to him:

> Husband, I come:
> Now to that name my courage prove my title!
> (V, ii, 289–290)

When she applies an asp to her breast, she does not forget her purpose to prove "great Cæsar ass unpolicied," but almost her last words are "O Antony!"

Obviously, an advocate who would have Shakespeare's Cleopatra enrolled in the catalogue of Cupid's saints can make a case for canonization. Having many times previously sworn her love for Antony, she dies with that "Husband, I come" and that "O Antony!" upon her lips. It may be argued that these words, spoken at the moment when she would naturally reveal whatever lies deepest in her heart, show that her love for Antony has come to be the center of her being. She seems to think of herself as winning the right to call Antony husband by demonstrating, in the face of defeat and threatened dishonor, the courage to make a Roman exit from life such as he has made. She visualizes Antony as rousing himself in the next world to praise her "noble act" and mock the "luck of Cæsar."

But, just as obviously, a Devil's advocate can make a case against canonization. Cleopatra seems to have thought of escaping Caesar's triumph by suicide before Antony gives her his Roman example of suicide. Before Antony dies she seems quite capable of deciding her fate independently. After he dies she prolongs her stay in the world that he has deserted, and she ends that stay only after she is absolutely certain that Caesar plans to lead her in triumph. As she makes her decision to end her life, she says nothing of a desire to rejoin Antony or a desire to do what Antony would approve, but talks only of being noble to herself. It seems that the self to which she is to be noble means far more to her than her children, and we may therefore all the more readily believe that it means more than Antony. As for the "Husband, I come" and the "O Antony!" of the death scene, it may be effectively argued by the heartless critic that in these words an ever-histrionic Cleopatra is dramatizing her exit from the world with a fine show of sentiment.

Perhaps it is the Devil's advocate who in the way of reason can make the better case. He has an advantage in that he argues from both words and actions of Cleopatra's, not merely from words, as his opponent does.

But by following reason coldly the Devil's advocate may arrive at a condemnation of Cleopatra that Shakespeare will not support. The beauty and sublimity of the poetry given to her upon more than one occasion when she speaks of what Antony means to her must be felt and duly taken into account by the critic if the Cleopatra whom he judges is to remain Shakespeare's. This beauty and this sublimity are parts of a certain splendor lent by Shakespeare to his heroine which persistently refuses to be written off as in every way false. If we are to understand that the love of Cleopatra for Antony, like her character, continues to be deeply flawed to the end of her life, we are nevertheless to understand that, like her character, it has its measure of nobility. If Cleopatra never comes to have a love for Antony to match his love for her, she at least comes to have magnificent visions of what it would be like to achieve such a love, and her climactic vision leads her to call him husband as she dies.

Shakespeare seems to have done his poetic best to make us feel that the full achievement of Cleopatra in love is a dark matter, dark perhaps even to her, but that though she very possibly does not attain to a noble constancy in love, she does attain to a noble aspiration in love. Also, Shakespeare seems to have done his poetic best to make us sense in the "immortal longings" of Cleopatra a paradox to cap the other paradoxes in her character—a paradox which gives her the visions of a daughter of the game at the same time that it gives her those of a constant wife. The waiting

woman Iras dies before her mistress submits herself to the
asp. Says Cleopatra, in haste to overtake her:

> This proves me base:
> If she first meet the curled Antony,
> He'll make demand of her, and spend that kiss
> Which is my heaven to have.   (V, ii, 302–305)

One may gather that for Cleopatra Elysium is to be an
eternity of faithfulness in love and yet somehow it is also
to be an eternity of delightful competition for kisses. Competition between the mistress and the maid is not to be
excluded. Cleopatra is very much the queen, but even more
she is the woman, and merely as a woman she is willing
to take her chances with any other woman in this world or
the next.

VII

As we pass from *Macbeth* to *Antony and Cleopatra* we see
the problem of evil suddenly lose urgency for Shakespeare.
In *Antony and Cleopatra* there are no villains. The hero
and heroine have nothing of true villainy in them, and their
ruin is not brought about, even in part, by villainy in others.
Shakespeare might, on the authority of Plutarch, have
given them much more strongly marked strains of cruelty
than they have, but he chose in the main to make their
vices the more amiable ones and to show them as destroyers
of themselves rather than destroyers of others. They are in
no sense trapped into doing what they do to themselves,
either by human or by supernatural opponents. They go
their own ways to destruction.

We may even gain the impression that outside forces are
often kind to Antony and Cleopatra and in general go so

far as to favor them until what the lovers create for themselves becomes too strong for benevolent powers to counteract. Before the Battle of Actium, friends do all they can to save Antony from making false judgments. At the battle, "vantage" appears "like a pair of twins," and that of Antony and Cleopatra even seems to be "the elder," until Cleopatra flees and Antony follows. Enobarbus turns renegade only when his leader's fortunes are completely hopeless, and the god Hercules waits even longer to remove his protection from Antony. The fate that works through human character is against Antony when he brings himself into competition with Octavius. Antony accepts without demur the soothsayer's judgment that the guardian spirit of Octavius has a mysterious power to reduce his own spirit to fear, and to dim the luster of it, when he and Octavius come together. But this fate nevertheless is generous to Antony. For his daemon is

> Noble, courageous, high, unmatchable
>
> (II, iii, 20)

when not near Caesar's.

In *Antony and Cleopatra* there is nothing to suggest that the order of life is in a state of decay or that medicine needs to be administered to a sickly weal. There is no one in the play who struggles idealistically against wrong. Octavius puts Antony down and becomes a better lord of the whole world than Antony could ever have been, but though he despises the sensualism of Antony he does not fight against him to free the world from that sensualism and its effects. He fights against him simply to work out his own imperial destiny.

As Shakespeare proceeds with the creation of his last tragic world, he comes logically to that view of the tragic scheme of things which we find in *Antony and Cleopatra*. Seeing tragedy more and more as a product of flaw in character, he sees less and less of mystery in its causation. Then suddenly the mysteries of evil and injustice cease to challenge him. This does not mean that he turns to a presentation of tragedy which has nothing in it of the enigmatic and that he does violence to life by reducing it to the neat form of a solved problem. In the amplitude of *Antony and Cleopatra* there are enigmas in abundance. But all of them that really matter are within the hero and heroine; they are enigmas of personal constitution. At last, Shakespeare's growing interest in the paradox he has discovered in deeply flawed yet noble character becomes very distinctly his sustaining interest in the writing of tragedy. This paradox, which in *Timon* and *Macbeth* has been for him one of the most challenging of tragic mysteries, becomes for him in *Antony and Cleopatra* the all-absorbing tragic mystery.

Chapter V

"CORIOLANUS"

IN *Coriolanus,* Shakespeare finds within deeply flawed yet noble human character the only tragic mystery that really matters, just as he does in *Antony and Cleopatra.* He also focuses attention narrowly upon a single example, as he does not in *Antony and Cleopatra.* The tragic flaw of the hero reveals itself at the very beginning of the action, and once we have seen it we never wonder whether we have seen it aright. It is constantly in evidence, first as Coriolanus rises to an eminence from which he can reach for the Roman consulship, then as he mars his fortune and enters upon a downward course, and finally as he goes to his destruction.

The hero does not merely stand at the center of the tragedy; he *is* the tragedy. He brings no one down with him in his fall, and his character is entirely sufficient to explain his fall. No supernatural forces are shown to be at work against him. The tribunes and Aufidius work underhandedly to entrap and undo him, but it seems that by taking advantage of the imperfections of his nature they only hurry him into making tragic errors which eventually he would have made of his own accord. The tragic flaw of Coriolanus is pride, as we are told by other characters in the play again and again. The paradox of Coriolanus is that in his pride, or closely connected with it, there is not only everything bad but also everything good by which he comes to be a subject for Shakespearean tragedy.

Shakespeare took from the moral Plutarch the conception of Coriolanus as a notable combination of good and bad qualities, but he changed radically the nature of the combination. He intensified the drama involved in the opposition between the two sets of qualities by binding them much more closely together than Plutarch had bound them. It was Shakespeare himself who created the paradox in Coriolanus, and he did so by making the good and the bad in his character into elements seemingly inseparable and even seemingly interdependent.

In the introduction to the biography of Coriolanus in North's translation of Plutarch's *Lives,* Shakespeare found his tragic hero presented as "a good proofe to confirme some mens opinions" that "a rare and excellent witte vntaught, doth bring forth many good and euill things together: like as a fat soile bringeth forth herbes & weedes that lieth vn-manured."[1] Plutarch makes out in his introduction that the essential nature of Coriolanus was excellent and that his faults were due to a lack of proper education. Coriolanus (to continue in the words of North), "being left an orphan by his father, was brought vp vnder his mother a widowe, who taught vs by experience, that orphanage bringeth many discommodities to a childe, but does not hinder him to become an honest man, and to excell in vertue aboue the common sorte." Because he was not meanly born and because he inherited eminently good qualities, Coriolanus had great natural virtue, but this virtue lacked cultivation at the hands of a painstaking father. His "naturall wit and great harte dyd maruelously sturre vp his corage, to do and

_____
[1] For notes to chapter v see pages 277–278.

attempt notable actes." But "for lacke of education, he was so cholericke and impacient, that he would yeld to no liuing creature: which made him churlishe, vnciuill, and altogether vnfit for any mans conuersation." Men marveled much "at his constancy, that he was neuer ouercome with pleasure, nor money, and howe he would endure easely all manner of paynes and trauailles: thereupon they well liked and commended his stowtnes and temperancie." Yet "they could not be acquainted with him, as one citizen vseth to be with another in the cittie" because of his unpleasant behavior and "a certaine insolent and sterne manner he had, which because it was so lordly, was disliked." In short, Coriolanus lacked "the greatest benefit that learning bringeth men vnto," for he had never been taught "by compasse and rule of reason, to be ciuill and curteous & to like better the meane state, then the higher."

Neither in this introductory character analysis nor in anything said later does Plutarch make innate pride the principal or underlying fault of Coriolanus. As he proceeds to tell the story of his rise and fall he uses the terms haughty and insolent to characterize him, but he thinks of his haughtiness and the insolence that went with it as issuing from untutored rudeness and roughness, that is, from a lack of education for which Coriolanus himself was not responsible. Also, Plutarch mentions more frequently than the fault of haughtiness the fault of choler, which, as he says, made Coriolanus excessively impatient with his fellows and helped to keep him from yielding to any living creature; and this fault likewise he thinks of as issuing from the same untutored rudeness and roughness. When the common people refused Coriolanus the consulship after having approved him for the office, he was "out of all pacience," says Plutarch, and proved that "he was a man to full of passion and choller, and to muche geuen to over selfe will and opinion, as one of a highe minde and great corage, that lacked the grauity, and affabilitie that is gotten with iudgment of learning and reason, which only is to be looked for in a gouernour of state." When the judgment of banishment came upon him, "he was so caried awaye with the vehemencie of anger, and desire of reuenge, that he had no sence nor feeling of the hard state he was in." He showed that the choleric man can be "so altered, and mad in his actions, as a man set a fyre with a burning agewe."

When Plutarch offers his final estimate of Coriolanus in the "Comparison of Alcibiades with Martius Coriolanus," he gives more attention to the fault of haughtiness than he has given before, but he still mentions the haughtiness in connection with that austerity or churlishness which he has described as resulting from lack of education. The basic flaw of Coriolanus seems to Plutarch, as he writes the "Comparison," to have been an austerity and a haughty obstinacy which amounted to the same thing: "And of all his misfortune and ill happe the austerity of his nature, and his hawtie obstinate minde, was the onely cause: the which of it selfe being hatefull to the worlde, when it is ioyned with ambition, it groweth then much more churlish, fierce, and intollerable. For men that haue that fault in nature, are not affable to the people, seeming thereby as though they made no estimacion or regard of the people: and yet on thother side, if the people should not geue them honour and reuerence, they would straight take it in scorne, and little care for the matter." Aside from his failings Coriolanus had a character worthy of the highest admiration: "Martius stowtnes, and hawty stomake, did stay him from making much of those, that might aduaunce and honour him: and yet his ambition made him gnawe him selfe for spite and anger when he saw he was despised. And this is all that reasonably may be reproued in him: for otherwise he lacked no good commendable vertues and qualities. For his temperaunce, and cleane handes from taking of bribes and money, he may be compared with the most perfect, vertuous, and honest men of all Græce."

Thus, as Plutarch sees it, there was nothing paradoxical about the nobility of spirit shown by Coriolanus. His good qualities were thoroughly good and his bad thoroughly bad, and the two sets of qualities were quite separate. His honesty, temperance, and valor had sufficient power in themselves and drew no strength from his insolent haughtiness, which was purely a failing. Plutarch very obviously thinks that these virtues could have existed in Coriolanus, and could have shown to better advantage, if the haughtiness had been absent, for the haughtiness was merely unpolished roughness and had a train of anger that was merely impatience. It was not this haughtiness but his "great harte" that stirred up the courage of Coriolanus and made him do notable deeds. The separation between his good and bad qualities was all the more distinct because they had separate origins: the good existed because of his heredity and the bad because of the environment of his youth. Certainly Plutarch wants his readers to see the faults of Coriolanus plainly and to draw a moral lesson from them, but he gives the impression that the good characteristics of Coriolanus are the natural man—the true man—and that the bad ones are accidentally acquired. The faults of Shakespeare's Coriolanus are much more deeply rooted than those of Plutarch's Coriolanus.

II

It was entirely possible for a man of the European Renaissance to be blind to the faults of Coriolanus and to see in his story an example of the envy and hatred that human mediocrity all too frequently feels toward those who are set apart in the world by greatness of spirit; for to one type of Renaissance mind it might seem that Coriolanus had the military genius of a Tamburlaine and yet was cast out of his native city by a spiteful Roman populace, who preferred to be ignominiously weak without him rather than gloriously strong with him. In the Renaissance the monarchic form of government was generally looked upon as best, the aristocratic as faulty but next best, and the democratic as bad; and Coriolanus might readily be seen as a staunch member of a ruling aristocracy who quite properly had no love for the hydra-headed, fickle multitude of Rome. His lack of love for the common people of his city could be made into an outstanding virtue—though not, be it noted, on the authority of Plutarch.

For example, the garrulous Welshman Ludovic Lloyd, one of the sergeants-at-arms and gentlemen in ordinary to Queen Elizabeth, who fancied himself for the way in which he could work shreds of classical learning into almost any kind of discussion, saw Coriolanus in that light. In *The*

Consent of Time (1590) Lloyd pictures him as a "rare man" who was banished for his virtues and who later, when he had it in his power to take revenge, spared Rome because of the compassion he felt for his family:

In *Rome* dwelt a rare man of great seruice in the warres of *Tarquine*, whom *Largius* the first *Dictator* knewe to be such as deserued great prayse then, being a young man: for he was crowned with Oken leaues according to the *Romanes* maners in *Tarquinius* dayes, and sithence profited *Rome* in diuers seruices, in subduing the *Volscans*, in winning the citie *Corioles*, he inuaded the *Antiates*, and often repressed the insolencie of the people, insomuch that the *Romanes* hauing many warres in those dayes, this *Coriolanus* was at them all: for there was no battell fought, no warre enterprised, but *Coriolanus* returned from thence with fame and honour. But his vertue and renowme gate him much enuie: for hereby hee was banished *Rome* by the *Ediles* & *Tribunes* of the people, against the Patricians will: but the *Romanes* made a rodde to beate them selues, when they banished *Coriolanus*: for he came in armes against his owne Countrie and Citie with the *Volscans*, being at that time their generall. . . . *Volumnia* his mother, and *Virgillia* his wife with their two young sonnes gotten by *Coriolanus*, with *Valeria* the sister of *Publicola*, and diuers other Ladies of *Rome* came to meete *Coriolanus*, to entreate for peace vnto the *Volscans* campe, and what time hee had compassion of his mother, of his wife, and of his two sonnes, and of the other Ladies being his neere kinswomen: then he withdrew his armie from *Rome*, and yeelded to the teares of his mother: but the fickle mindes of the people by the conspiracie of *Tullus Aufidius* were such, that *Coriolanus* was murdered in the Citie of *Antium*, at his very returne from that voyage.[2]

In *The Stratagems of Ierusalem* (1602) Lloyd has more to say about the high deserts of Coriolanus and the great injustice of his banishment. Here again Lloyd does not mention his faults. Coriolanus was one of the "best deserued men in *Rome*." Like Scipio Africanus, Metellus, and "diuers others of the best Romanes," he was "vniustly banished." Yet he was capable of "sparing to destroy his vngratefull countrey" because of the tears shed by his mother and his wife. For this act of mercy he was slain by the Volscians; "he might well haue said as *Scypio Affrican* said at *Linternum* after he was banished, *Ingrata patria non habebis ossa mea,* Oh vngratefull countrey, thou shalt not possesse my bones."[3]

The French dramatist Alexandre Hardy wrote his *Coriolan* early in the seventeenth century, perhaps just before Shakespeare wrote his *Coriolanus.* Hardy's conception of Coriolanus is more like Lloyd's than like Shakespeare's, though Hardy, however lacking in distinction he may be as a dramatist, is not to be put in a literary class with the unimaginative Lloyd. Hardy shows great admiration for Plutarch in the "Argument" prefixed to *Coriolan* and yet he mentions there none of the faults of Coriolanus that Plutarch dwells upon as the cause of his fall. The tragedy, as Hardy offers it to the reader in his "Argument," has to do with a "grand Personnage" exiled from Rome most unjustly. Hardy begins his summary of the action thus: "Coriolan apres plusieurs signalez seruices rendus à sa patrie, est en fin contraint de ceder à l'enuie du peuple Romain, qui sur des crimes supposez le condamne à vn exil perpetuel. Injure tellement sensible & incompatible à ce grand courage, qu'il se resoût à la vengeance, à tel prix que ce fût."[4] We are led to expect a tragedy in which the faults of Coriolanus play no essential part and in which the main cause of his misfortune is the Roman people's envy of his greatness.

This, as a matter of fact, is the sort of tragedy that Hardy writes. He does not show any of the course of action by which Coriolanus excites the anger of the populace. At the beginning of the play Coriolanus is about to be condemned by the people, and before the end of the first act he is exiled, after he has talked eloquently through two scenes about the great wrong that is being done him and after he has been given every chance to make us feel that he is indeed suffering a grave injustice. As the act concludes, a chorus of Romans engages in a triumphal chant opening with the words: "Va, va, monstre orgueilleux." This must be taken as revealing the malice of the people and not as indicating a pride in the hero that may be called a tragic flaw. After leading the Volscians against Rome, Coriolanus spares the city out of dutiful love for his mother. For his *piété* he sacrifices his honor and his life. When his mother learns that he has been killed by the Volscians, she laments that in order to save her country from destruction she has been forced to immolate her "innocent" son. In the course of her lament she addresses herself in these terms:

> O Mere parricide! ô Mere criminelle!
> De ton sang innocent execrable bourrelle.[5]

This lament of Volumnia's ends the play. For Hardy the most moving circumstances of the tragedy seem to be the dutiful sacrifices made by Coriolanus and his mother.

But if it was possible for the Renaissance sometimes to be blind to the faults of Coriolanus, it was also possible for it sometimes to see them as plainly as Plutarch had intended them to be seen, though in a Christian rather than a pagan

light. The haughtiness and angry impatience that Plutarch
had found in Coriolanus and had attributed to faulty education could be made into instructive examples of moral
failings that should be severely condemned by all followers
of the Christian tradition. They could be taken as pride
and wrath by an age that had by no means forgotten the
spiritually destructive qualities of these two deadly sins.
They could be thought of as pernicious vices or ruinous
passions. In the *Politicke, Moral, and Martial Discourses.
Written in French by M. Iaques Hurault ... and translated
into English by Arthur Golding* (1595) Coriolanus is named
in one context as a "man of valour" who like some others
of his nature had been hindered in all "well doing" by the
"only vice" of pride. Plutarch is the authority quoted:
"*Plutarch* in the life of *Coriolane,* saith, That the proud and
stoure nature of *Coriolane,* was the cause of his ruine, not-
withstanding that therwithall he was one of the absolutest
men of all the Romanes. For whereas pride of it selfe is
odious to all men, surely when it is matched with ambition,
then becommeth it much more sauage and vntollerable."[6]
In another context in the same work Coriolanus is named
as a "great personage" and "but for his choler, one of the
forwardest in Rome." Choler "did raigne so sore in him,
that it made him of small account, and vnmeet to liue and
be conuersant with men." Again Plutarch is the authority
quoted: "And as the same authour [Plutarch] saith in the
life of *Coriolanus,* Anger seemeth to be magnanimity, because it hath a desire to ouercome, and will not yeeld to any
man: and yet for all that it is but a feeblenes, the which
thrusteth the choler forth, as the weakest and most pas-

sionate part of the soule, no less than a corrupt matter of
an imposthume. They that have vpheld, that cholericke
persons are apt to learne, haue added that they were not fit
for gouernement, and therefore that the Lacedemonians
praied dayly vnto God, to inable them to beare wrongs:
esteeming that person vnworthie to be in authoritie, or to
deale in great affairs, that is subiect to anger."[7]

III

Shakespeare is so far from being blind to the faults of Coriolanus that he makes them as pernicious as any moralist
of his age makes them. He gives them, with regard to their
effects in this world, the destructive powers of deadly sins,
and he allows them to wear the aspects of deadly sins. Out-
wardly the Coriolanus of Shakespeare is much like the
haughty and angrily impatient Coriolanus of Plutarch, but
inwardly he is a very different man; for as Coriolanus
passes through the hands of Shakespeare, the overlying
haughtiness, the "hawtie obstinate minde," given him by
Plutarch becomes an underlying pride, a spiritual flaw
reaching to the depth of his being, and this deep-going
pride has deep-going wrath in its train instead of mere
angry impatience. Moreover, the wrath of Shakespeare's
Coriolanus is much more clearly subsidiary to pride than
the angry impatience of Plutarch's Coriolanus is subsidiary
to haughtiness. Shakespeare's Coriolanus is often a wrathful
man, but always and before all else he is a proud man.
Whenever we see his wrath, we know that it is fed by pride.

The tragedy made by Shakespeare out of Plutarch's story
of Coriolanus is not that of a noble spirit ruined by lack of

education, which is the tragedy that Plutarch outlines. It is the tragedy of a noble spirit ruined by something in itself which education cannot touch, or at least does not touch. We do not hear anything in Shakespeare's play about the hero's lacking instruction because of his father's death and thus acquiring a faulty character. On the contrary, we learn that Volumnia, the strong-willed mother of the hero, has been both father and mother to him, has devoted herself, according to her lights, to the education of his character, and has certainly not failed to teach him how to be manly. By her precepts and her praises she has stimulated his valor. We have her own word for it that she does not approve of his unbending pride, and presumably she has done what she could to check it when she saw it standing in the way of his advancement. She is not the best of teachers to show him how to overcome his pride, but at least she can condemn it as something not drawn from her:

> Thy valiantness was mine, thou suck'dst it from me,
> But owe thy pride thyself.   (III, ii, 129–130)

The pride she condemns is what she says it is, a thing of his own, fixed in his nature. It is in the original substance of his character and is not an untutored churlishness acquired through the accident of his father's death.

But there is that about the pride of her son which Volumnia is quite incapable of understanding. Though she sees clearly that it can keep him from gaining the highest honors in Rome, she does not see that it can also keep him from base timeserving. It is more worthy of condemnation than she knows, but at the same time it is worthy of praise in a way that she does not even suspect. Her pupil shows reaches of nobility for which she is not responsible, and he shows them even in his valor, which is not a virtue of her creation, as she seems to think, but a virtue grounded in his natural pride. This valor has been developed but not called into being by her instruction.

The pride of Coriolanus has two very contradictory faculties. It is the tragic flaw in his character and therefore has the well-known power of pride the preëminent deadly sin to produce other faults and destroy good in the spirit of its possessor; but it is at the same time the basis of self-respect in his character and thus has power to produce good in his spirit. Whether destructive of good or productive of good, it is a fierce pride, accompanied by a wrath that makes it work at white heat. The wrath is like the pride it accompanies in not always having the qualities of a deadly sin; it can at times be righteous wrath, directed against human baseness. Hence both the pride and the wrath of Coriolanus can be admirable as well as detestable. Just as taints and honors "wage equal" with the sensualistic Antony, so do they with the proud Coriolanus.

Shakespeare lets us know in the first scene of the play that even among the worst enemies of Coriolanus his honors ask to be balanced against his taints. It is with praise alone that Shakespeare surrounds a deeply flawed but noble hero at the opening of *Macbeth*, and it is with scorn alone that he surrounds such a hero at the opening of *Antony and Cleopatra;* but it is with praise and scorn together, set one against the other, that he surrounds such a hero at the opening of *Coriolanus,* and if the praise does not receive so much dramatic emphasis as the scorn, it is nevertheless honest praise and weighs all the more when we consider that it is offered in defense of Coriolanus by a fair-minded man who has no reason to love him.

When the mob of citizens riot for bread in the beginning lines of the play, First Citizen, who is the leader, makes a case against Coriolanus, and Second Citizen, at some disadvantage because of his secondness, makes a case for him. First Citizen maintains that Coriolanus is the chief enemy of the people among the patricians and that if the people kill him they will have corn enough at their own price. All the citizens except Second Citizen agree that Coriolanus should be killed, for he is "a very dog to the commonalty." Second Citizen shows courage when he asks his starving fellows to think of the patriotic services rendered by Coriolanus to his country. First Citizen argues somewhat subtly that Coriolanus deserves no "good report" as a reward for what he has done to benefit his country because for "what he hath done famously" he pays himself well enough: he pays himself "with being proud" and with pleasing his mother. Coriolanus is proud, declares First Citizen, "even to the altitude of his virtue." The implication is that the pride Coriolanus takes in his ability to fight for his country and the happiness he takes in pleasing his mother with his exploits make his patriotic valor into something so completely selfish that it does not really deserve the name of virtue.

Second Citizen thinks this is speaking "maliciously" about Coriolanus and excuses him by saying, "What he cannot help in his nature, you account a vice in him." It is

to be remembered that exactly the same defense of a deeply
flawed tragic hero is made in *Antony and Cleopatra* by the
tender-minded Lepidus when the tough-minded Octavius
passes judgment upon Antony with extreme severity.
Lepidus, like Second Citizen, implies that great faults possessed by a great spirit are simply to be accepted when they
are so much a part of his essential nature that the great
spirit cannot remove them. Lepidus says that the faults of
Antony are

> hereditary
> Rather than purchas'd; what he cannot change
> Than what he chooses;   (I, iv, 13–15)

and he thinks that in Antony one cannot find

> Evils enow to darken all his goodness.
>   (I, iv, 11)

Second Citizen does not defend Coriolanus so enthusiasti-
cally as Lepidus defends Antony, but he defends him
stoutly. He urges in conclusion that though Coriolanus can
be accused of pride, he must in no way be accused of covetousness. First Citizen replies tartly that nevertheless plenty
of accusations can be made, for Coriolanus "hath faults,
with surplus, to tire in repetition." We are reminded that
the Antony in whom Lepidus finds much undarkened
goodness is seen by Octavius as

> the abstract of all faults
> That all men follow.   (I, iv, 9–10)

As the action of the opening scene progresses, we find
that First Citizen is not a man to back down when he comes
up against more formidable opposition than that provided

by Second Citizen.[8] He stands up to Menenius when that affable patrician justifies the Senate in characteristic fashion by telling the "pretty tale" of the good belly and the rebellious members of the body. What is even more to his credit, he stands up to Coriolanus when that patrician the reverse of affable justifies the Senate in equally characteristic fashion by pouring vilification upon the common people. First Citizen argues with Menenius. He does not have an opportunity to argue with Coriolanus, but he is briefly ironic when Coriolanus begins his tirade by calling the citizens "dissentious rogues." "We have ever your good word," says First Citizen in reply to this name calling. It is the last we hear from him. He has served his purpose, and not the least of the things he has done is the making of this last remark.

The phrase "good word," spoken by First Citizen in scorn, is a spur to Coriolanus that sets him off upon a most revealing course of argument. His good word for the citizens! Why, begins Coriolanus,

> He that will give good words to thee will flatter
> Beneath abhorring.   (I, i, 173–174)

There is no virtue whatever in the citizens, he declares, and any man who tells them they have virtue is a base, flattering politician. This, as we shall learn, is not mere sound and fury, pumped up by Coriolanus as a means of cowing the mob. It is honest passion. The idea that to flatter the common people is a supremely detestable thing is fixed in his mind and insistently appears in his speeches throughout the first half of the play. Here, in what he says to the rioters, he is expressing the idea for the first time. The words "flatter" and "beneath abhorring" look forward to the soul struggle he is to experience as he becomes convinced that to get the consulship he must somehow canvass for votes from the populace.

Under one aspect *Coriolanus* is the tragedy of a great spirit who cannot stoop to flattery in the way of the world. But the nobility of Coriolanus is never simple or outright; one may be led to qualify, or even reject, the praise of his nature offered by the loquacious Menenius in these well-known lines:

> His nature is too noble for the world:
> He would not flatter Neptune for his trident,
> Or Jove for's power to thunder.
>
> (III, i, 254–256)[9]

It is of course Coriolanus' pride with all its viciousness, the same pride that First Citizen sees as the impelling force behind his valorous patriotism, which makes him "too noble" to stoop to flattery. Yet this pride, which can paradoxically be good as well as evil, makes him react not only with anger but also with horror to that ironic remark of First Citizen, "We have ever your good word." Coriolanus, it would seem, has had the shocking thought before the play opens that he might sometime be tempted to flatter the populace, and thus be completely false to his "own truth," in order to win the consulship.

That Coriolanus has thoroughly honest principles and thoroughly honest reasons for detesting the citizens, it may be hard for us of a democratic age to believe; but we are certainly meant to understand that he does have them and that they are well based according to his view of things. They are put before us clearly in the speech with which he answers the ironic remark of First Citizen. The citizens, says Coriolanus, are good for nothing, either in war or peace, since war "affrights" them and peace makes them "proud." It is entirely characteristic of Coriolanus to divide all life into war and peace and to judge any man by asking first whether he is a true man of war. The true men of war are of course the warrior aristocrats, who are bred through generations to bear arms, to strive for honor, and never to show cowardice. Coriolanus thinks that these have an absolute right to rule the state because without them to defend it the state could not exist at all in a world where dog-eat-dog conflict is recurrent. The common people, who are not true men of war, could be true men of peace if they were not corrupted by peace into thinking that they should have power in the state. It is abundantly plain that they are thus corrupted, says Coriolanus, and thus that they are proud. It is ironic that he should make this statement so soon after he himself has been accused by First Citizen of being proud.

If Coriolanus had heard First Citizen accuse him of pride, he might have said in reply that trustworthy patricians have a right to be proud. What he says as he accuses the citizens of pride is that mere plebeians are never under any circumstances trustworthy and therefore, by implication, do not have any right to be proud. One who trusts them to show courage finds them hares instead of lions, and one who trusts them to show intelligence finds them geese instead of foxes. They discover worthiness in the offender condemned by justice and curse the justice that condemns him.

The man who deserves greatness deserves their hate, and the man who would achieve greatness by depending upon their favor "swims with fins of lead." They are so fickle that with every minute they change their minds, now swinging from hatred to adoration, and now from adoration to hatred. And these untrustworthy commoners are crying out against the trustworthy noble Senate, against an aristocracy who may be counted upon in time of war to save the state from destruction by forces without and in time of peace from destruction by forces within. For in peace as in war there is dog-eat-dog conflict which can ruin the state; freed from the control of the Senate, the commoners, "curs" that they are, would devour each other. "What's the matter," he asks them,

> That in these several places of the city
> You cry against the noble senate, who,
> Under the gods, keep you in awe, which else
> Would feed on one another? (I, i, 191–194)

Coriolanus does not offer the citizens a picture of the patrician Senate gathering up the goods of life and distributing them to the commoners, a picture such as Menenius offers when he tells the fable of the belly and the members. The amiable food-loving and wine-loving Menenius very naturally sees the good commonwealth as a body in which there is plenty of nourishment flowing out to all its parts, though of course as a patrician he believes that the Senate should control according to its wisdom the distribution of good things. Coriolanus, on the other hand, just as naturally sees the good commonwealth as something austerely negative rather than something gratifyingly positive. We may be sure that Coriolanus is no more subject to the deadly sin of gluttony than to the deadly sin of covetousness, and that his thoughts are always above sensual delights as much as they are above material rewards. He has reached spiritual heights of which Menenius, the amiable feeder and drinker, knows nothing. But his spirit is so bleak that he can only picture the good commonwealth as one in which the many who are brutish are properly restrained from eating each other up by the few who are their betters. And he tells the citizens that under the beneficent restraint of the Senate they are fortunate brutish members of a well-ordered commonwealth.

We understand from these lines which Coriolanus speaks thus early in the play, in justification of all he stands for, that for him the virtue of all virtues is trustworthiness. The good man is the trustworthy man, and the trustworthy man is the complete aristocrat, who not only is born with blue blood but also lives in accordance with inherited principles and thus by rules of conduct well established. Such a man, thinks Coriolanus, runs true to form. You know what he will admire and what he will detest, and you know that he will not change his mind except for solid cause. Naturally, a part of the trustworthiness acquired from aristocratic warrior ancestors is his courage. He can be counted upon in battle to do credit to his noble blood. Since he is not a coward, he does not tell lies, for the liar is a coward afraid to tell the truth; and since he does not tell lies, he flatters no man. Flattery is the weakling's way of gaining favor and advantage in the world, and the trustworthy man will not stoop to it. Especially will the noble trustworthy man, the aristocrat, not stoop to flattery when he deals with the base, untrustworthy man, the commoner. Commoners are

> no surer, no,
> Than is the coal of fire upon the ice,
> Or hailstone in the sun. (I, i, 178–180)

To say good words to them is to "flatter beneath abhorring," and to give them tribunes who will "defend their vulgar wisdoms," as has just been done, is to "break the heart of generosity." By this condemnation of the citizens for their lack of trustworthiness and by the attendant revelation of his faith in an aristocratic ideal of trustworthiness Coriolanus asks to be judged according to the measure of his own trustworthiness. That measure, as we shall see, is in one direction admirably large and in another pitifully small.

IV

Thus the drama begins in a way that makes us ask at once whether its author puts himself on the commoners' or the patricians' side. A part of the answer, I think, is that Shakespeare shows a singular detachment in his ability to find human faults on both sides and a singular breadth of sympathy in his ability to find human virtues on both sides. Another part of the answer is that he does not have such superhuman detachment that he never favors one side. The plain fact is that he is on the side of the patricians whenever they are to be taken as representing a theory of government, and that he gives them an advantage even in the first scene of the play.

In the first scene, as we have found, Shakespeare provides the patricians with two arguments in favor of the aristocratic form of government: the argument of Menenius that an aristocracy is a source of nourishment for the state, and the argument of Coriolanus that an aristocracy is a bulwark for the state. Both of these arguments are set forth with skill, and both are emphasized. Whatever a modern democratic mind may think about their validity, their mode of presentation makes them carry weight in the drama.

While Shakespeare is giving the patricians these two effectively presented arguments in favor of aristocracy, he gives the commoners not even one such argument in favor of democracy. We hear much from the commoners to make us sympathize with them for their sufferings, and much to make us think that they have been unjustly treated by the patricians; yet we do not find their leader, or any other member of their group, setting democracy up against aristocracy as a better form of government and explaining it vividly and eloquently, as Menenius and Coriolanus explain aristocracy. First Citizen shows a burst of eloquence when he implies that the "cormorant belly," the "sink o' the body," has no right to restrain the "kingly crowned head," the "vigilant eye," and other admirable "muniments" of the body, but after Menenius tells him the belly's answer to rebel muniments, he trails off into the weak comment, "It was an answer." Apparently he cannot reply to the justification of aristocracy given by Menenius. And when he comes up against Coriolanus, he never gets beyond his few words of irony.

One is forced to believe, not only by political passages in *Coriolanus* but by such passages in Shakespeare's work generally, that the reason why Shakespeare does not provide these opponents of Menenius and Coriolanus with an effective argument in favor of democracy is simply that he does not think any can be offered. After all, Shakespeare's age was a time when men were little disposed to think that such an argument could or should be made.

Usually in the Renaissance we find democracy condemned out of hand. An Elizabethan writer who condemns it but first notes briefly that something has been said in favor of it is John Barston. In his work called *The Safegarde of Societie* (1576), dedicated to Robert Dudley, Earl of Leicester, he says that of the sundry kinds of government there are three which "chiefly out of Plato may be noted," and these three are *"Monarchia, Aristocratia, & Democratia."* He discusses them at some length.[10] Monarchy he thinks to be unquestionably the best of governments, most conformable to the laws of God and nature. It is "ye state of empire and rule where one onely ruleth as most loyal prince and gouernor and no more." It is the most stable form of government. Aristocracy is less stable, but it places men of the best sort at the head of the state: *"Aristocratia,* the soueraine rule, not of one but many, and that of the best sort and condition, as we may say, of the peeres and nobles, is thought to be most necessarie of al such, as imagine nothing well done, that cōmeth vnder name of one, bicause say they, many wits will easily find y^t, wherin one may be deceiued: & in no one man are all good qualities, though among many not one perhaps is lacking." As for democracy, it has been defended by some: "In the iii. that is *Democratia,* or popular regiment, where neither prince alone, nor nobles only shall rule, but ye cōmon people strike the stroke togither, some reason is made, that all men will be one for other in cōmon, when none is to bee charged or preferred aboue yᵉ rest, alluding also to the cōmon prouerbe, *Vox populi, vox Dei:* that which al agree upon, is no doubt yᵉ speeche of God." But, continues Barston, there is a saying contrary to that: "*Vulgus est bestia multorū capitū,* The vulgar sort is a beast with many heads." And as a matter of fact, according to Barston, democracy has been proved by history to be a bad form of government.

Both the Romans and the Athenians knew democratic rule and found it pernicious, says Barston. The Romans first had a monarchy, then an aristocracy with the "whole iurisdiction ... in the senators," who were "the nobles or auncient peeres," and then a democracy. Disorders happened under the rule of the Senate, and matters went from bad to worse. And so, "by the dayly seditions, priuie mutinies and conspiracie of the common sort, began that disordered and vnruly gouernement of *Democratia,* by the vulgar people and base commons. For ... the tribunes or prouosts of the people, at their earnest suite, caused the highe promotions to be permitted to inferiour persons, by which occasion all was almost on vprore, & authoritie began to be defaced and adnulled to al licentious libertie of the meanest sorte." Then monarchy was restored at Rome, and it was continued by the Caesars. The Athenians, before they were conquered, gave equally good proof that democracy, with its "equall authoritie in al degrees of persons" is a "most pernicious state." For "then, as verie well they might be termed the monstrous beast of many heades, they did all things so headily, without counsell, good aduise, or reasonable discretion, in theyr furious outrage and follies, that moste wrongfully they did to deathe, and by moste grieuous tormentes, manye moste innocente persons, high Clerks and noble Counsellors, as *Socrates, Solon, Aristides, Phocion.*" The only way for a state to avoid the kind of decay that leads to democracy, thinks Barston, is for it to have a prince at its head. For even aristocracy, "that rule of the honorable and auncient nobles," by being a government "without a certayne and vndoubted Prince" can bring on "perillous commotions," as was shown at Rome.

Writer after writer of the Elizabethan age calls the common people the beast with many heads, as Barston does.[11] Shakespeare's Coriolanus is made to use language excessively familiar to the Elizabethan theater audience when he refers to the people as "Hydra" and scorns the threatening tribune Sicinius as "the horn and noise o' the monster's" (III, i, 92–94), or when he says to those who bid him farewell as he leaves the city to go into banishment:

> Come, leave your tears: a brief farewell: the beast
> With many heads butts me away.   (IV, i, 1–2)

The groundlings in Shakespeare's audience were well used to hearing characters in plays condemn the common people for their lack of political stability, and probably most of them accepted the condemnation as entirely just. Probably they did not find it at all strange that a citizen in *Coriolanus* should be made to declare that the hero of the tragedy had some basis in reason when he "stuck not to call" the Roman populace "the many-headed multitude." The citizen speaks as follows.

We have been called so of many; not that our heads are some
brown, some black, some abram, some bald, but that our wits are so
diversely coloured: and truly I think, if all our wits were to issue out
of one skull, they would fly east, west, north, south; and their consent
of one direct way should be at once to all the points o'the compass.

(II, iii, 19–26)

In translations of two French works that had a reputation
in their own day the Elizabethan reader could find commonwealths classified into three good kinds and three corresponding bad kinds—more in accord with Aristotle than
with Plato,—and could find democracy given as one of the
bad kinds.[12] The better known of these works was *L'Aca-
démie françoise* (1577), by Pierre de la Primaudaye, translated by "T. B." as *The French Academie* (1586). The
other was *Le Miroir politique* (1555), by Guillaume de la
Perrière, translated anonymously as *The Mirrour of Policie*
(1598). Both works list the good commonwealths as monarchy, aristocracy, and timocracy, and the bad as tyranny,
oligarchy, and democracy.

In *The Mirrour of Policie* there is a schematic presentation of the six kinds of commonwealths.[13] In right
Aristotelian fashion this presentation makes each bad commonwealth a corrupt form of a good commonwealth, so
that the three kinds of "a depraued Commonweale" are
"diametrically contrarie vnto the three former kindes of a
good and right Commonweale." Tyranny is a corruption
of monarchy. In tyranny, "power is put into the hands of
one alone, who beareth rule, or rather ... tyrannizeth according to his disordinate will, not obseruing the laws or
precepts of Iustice." The opposite of the tyrant is "the good
King or Prince, who gouerneth and ruleth his people, not

according to his sensuall appetite and will, but by ripenesse
of counsell, obseruation of lawes, and right of iustice." Oligarchy is a corruption of aristocracy. "This maner of Commonweale taketh place, when as a few rich men, or of the
Nobility, doe occupie the politicke gouernement, bending
all their endeauours, and aiming at their owne priuate gaine
and commodity, hauing no care of the common profit."
This kind of government is "directly contrarie to the Commonweale of the best men, called by the Grecians *Aris-
tocratie,*" in which rulers have regard for justice and "seeke
the common profite." As for democracy, "the last kind of a
depraued Commonweale," it is a corruption of timocracy. It
is "a Popular gouernement" in which "mechanicall Hand-
icraftsmen, and men of the baser sort beare rule, not seeking the publicke profite, but either their owne priuate, or
their equals." Those to whom a democratic government is
committed "are called Plebeians," and they "doe alwaies
persecute such as are rich, and of noble discent, fauouring
alwaies the vulgar base sort, as they themselues are." Democracy, it is said, is directly contrary to that form of government called by the Greeks *Timocratie* and by the Latins
Censu potestas, in which rule is committed to men of middle
degree, that is, to such as hold a mean between the rich and
the poor, the noble and ignoble, and in which regard is had
for the poor as well as the rich. Just as "the power of men
meanely rich is of least value and worth," so the corruption
of the government in which they bear the rule is of least
depravity. Democracy is always bad, but it is not so bad as
oligarchy, and oligarchy is not so bad as tyranny (which,
we may note, is an idea emphasized by Aristotle).

In *The French Academie* the presentation of the six kinds of government is made with less attempt at schematic arrangement.[14] But there is the same basis of distinction between good and bad commonwealths which goes back to both Plato and Aristotle: "That is a good common-welth, wherin the gouernours seeke the publike profit of the citizens, & the benefit of the whole ciuil societie," and "a corrupt common-wealth is that which repugneth and is directly contrary to that which is good and iust," for "it seeketh only the increase of priuate commoditie, hauing no care of publike profit." A monarchy becomes a tyranny when the single ruler selfishly looks "vnto his particular benefit," and other good governments may be corrupted into bad governments in like fashion. An aristocracy may be corrupted into an oligarchy, in which a few men rule selfishly, and this oligarchy in turn may be corrupted into a tyranny. Democracy is a corrupt form of government which, like oligarchy, may be brought into being where "many are passing rich, or extreme poore." It is a commonwealth "where free and poore men being the greater number, are lordes of the estate." In *The French Academie* it is allowed that some democracies are not so bad as others and even that it is possible for a combination of oligarchy and democracy to produce timocracy, a good form of government, but it is not allowed that oligarchy and democracy are "of themselues" anything but "vicious and corrupt."

It seems that as Shakespeare wrote *Coriolanus* he proceeded upon an assumption, made often enough in his day, that the common people were unfit to have ruling power in a state, not only because they were many-minded and had no stability, but also because they were shortsighted and had no power to see the interests of any other group than their own. A democratic government, then, was an evil government, and it might upon very good authority be called no true government at all but only a perversion of government. Of course, the governments that upon good authority could be called true governments were by no means always perfect. The aristocratic government presented in *Coriolanus* is obviously an imperfect one, and the common people who rebel against it are shown to have grievances. But it is significant that although, as the drama develops, we are often invited to sympathize with individual ordinary citizens, we are rarely if ever invited to sympathize with the tribunes, who are the means by which the citizens as a body are becoming a political power and challenging the authority of the patricians—the means, in other words, by which Rome is bringing democracy into being.[15]

The deeply flawed Coriolanus, as Shakespeare sees him, is one of the chief reasons why the government headed by the patricians is imperfect, and yet he is also one of the chief reasons why that government has virtue in it. His pride is patrician pride grown to a self-contradictory greatness that makes it at times a monstrous liability and at other times a magnificent asset to the state. It forces him to set himself off from other men, as better than they—so far off, indeed, that he lacks an understanding of humanity and cannot make any truly unselfish contribution to the public weal; but though it keeps him at all times from knowing what true self-sacrifice for the state can be like, it paradoxically drives him to give himself to the state completely, and heroically, in time of war. In battle Coriolanus is an eminent possessor of the virtue of trustworthiness.

v

When we see Coriolanus in battle against the Volscians, we are able to judge for ourselves the quality of service which he renders his country with his sword. As he goes to make preparation for the Volscian campaign, the tribunes analyze his character and decide that in pride he has no equal. From them we hear once more what we have already heard from First Citizen, that Coriolanus is a self-centered seeker after fame, driven by excessive pride to show outstanding valor. From them we hear further that his pride is a scheming pride which makes him willing to serve under Cominius in the Volscian campaign in order that he may have the opportunity of winning fame as a warrior without any risk of losing fame as an unlucky commander-in-chief. As Coriolanus sweeps all before him in the campaign, moving with the ease and surety of genius in an element seemingly made for him, we see that he is indeed a man driven by inordinate pride, but not so ignobly driven, by any means, as the tribunes think.

In making out that Coriolanus is a schemer as he prepares to serve under Cominius against the Volscians, and in attributing to him the deviousness of a politician, the tribunes only betray that they themselves are schemers and that political deviousness is to them second nature. They believe that any man with the pride of Coriolanus will of course desire the highest position of power in any undertaking of which he is a part unless he finds that by accepting a lower position he stands to profit later. Coriolanus never at any time shows the political sense and the ability to calculate advantage for himself that the tribunes credit to him. This, quite obviously, is one reason for his tragic fall. Also, Coriolanus never at any time shows a desire for power as power. This it is most important to realize if we are to understand the nature of the ambition engendered by his pride.

For Coriolanus is not a Julius Caesar or an Augustus, with an intelligent craving for supreme executive power, and neither is he a Tamburlaine, with a blind lust for supreme conquering power. What he yearns for ambitiously is recognition in Rome of his supreme worth as a valorous and entirely trustworthy patrician warrior, and he wants power only as it stands for that recognition. In short, he wants power only so far as it is honor. This is seen clearly when he becomes a candidate for the consulship. Moreover, he is completely scrupulous according to his lights and does not want to be dishonorable in gaining the power that for him is honor. By turning traitor to Rome he shows a tragic blind spot in his aristocratic perception of the honorable, but as he fights against the Volscians, and as he lets himself be put forward for election to the consulship, his eye for the honorable is that of a thoroughly upstanding Roman patrician; his vision is limited by the traditions of his class, but within limits it is admirable.

When Coriolanus agrees to serve under Cominius, he is keeping a promise which as a man of honor he cannot break. "It is your former promise," Cominius reminds him.

Coriolanus replies: "Sir, it is; / And I am constant" (I, i, 244–245). His service under Cominius proves that he is a great soldier, not that he is a great general. In warfare he is an invincible champion, an inspiring example of what one brave man can do with a sword, rather than a wise and skillful leader of men. On the battlefield, pride leads him to show the very finest of his noble qualities, but, as one might expect, it tends to cut him off from those around him even while it makes him win their praises. In Shakespeare's eyes, Coriolanus is the complete opposite of that happy warrior Henry V in his attitude toward the mass of common soldiers. He can curse them effectively and shame them effectively, for he never commands them to do anything that he himself cannot and will not do better than they, but never in the least does he make himself one with them, as Henry does when he says to his men before the Battle of Agincourt:

> For he today that sheds his blood with me
> Shall be my brother; be he n'er so vile
> This day shall gentle his condition.
> (*Henry V*, IV, iii, 61–63)

Gentle the condition of the common file? It is flattery, demagogic flattery, for a general to use such words, Coriolanus would say. His faith is firm that only "our gentlemen" are brave and that common soldiers are always ready to run "from rascals worse than they" (I, vi, 42–44). It is typical of him that he performs prodigies of valor to enter the gates of Corioli and then, because he is not followed by his men, who of course have no love for him and think him foolhardy, has to perform more prodigies of valor to get out of the city again and shame the Romans into making a victorious assault upon it. "Mark me, and do the like," he cries as he storms the gates.

In the main, Shakespeare follows Plutarch closely as he shows the nobility of Coriolanus on the Volscian battlefield. Like Plutarch he presents a superbly valorous hero who is above any desire for material reward and who scorns to take a share of the Volscian spoils but is quite willing to accept— in the way of honor—such gifts as a war horse and the commemorative name of Coriolanus. But because Shakespeare is giving a paradoxical side to the nature of Coriolanus, something of which Plutarch has no conception, he makes a notable change in one of Plutarch's incidents. This incident, offered to show magnanimity in the conqueror of Corioli, is given the following form by the biographer. Coriolanus, after rejecting mercenary reward for what he has done in the battle, begs to be granted one boon. He requests freedom for a Volscian, "an olde friende and hoste" of his, "an honest wealthie man, and now a prisoner, who liuing before in great wealth in his own countrie, liueth now a poore prisoner in the hands of his enemies" and is about to be "solde as a slaue."[16] In Shakespeare's hands this Volscian host of Coriolanus's changes from a rich man to a poor man, and Coriolanus is given an extra measure of magnanimity when he is made to plead not only for an enemy but for an enemy who stands far down in the social scale. Yet along with this extra measure of virtue goes an extra measure of defect, and the virtue seems inseparable from the defect. When Coriolanus is asked for the name of the poor Volscian whom he wants to benefit, he cannot remember it!

Nor does he seem concerned that he cannot remember the man's name. After all, we are to infer, this was a lowly Volscian and hence one of no importance, even though he once put Coriolanus in debt to him for friendly services. Who could expect that his name would be remembered? Because Coriolanus is spurred by pride to stand out among men as the most virtuous of great-spirited soldiers, he is also spurred by pride to be magnanimous to an enemy, even a plebeian enemy. But his pride is always a passion which cuts him off from true sympathy with, and true interest in, any other human being.

The pride of Coriolanus leads him to be gratified by praise given to his prowess and magnanimity, but—to complete the paradox of his nature—it also leads him to have contempt for such praise. Mr. John Palmer makes the just remark that the qualities in Coriolanus which "claim our admiration in these battle scenes are inherent in his defects," and hence that we think "his contempt of praise is rooted less in modesty than in pride."[17] The pride of Coriolanus makes him impatient when he is praised because it makes him think himself greater than any praise can indicate, and for this his pride is certainly not commendable. But just as certainly it is commendable because it makes its immodest possessor strive honestly to be more and more worthy of praise—even, be it noted, of praise for modesty.

Coriolanus is morbid upon the subject of flattery, whether flattery expected from him or flattery offered to him. When he is honored on the battlefield with a flourish of drums and trumpets and with cheers, he replies to his generous companions in a speech that should be regarded by them as insulting, though they are good enough not to take it that way. Their acclamations are "hyperbolical," he says, and imply the existence in him of a base yearning that his "little should be dieted / In praises sauc'd with lies" (I, ix, 52–53). It is the next thing, of course, to calling his praisers liars. Matters are brought to such a pass, says Coriolanus to his kind friends, that drums and trumpets, noble instruments of war, must "i' the field prove flatterers" and be guilty of the "false-fac'd soothing" found in courts and cities. In any situation, Coriolanus is a most difficult person for his associates to bear with, but Cominius deserves special credit for showing restraint in his answer to this wild talk about lying flattery. His reply is merely that the "too modest" Coriolanus is more cruel to his good report than grateful for it.

After the victory of Corioli it is inevitable that Coriolanus will stand for the consulship, since both he and his mother now think of that position as rightfully belonging to him in the way of honor. It thus becomes inevitable that Coriolanus will be tempted to use the flattery which he has so much despised. Because he comes to be thus tempted, the theme of flattery has very different proportions and very different qualities in Shakespeare's tragedy from those it has in Plutarch's biography.

Let us look at the theme of flattery in the biography. Plutarch speaks of "flatterers of the people" that stirred up sedition in Rome, "busie prattlers that sought the peoples good will by flattering words," and it turns out that among these were Sicinius and Brutus, who were not only "seditious tribunes" but also "flattering tribunes." Coriolanus, Plutarch says, rebuked all such "people pleasers" in delivering his speech against the free distribution of corn to the citizens, and he gained the reputation among certain patricians of being the only man in the city who "stoode out against the people, & neuer flattered them."[18] But apparently Plutarch is not so thoroughly on the side of the people-hating Coriolanus as these words might lead us to expect. In the "Comparison of Alcibiades with Martius Coriolanus" he declares that Alcibiades was extremely given to flattery of the people and Coriolanus extremely averse to it, and he then goes on to make the comment that though in this respect "neither the one nor the other was to be commended," Coriolanus was the more blameworthy. For "he is lesse to be blamed, that seeketh to please and gratifie his common people than he that despiseth and disdaineth them, and therefore offereth them wrong and iniurie, because he would not seeme to flatter them, to winne the more authoritie."[19]

It is to be noticed that in Plutarch there is nothing at all about flattery of the people in connection with Coriolanus's standing for the consulship. After describing the custom according to which a candidate appeared before the citizens clad only in a "poor gowne," perhaps "to moue the people the more," perhaps to make it possible to show them wounds gotten in the service of the commonwealth, Plutarch says quite simply that Coriolanus followed the custom, showed his many wounds, and immediately won the promises of the people to vote for him. He allows us to understand that Coriolanus followed the custom without hesitation and that neither at this time nor when the people afterward went back on their promises did Coriolanus feel that in dealing with them he was in any way called upon to be false to his principles. Apparently, then, Plutarch's Coriolanus suffered no temptation to use flattery. Plutarch is careful to explain that, in the time of Coriolanus, offices of dignity in Rome were not given by favor or corruption, and he implies that when a candidate of that period asked for votes he did not have to abase himself but could keep a dignity worthy of the office he sought.

It is patent that in *Coriolanus* Shakespeare develops the theme of flattery *con amore*. He takes from Plutarch the people-flattering demagogues and the demagogue-hating Coriolanus, but he goes beyond Plutarch to invent a trial of the hero's integrity as a demagogue-hater and to make this trial of integrity more important than all else in the theme. Like many others of the Renaissance, Shakespeare was able to find dire evil in the practice of flattery, and the theme of flattery appears often in the tragedies of his maturity.[20] In *Coriolanus* he has his Roman hero undergo a Renaissance temptation to practice flattery in the evil way of a Machiavellian "politician," and has him meet this temptation with an instinct against the use of flattery so ineradicable that by one Renaissance standard it is an essential virtue of the most admirable quality. To Shakespeare's Coriolanus flattery is as hateful and debasing as it was to the strictest of Renaissance moralists, who in their frequent condemnations of it might go so far as to call it "the sweete bayte of enuie, the cloake of malice, the onelye pestilence of the worlde."[21] It is true, of course, that he does not see its evil in the large, with the eye of a man concerned for the good of his fellows. Yet he reacts against flattery with a kind of moral passion, and this passion saves him in the end from his temptation to use flattery. We are not to forget, though, that behind the moral passion there is always pride, which has every appearance of being its only support. Just as the fiercely valorous Coriolanus is always the proud Coriolanus, so is the fiercely nonflattering and honest Coriolanus. There is no sign that this man of proud virtue is ever led to be noble in spirit by a natural love for all that constitutes nobility of spirit. Thus is raised the delicate question whether the virtue of Coriolanus is in truth worthy of admiration, since it is dependent upon something so vicious as his pride. But who knows, Shakespeare seems to be asking as he presents the paradox of his hero's character, to what degree there may be an admixture of selfishness in the finest of human virtue, the world being as imperfect as it is? Is it not even possible for a virtue to draw supporting strength from a vice that cannot be separated from it? Is not this a way in which good may come from evil in a world infinitely subtle and self-contradictory?

To the victorious Coriolanus returning from Corioli his mother says that the consulship is the one thing wanting among his honors and that she does not doubt it will be given him. Coriolanus makes answer out of his pride. His answer does not come from the pride that leads him to think of the consulship as rightfully his, but from a deeper pride, which makes him value his integrity above anything else. It is made in these words:

> Know, good mother,
> I had rather be their servant in my way
> Than sway with them in theirs.
>
> (II, i, 220–222)

He foresees something at least of the temptation that will be offered him and characteristically merges a conception of honorable integrity with one of individual integrity. In the excess of his pride he assumes as a matter of course that being most himself will be the same thing as being most noble and virtuous.

The test of integrity forced upon Coriolanus when he becomes a candidate for the consulship does not at first seem to him a very serious matter. Indeed, he thinks he can avoid it. After he is approved by the Senate for the consulship, he is told that he must speak to the people and ask them for their voices in the usual manner. He requests that he be excused from following the custom, but he does not make an issue of his request. When the tribune Sicinius declares bluntly and provocatively that the people will not bate one jot of ceremony, and Menenius urges him to conform to the custom, Coriolanus surprises us by giving in without a struggle, albeit ungraciously. He lets it be known that he will act the part of a pleader for votes before the people, though he will blush to do it. He seems to have yielded ignominiously to a temptation to buy the consulship with flattery and to have yielded with indecent haste, as soon as the temptation was presented.

But it turns out that he has not yielded at all, according to his view of the matter. Though he acts the part of a flatterer of the people, he does so in a supercilious way and thus serves notice as he performs his role that he really is not a flatterer. He makes no attempt to deceive the citizens. On the contrary, by insulting them he takes pains to keep them from being deceived. Says he to one of them: "I will, sir,

flatter my sworn brother the people, to earn a dearer estimation of them; 'tis a condition they account gentle: and since
the wisdom of their choice is rather to have my hat than
my heart, I will practice the insinuating nod, and be off to
them most counterfeitly" (II, iii, 101–106). Though there is
irony here, the speech is plain-spoken enough in all conscience. Coriolanus has the feeling that even as he "begs"
votes he remains openly and honestly himself, every inch a
scorner of the people, and that because he hides none of his
scorn he suffers no damage to his inner man.

The trouble is that the slow-witted citizens are deceived
even while Coriolanus is scornfully warning them not to
be deceived. They have a sense of justice and want to give
him the consulship as a reward for his victories. They have
some doubts that what he has been saying to them as he has
solicited their votes is exactly as it should be, but they do
not understand it fully and they promise him the consulship. When they change their minds, after being prompted
to do so by the tribunes, Coriolanus finds himself faced
anew with a problem which he thought he had put aside.
In his anger that the people should change their minds, he
berates the "mutable, rank-scented many" who cannot rule
and will not suffer themselves to be ruled. Let them, he says,

> Regard me as I do not flatter, and
> Therein behold themselves. (III, i, 66–67)

No voice in public affairs, he lets it be known, should ever
have been given them. When Sicinius calls him a traitor, his
passion becomes blind rage. As an aristocrat who believes
proudly that aristocracy justifies itself by defending the

state from all harm, and who thinks of himself as the foremost of state defenders, Coriolanus takes the word "traitor" as a fighting word. As we shall see, this is not the only time he does so. Both as a potential traitor and as an actual one he is painfully sensitive to the accusation of treason.

The riot precipitated by Coriolanus when Sicinius calls him traitor leaves his problem clearly defined and makes it urgent. Coriolanus now sees that he cannot avoid a test which he once thought he could avoid easily. As soon as he sees that the test must really be met, his instinct is to adopt a course of complete honesty by defying the people and declaring with all the scorn he has for them that even though they seize him to cast him from the Tarpeian Rock he will still "be thus to them." Since he is truly brave, he does not fear to follow this instinct. But his mother, assuming a role of which there is no hint in Plutarch, plays the tempter and succeeds so well in confusing his judgment that he decides to go contrary to all his principles. On this occasion, as always, the principles of the individualistic Coriolanus are nothing more than his instinct. To do right seems to him only a matter of being his natural self. He is amazed that his mother does not approve of his honest desire to defy the upstart "woollen vassals" and he demands of her:

> Would you have me
> False to my nature? Rather say I play
> The man I am.   (III, ii, 14–16)

The honesty of Coriolanus, which has regard for nothing but this precious "nature" of his, is thus a selfish honesty; but it is just as insistent in the demands it makes upon him as any unselfish honesty could be, and just as uncompromising in its conception of truth. It is never a doubtful or halfway virtue. This is more than can be said, certainly, of his mother's honesty. When she explains her disapproval of his plan for honest defiance of the people, Volumnia shows herself perfectly capable of juggling with truth according to expediency and of letting the despised commoners force her to play fast and loose with the concept of honor.

Thus Volumnia proves a very different patrician from her son, despite the spiritual bond between them. She is a political-minded patrician with something of the Machiavellian in her character. One may say that she is a most necessary kind of person for the aristocrats to have in their number when the common people begin to acquire power and become a threat to aristocracy, but, to use a word of her own, she is not "absolute" in her aristocratic pride. At a certain point she will compromise with the nonaristocratic part of the world and do so even at the cost of being ignoble, in the belief that nobility must at times save itself by ignoble means. The aristocratic nature of Coriolanus which leads him to be arrogantly truthful wins high praise from her, but when he asks whether she would have him be false to that nature, her answer is an unhesitating yes:

> You are too absolute;
> Though therein you can never be too noble,
> But when extremities speak. (III, ii, 39–41)

In other words, to be fearlessly honest would now, she thinks, be for Coriolanus a noble luxury that he could not afford. She tells him that he should dissemble.

> I would dissemble with my nature where
> My fortunes and my friends at stake requir'd
> I should do so in honour. (III, ii, 62–64)

This dissembling "in honour" is not like plain dissembling. It is "policy." There is a kind of sharp practice which, as he very well knows, can be used honorably to deceive an enemy in time of war. Why can it not be used honorably to deceive an enemy in time of peace, especially when the fortunes of himself and his friends, of the whole aristocratic class, are at stake?

Coriolanus goes down before his mother's assault, which is supported by Menenius and Cominius, but he yields only after a struggle. As his mother very well says, he would rather follow his enemy in a fiery gulf than flatter him in a bower. He promises to go back to the people and flatter them, not superciliously as he has done before, but with real intent to deceive.

Coriolanus yields to Volumnia and yet is not fully corrupted by her. He retains his conscience. He cannot answer her argument and cannot keep his judgment from being confused by it, but in his heart he knows perfectly well that flattering the people in downright fashion will for him be heinous wrongdoing. It will mean letting himself be possessed by "some harlot's spirit." For his mother the end will justify the means, but not for him. He has no sooner yielded to his mother than he changes his mind and says that he cannot and will not go through with what is wanted of him, because to do so might make him go so completely against his inner sense of truth that he would convert his inherent nobility into inherent baseness.

> I will not do 't,
> Lest I surcease to honour mine own truth
> And by my body's action teach my mind
> A most inherent baseness.   (III, ii, 120–123)

Volumnia finally prevails over Coriolanus by using tactics which, as we shall see later when she stops him from burning Rome, are not to be resisted under any circumstances. What Volumnia does as a last resort to make sure that her son will placate the people is simply to tell him that he must flatter them *for her sake*. She has asked him to flatter them in order that general ruin may be avoided—not, she would have him know, because she has a heart less stout than his and therefore fears them. He finds dishonor in flattering them and begging the consulship from them. Very well, she counters:

> At thy choice then:
> To beg of thee it is my more dishonour
> Than thou of them.   (III, ii, 123–125)

Volumnia is as shrewd as her son is lacking in shrewdness, and she is never more shrewd than when in desperation she appeals to him thus, by demanding that he dishonor himself in order that he may not dishonor her. She does not base her appeal upon his love for her, though this love is greater than that he has for his wife, or his son, or anyone else. She bases her appeal upon his loyalty to her. Coriolanus the self-centered individualist is not capable of sacrificing himself for any other human being—even his mother—in the way of love. But Coriolanus the self-centered worshiper of honor is capable of sacrificing himself for one other human being—his mother—in the way of loyalty. The loyalty felt by him for his mother is the only true loyalty he has, and only where she is concerned can he place the honor of another above his own honor. Coriolanus knows well enough that the honor among his fellows which he proudly wants to maintain for himself demands that he have loyalty to others. He counts himself a good patrician and a good Roman, two things which in his mind amount to the same thing, and he knows that he is called upon to be loyal to his class and to Rome. Yet though he *knows* the need of such loyalty, he does not *feel* it. His loyalty to his mother is his only true loyalty because it is the only one whose need is for him an emotional reality.

We see in the proudly self-centered Coriolanus a man who has almost but not quite achieved spiritual isolation and has been saved from it largely because he honors his mother. He has almost but not quite come to the point of finding no compulsion outside himself and holding nothing sacred outside himself. To be a good Roman patrician he must have reverence for his class and its traditions and have veneration for Rome itself as a body politic created and supported by his class, but for him everything sacred about his class and about Rome, everything in the way of tradition and substance that must absolutely remain inviolate, is gathered in his mother. She is the one holy vessel in his Roman temple. She prevails over him not by making him accept her version of truth, but merely by making him feel the sheer weight of her matriarchal dominion. One may say that she treats him as a bad boy and scolds or browbeats him until he surrenders, but one must go farther to explain her power over him.

Thus, because Coriolanus agrees with Volumnia that it is more dishonor for her to beg of him than for him to beg of the people, he finally agrees to "mountebank" the loves of the people, though he continues to feel, as she does not feel, that to dissemble in this way is inherently base. The result is a very unstable solution of his difficulties. Try as he will, he cannot be a fulsome political mountebank, but he really steels himself to placate the citizens by telling them an untruth. He appears before them and announces, without giving any sign of having mental reservations, that he is "content" to submit himself to the people and their officers and to suffer lawful censure for faults proved upon him. This is as far as he can go with his flattery. By this simple statement he acknowledges, though his heart denies each word of what he says, that the people are entitled to their tribunes and have the right to pass judgment upon him. It is only momentarily that he is able thus to dishonor his own truth. As soon as the tribune Sicinius, knowing very well what the effect will be, charges that Coriolanus has contrived to gain tyrannical power and has become a "traitor to the people," Volumnia's work is all undone. Pride and wrath surge up in Coriolanus to overwhelm the respect he has for his mother, and make him throw the lie in the tribune's teeth. The accusation that he has schemed to win tyrannical power is of course utterly unfounded, but what really stirs his wrath is the word "traitor." He has had trouble enough over a loyalty to his class which his mother has urged him to recognize, and now he must be told that he owes loyalty to the people and has betrayed them—the people, who are so detestable that they can make no call upon anyone's loyalty, his least of all. From the dishonesty of flattery he turns to the honesty of curses and finds relief for his spirit as he cries:

> The fires i' the lowest hell fold-in the people!
> Call me their traitor! (III, iii, 67–68)

This is the turning point of the tragedy. Coriolanus has reached the pinnacle of his fortune and as he leaves Rome to go into banishment he begins his descent to destruction. Because we can see very well that he brings misfortune on himself by his pride, and because we can see equally well that his pride is a vicious defect, we may feel that when misfortune comes to him he thoroughly deserves it. Nevertheless, there is irony in the fact that he is banished and started on his way to ruin because his pride keeps him from being false to the truth. One of his heroic aspects is that of a martyr to honesty.

Such instinctive honesty as that shown by Coriolanus, the England of Shakespeare's day was ready to commend in high terms whenever it thought, as it often did think, that matters had come to the dangerous pass described in the jingle:

> Good policy hath lost commended vse,
> Bad politicks, boast in that words abuse.
> A faithlesse wit, is wisdom which excells,
> They are best wise, that most are Machiuiles.[22]

The fact that, for the sake of his mother, Coriolanus earnestly tries to be a practicer of "policy" in the Machiavellian way and fails only because his hot temper betrays him into truthtelling does not, of course, make him any less naturally incapable of dishonesty. For the more knowing among

Shakespeare's audience, Coriolanus, because of his antipathy to flattering the people, could take on some resemblance to the virtuous Cato. As the Elizabethan might read: "Cato the elder suing for the office of Censorship in *Rome,* and seeing that many did curry fauour and flatter with the people to obtaine it, with an high & loftie voice, said vnto them: that the people of *Rome* had as much neede of a seuere, speedie, and sharpe Phisition, as they had of a strong purgation."[23] Or, Coriolanus could have some resemblance to other virtuous nonflatterers of the ancient past. As the Elizabethan might also read:

> In Rome such polycies were practised, such sutes were made to become eyther Consull, Pretor, Tribune, Censor or Aedile, that the 35. Tribes were so flattered and followed in *Martius* field with money, with friends, and with all meanes possible to become Magistrates and officers within the City of Rome, and at that time the Arte of Flattery was there to be taught and learned. . . .
>
> This kinde of election continued but a short time, yet flattery endured longer, and was practised at any change of Magistrates or Officers, yet *Lu. Crassus* could not be brought before *Q. Scæuola* to giue thankes vnto the people; lest hee should seeme to haue the name of a flatterer. . . .
>
> Such was *Phocion* in Athens. . . .
>
> Such was *Aristides,* a man most iust and most quiet among the Athenians: but these were rare men to be found.[24]

Members of Shakespeare's audience might at first be led to condemn Coriolanus, in the light of contemporary ideas about the viciousness of the man guilty of pride, and then be led to reconsider their condemnation, in the light of contemporary ideas about the virtuousness of the man incapable of flattery. The virtue of the nonflatterer could only too easily, in a corrupt world, be mistaken for envy or pride, as

they might remember having been told in some such words
as these: "The world is growne to that corruption that he
that cannot flatter is either accompted enuious or reputed
proud and arrogant."[25] So one might have second thoughts,
or even third and fourth thoughts, about the degree to
which Coriolanus should be condemned for that pride
which leads to his banishment.

VI

As Coriolanus says farewell to his family and friends and
goes into exile, he makes this promise:

> While I remain above the ground you shall
> Hear from me still; and never of me aught
> But what is like me formerly.   (IV, i, 51–53)

There is unconscious irony in his words, for it fortunes
that he lives up to them in a way he does not think of when
he utters them. He does not continue to make his mark in
the world by continuing to be the honorable man he has
been formerly, which is what he means to say he will do.
He continues to make his mark in the world only by becoming a traitor. And yet when he follows the course of
treason there is nothing in him which is essentially not like
him formerly, because with his inordinate love of self and
his total lack of any loyalty except that to his mother he has
always been potentially a traitor.

Only after a severe soul struggle has Coriolanus undertaken to be a dissembling politician and flatter the people.
He undergoes no soul struggle at all as he prepares to
become a traitor to his country. His pride gives him a conscience to support in him the virtue of plainspoken honesty,

but it does not even intimate to him that for the kind of patrician he has taken himself to be, namely, a trustworthy man born to rule and defend his country, treason is an unforgivable sin. Suddenly, quite without warning, we find him saying in a soliloquy that he hates Rome and will turn to Corioli to do it what service he can. He has the idea that his change of allegiance is entirely natural in a world of "slippery turns," where fast friends can in a moment become bitter enemies. Later he shows no sign of compunction as he tells Aufidius that he is offering his sword to the Volscians "in mere spite," to be revenged upon his banishers. He implies by what he says to Aufidius that he owes no more consideration to his own class, the "dastard nobles" who have not been able to keep him from being banished, than to the Roman plebeians, the "slaves" who have decreed his banishment.

Once Coriolanus has perpetrated treason, there is really nothing new to be learned about him, since the remainder of his tragedy is a second perpetration of treason brought about by the same deficiency in his nature that is responsible for the first. Everything that happens when he betrays the Volscians has a completely familiar quality. It is true that he does not betray them as he has betrayed the Romans, to get revenge for an insult to his ego; but he betrays them for a purpose sufficiently characteristic—to please his mother. When Coriolanus appears before Rome with his army of Volscians, he seems so fiercely bent upon taking the city and reducing it to fire-blackened ruins that he cannot possibly be turned from his destructive course, and yet his mother, pleading successfully after he has proved deaf to other Roman suppliants, saves the city. She does so by making him feel once more the full power of that authority which to him is her matriarchal sacredness.

At the beginning of her plea Volumnia shocks him by kneeling to him. "What is this?" he asks:

> Your knees to me! to your corrected son!
> Then let the pebbles on the hungry beach
> Fillip the stars.   (V, iii, 57–59)

The deep respect he shows her promises well for her efforts, but as she proceeds with her plea she finds it useless to search for patriotism in him or to confront him with his wife and child and appeal to his love for them. She also finds it useless to argue deviously, in a manner of which she has once before shown herself a master, that he is too inflexible in his conception of honor. Her argument is extremely plausible. He should realize, she says, that though it would be "poisonous" to his honor to save the Romans by destroying the Volscians, it would greatly increase his honor to make a peace in which the Volscians and the Romans could enjoy reconciliation and in which the Volscians could acquire merit by showing mercy to the Romans. The truth is that, no matter how good it might be for all concerned if the Volscians could show mercy, Coriolanus has got himself into a position where the decision to grant mercy or withhold it is simply not his to make. Indeed, where there is any question of foregoing a part of the Volscian victory over the Romans, he needs, if he is to be honorable, to lean backward. Coriolanus himself is quite aware that this is the way things stand. He has told Menenius that his affairs are now "servanted to others" and that any "remission" for the Romans must come from "Volscian breasts." Again we see that Coriolanus has a sense of honesty far more surely grounded than his mother's.

Volumnia finally has success by bringing against Coriolanus the accusation that he is not being honorable so far as *she* is concerned, since he is restraining from her "the duty which / To a mother's part belongs" (V, iii, 167–168). There is no man "more bound to 's mother" than he, she would have him know. It is not of any bond of love between her son and herself that she speaks, but only of a bond of duty. Once more she kneels before him, together with the ladies who accompany her. "Let us shame him with our knees," she cries. As he remains obdurate, she rises to lead her fellow petitioners back to Rome, but turning to leave she lets him understand that when the city is afire he must be put to further shame by his dishonored mother, for at that time she will yet again "speak a little." It is only after this parting shot is delivered that Coriolanus at last gives way.

Thus Volumnia demands that Coriolanus spare Rome at the cost of dishonoring himself, just as she has demanded that he win the Roman consulship at the cost of dishonoring himself. Both times, she gets him to dishonor himself by asking him to honor her. It is true, of course, that in bringing upon him the dishonor of betraying the Volscians she saves him from the dishonor of destroying his native city and keeps him from proceeding to the ultimate violation of the allegiance to which he was born. But the good she does for her son comes far short of balancing the ill, because, though she brings him to the point of saving his native Rome, she cannot bring him to the point of saving his soul as a Roman. She cannot make him reaccept the old allegiance after she has made him turn false to the new, and she cannot even make him feel repentance—not the smallest—for having betrayed Rome in the first place. Hence the result for Coriolanus spiritually is that he is left unmitigatedly guilty of compound treason.

This time, Coriolanus yields to his mother without any sense of losing his integrity. Breaking faith with the Volscians is to him a very different matter from flattering the Roman plebeians, for it leaves his inner being quite untouched. He knows that such faith-breaking is wrong, but his knowledge of its wrongness is so superficial and so unimportant that it is not what keeps him so long from granting his mother's petition. The struggle within him is between his desire for revenge against Rome and his respect for Volumnia as the "honour'd mould" wherein he has been formed. Once he has decided to put his respect for his mother ahead of his desire for revenge, his spirit is at rest. As for the wrongness of his breaking faith with the Volscians, he feels that he must acknowledge it but not brood over it; and acknowledge it he does, to Aufidius:

> Aufidius, though I cannot make true wars,
> I'll frame convenient peace. (V, iii, 190–191)

His mother, as we have seen, has tried to make him think that by neglecting to press home the Volscian victory he would be working not against the Volscians, but for them, since he would be allowing them to show mercy and thus act nobly. This specious reasoning makes no impression on him. Bluntly he lays his sparing of Rome to his inability to "make true wars" for the Volscians, and calls the peace he is about to procure nothing more than "convenient." To the very end of his career the pride of Coriolanus gives him brave hatred for all paltering, and this virtue his mother is never able to corrupt, however hard she tries. But to do Volumnia justice, she is by no means villainous when she works to corrupt her son. She is a person of strong character who has succeeded in bending truth to her will and has succeeded so well that she has deceived herself about the nature of truth.

When Coriolanus says to his mother that she has won a happy victory for Rome, but that for him her success is most dangerous, "if not most mortal," he is looking at the on-coming shadow of his catastrophe. The Volscians are to exact his life in payment for his offense against them, after Aufidius has played out his role of villain. Aufidius is not without generous instincts. Though he can hate Coriolanus as an enemy, he can respect him as a glorious opponent and, when Coriolanus joins the Volscians, can embrace him as a "noble thing" that he can truly love. Even when Aufidius begins to grow jealous of his too successful associate, he can say, after talking about the pride of Coriolanus and his defects in general, "But he has a merit / To choke it in the utterance" (IV, vii, 48–49). Yet when Aufidius is confirmed in his jealousy and feels that the time has come to ruin Coriolanus, he stops at nothing, either to justify his aim or accomplish it. To justify his aim he goes so far as to make the accusation that Coriolanus has worked against him underhandedly among the Volscians by the seductive use of flattery. This, of course, is simply not to be believed. No such use of flattery is shown in the play, and everything we see of Coriolanus early or late in his career makes him seem incapable of it. Moreover, there is the admission by Aufidius that he is putting "a good construction" on his "pretext to strike" at Coriolanus. To accomplish his aim Aufidius forms a conspiracy and traps Coriolanus to his destruction. The scheme of entrapment is exactly the same as that used by the Roman tribunes, namely, to call Coriolanus traitor and thereby make him so angry that he must throw all caution to the winds and expose nakedly whatever is most offensive in his pride.

Upon his return to Corioli from his victory against Rome, Coriolanus appears before the Volscians with the declaration that he is still their soldier and that he is "no more infected" with love of his country than when he set forth to fight against it. This is quite true, and to him it seems to be all that really matters, but it is also true that (to use the words of Aufidius) he has sold the blood and labor of the Volscians and has denied them the full measure of victory which was rightfully theirs. By admitting his inability to "make true wars" for the Volscians, Coriolanus has acknowledged the wrong he has done them, and yet he has never seen the true quality of that wrong. He has never been infected with patriotism and has betrayed his own country without compunction; one would not expect him to acquire among the Volscians a sure understanding of treason. He knows that he has not kept faith with the Volscians, but, because of his pride and his consciousness that he is still ready to serve them heroically in any way short of delivering Rome into their hands, he cannot abase himself to the point of thinking himself their traitor. Traitors are scorned as ignoble. How can he, the noble Coriolanus, be scorned as ignoble by the Volscians, upon whom he once proved his nobility with his sword? Moreover, he has done the Volscians a great favor by fighting for them, even if he has done them wrong by not giving them Rome to loot and burn. What he has done for them and is still willing to do for them weighs much more, he thinks, than anything he has promised to do and not done.

Thus, when Aufidius brings out the word "traitor" in accusing him before the assembled Volscians, Coriolanus is like a man struck in the face by an unexpected blow. He is ludicrously unprepared to meet the attack and is ludicrously thrown off balance. He can only bluster: "Traitor! How now!" When Aufidius presses the attack and loads him with calculated insults, Coriolanus is toppled into the pit dug for him. Raging against the Volscians and boasting of his singlehanded conquest of their city of Corioli, he turns the Volscian common people against him and falls under the conspirators' swords.

But even as the Volscian people call for his blood a Volscian lord tries to save him from "outrage" and pays tribute to his nobility in these exalted words:

> The man is noble and his fame folds in
> This orb o' the earth. (V, v, 126–127)

There is another Volscian lord who calls the dead hero the "most noble corse" that herald ever followed to his urn.

And Aufidius himself ends the play with a speech declaring that Coriolanus, despite the injuries he has done to the Volscians, "shall have a noble memory."

VII

Coriolanus, then, can be thought of as greatly noble, and a chorus of Volscians urges us at the end of the tragedy to remember him thus. He is probably the last of the paradoxically noble heroes of Shakespeare's last tragic world. It is likely that few of us would call him the best of those "rare spirits" and that many would call him the worst. He is monstrously deficient as a human being, and his deficiency is the more unfortunate because it tends not to foster pity for him but to destroy any that we might give him. As a tragic hero he therefore has a marked disadvantage which is not shared by Timon, Macbeth, or Antony. Each of these others asks for our pity in a manner not to be denied—even Macbeth, who himself is pitiless but comes to know pitifully that by being pitiless he has lost "honour, love, obedience, troops of friends." Coriolanus, the fanatical lover of himself who never knows disillusionment, whose pride is so great that his spiritual self-sufficiency is never shaken, repels pity at any time, and when he does not inspire admiration, he is apt to inspire such detestation as to leave no room for pity.

As Shakespeare gives form to his last tragic world, he is always daring in his efforts to make the paradox of the deeply flawed noble hero yield subtle truth. In *Coriolanus* he pushes this paradox to its limit of tragic validity, and sometimes even beyond, with the result that he makes it more acceptable to the mind than to the heart. The deeply flawed Coriolanus who repels pity is too deeply flawed for Shakespeare's tragic purposes. Most of us who perceive nobility of spirit in him would doubtless rather praise it than associate with it.

In *Coriolanus* the problem of evil, once terribly urgent for Shakespeare, is almost completely absorbed within the dramatic hypothesis of a man who is supremely guilty of pride the vice and at the same time supremely noble in pride the virtue. Shakespeare constructs the hypothesis with mathematical precision. He uses the very greatest care to strike a balance between the repellent Coriolanus and the admirable Coriolanus, and he keeps the balance in a spirit both ironically superior and dispassionately just. The achievement, though delicately beautiful, has a quality that can only be called forbidding. About the play as a whole there is a lack of essential warmth amounting even to bleakness, and it is not for nothing that the verse is often eloquent but seldom deeply moving, often impressive but seldom sublime. *Coriolanus* is a magnificent failure in which Shakespeare seems to have brought his tragic inspiration to an end by taking tragedy into an area of paradox beyond the effective reach of merely human pity.

NOTES

TAINTS AND HONORS

(Pages 1–38)

1 Quotations from Shakespeare are from the Oxford text, edited by W. J. Craig.
2 This order is that given by E. K. Chambers, *William Shakespeare: A Study of Facts and Problems* (Oxford, 1930), I: 270.
3 I have said something about the world of early Elizabethan tragedy in *The Medieval Heritage of Elizabethan Tragedy* (Berkeley, 1936). See particularly chaps. ix and x.
4 In dating these four plays I follow Chambers, *op. cit.*, I: 397, 423, 462, 470.
5 See A. C. Bradley, *Shakespearean Tragedy* (2d ed.; London, 1920), pp. 246, 443 ff., 470, 477 ff.
6 See Chambers, *op. cit.*, I: 86, 273–274, 482–483.
7 For the argument that what has often been taken to be evidence of divided authorship in *Timon* is merely evidence of rough incomplete drafting on the part of Shakespeare, see Chambers, *op. cit.*, I: 482–483; R. A. Haug, "The Authorship of 'Timon of Athens,'" *Shakespeare Association Bulletin*, XV (1940): 227 ff.; Una Ellis-Fermor, "*Timon of Athens:* An Unfinished Play," *Review of English Studies*, XVIII (1942): 270 ff.
8 This, it may be said, is the generally accepted chronology for these three plays. It is that of Chambers, *op. cit.*, I: 475, 477, 480.
9 *Shakespeare's Satire* (New York, 1943), pp. 168 ff., 198 ff.
10 As is well said by U. M. Ellis-Fermor, *The Jacobean Drama* (London, 1936), p. 63.
11 *Bussy D'Ambois: A Tragedie* (1607), p. 40 (III, ii).
12 *Ibid.*, p. 41 (III, ii).
13 *Ibid.*, p. 11 (I, ii).
14 *Ibid.*, pp. 33–34 (III, ii).
15 *Ibid.*, p. 34 (III, ii).
16 *Ibid.*, p. 19 (II, i).
17 See Hardin Craig, "Ethics in the Jacobean Drama: The Case of Chapman," *Essays in Dramatic Literature: The Parrott Presentation Volume,* ed. Hardin Craig (Princeton, 1935), p. 42. See also H. Perkinson, "Nature and the Tragic Hero in Chapman's Bussy Plays," *Modern Language Quarterly*, III (1942): 266.
18 Edition cited, p. 19 (II, ii).
19 See F. S. Boas, "The Source of Chapman's 'The Conspiracie and Tragedie of Charles, Duke of Byron,' and 'The Revenge of Bussy D'Ambois,'" *The Athenaeum*, January 10, 1903, pp. 51–52.
20 See E. K. Chambers, *The Elizabethan Stage* (Oxford, 1923), II: 53–54 and III: 257–258.
21 Edition of 1607, p. 992.
22 *Ibid.*, p. 959.

[23] *Ibid.*, p. 993.

[24] *Ibid.*, p. 990.

[25] *The Conspiracie, and Tragedie of Charles Duke of Byron* (1608).

[26] *Ibid.*, sig. Q 3.

[27] *Ibid.*, sig. Q 3^v.

[28] *The Lion and the Fox: The Role of the Hero in the Plays of Shakespeare* (New York and London, Harper, 1927), pp. 269–270.

[29] Henry de Vocht, *Ben Jonson's Seianus His Fall, Edited from the Quarto of 1605* (Materials for the Study of the Old English Drama, XI; Louvain, 1935), p. 10.

[30] *Chapman* (Bloomsbury, 1934), p. 52.

[31] *Andromeda Liberata* (1614), sig. F^r.

[32] *Ibid.*, sig. ¢ 3^r.

[33] *Ibid.*, sig. B^r.

[34] Edition of 1612, sig. F^r (III, ii).

[35] *Ibid.*, sig. G 4^r (IV, iii).

[36] *Ibid.*, sig. M^v (V, vi).

[37] *The Complete Works of John Webster* (London, Chatto & Windus, 1927), I: 98.

[38] *Ibid.*, I: 94.

[39] *Themes and Conventions of Elizabethan Tragedy* (Cambridge Univ. Press, 1935), p. 187.

[40] *Op. cit.*, I: 93, 96.

[41] *Essayes or rather Encomions* (1616), sig. G. For the indebtedness of Cornwallis's paradoxes, and of the Renaissance English paradox in general, to the *Paradossi* (1543) of Ortensio Lando, see R. E. Bennett, *Four Paradoxes by Sir William Cornwallis, the Younger* (Harvard Studies and Notes in Philology and Literature, XIII [1931]), pp. 221 ff. Bennett notes (p. 221, note) that one of the manuscripts of Cornwallis's "the Prayse of Richard the Third" contains an unpublished dedication to John Donne that speaks of the author's friendship with Donne as "now of some continuance." This dedication was perhaps written while Donne was writing his own *Paradoxes and Problems*.

[42] See Mario Praz, "Donne's Relation to the Poetry of his Time," in *A Garland for John Donne*, ed. Theodore Spencer (Cambridge, Mass., 1931), pp. 60–61.

[43] For the dating of *Paradoxes and Problems* and *Biathanatos* see Evelyn M. Simpson, "Donne's 'Paradoxes and Problems,' " in *A Garland for John Donne*, pp. 23–24; *Iuvenilia or Certain Paradoxes and Problems . . . Reproduced from the First Edition*, ed. R. E. Bennett (New York, 1936), preliminary bibliographical note; Evelyn M. Simpson, *A Study of the Prose Works of John Donne* (2d ed.; Oxford, 1948), pp. 146–148, 120, 159; and *Biathanatos, Reproduced from the First Edition*, ed. J. W. Hebel (Facsimile Text Society; New York, 1930), p. v.

[44] See Evelyn M. Simpson, "Donne's 'Paradoxes and Problems,' " in *A Garland for John Donne*, pp. 39–40.

[45] Edition of R. E. Bennett, as cited, sigs. C^r–C 2^r.

[46] *The Poems of John Donne*, ed. H. J. C. Grierson (London, 1929), p. 287.

[47] See Evelyn M. Simpson, *A Study of the Prose Works of John Donne* (Oxford, 1948), p. 160.

[48] Edition of J. W. Hebel, as cited, pp. 25–26.

[49] *Ibid.*, p. 34.

[50] *Ibid.*, p. 35.

[51] In chapters to follow, as in this chapter, I do not make use of the term "baroque." But the reader may find it worth while to consider the recent development of the concept of the literary baroque, including the concept of baroque paradox. See, for example, René Wellek, "The Concept of the Baroque in Literary Scholarship," *Journal of Aesthetics and Art Criticism,* V (1946): 77 ff., and Helmut Hatzfeld, "A Clarification of the Baroque Problem in the Romance Literatures," *Comparative Literature,* I (1949): 113 ff. For an application to Elizabethan tragedy see L. L. Schücking, "The Baroque Character of the Elizabethan Tragic Hero" (Annual Shakespeare Lecture of the British Academy, London, 1938).

Notes to Chapter II

"Timon of Athens"

(Pages 39–77)

[1] *Coleridge's Shakespearean Criticism,* ed. T. M. Raysor (London, 1930), I: 238, 108–109.

[2] For what A. C. Bradley has to say about the bond of substance between *Timon* and *Lear,* see his *Shakespearean Tragedy* (2d ed.; London, 1920), pp. 246, 443.

[3] I have commented upon Shakespeare's use of the pyramidal tragic form in *The Medieval Heritage of Elizabethan Tragedy* (Berkeley, 1936), pp. 99 ff., 329 ff., 414 ff., 446 ff.

[4] *Shakespeare's Satire* (New York, 1943), pp. 168 ff.

[5] *The Shakespeare Papers of the Late William Maginn,* ed. Shelton Mackenzie (New York, 1856), pp. 132, 134.

[6] *Shakespeare as a Dramatist* (London, Cassell, 1935), p. 82.

[7] *Shakespeare* (London, 1929), p. 179.

[8] *The Wheel of Fire* (London, Oxford Univ. Press, 1930), pp. 250, 248, 241.

[9] "Timon of Athens," *Theatre Arts Monthly,* X (1926): 455.

[10] *Shakespeare's Life and Art* (London, Nisbet, 1939), pp. 184, 185, 183.

[11] See W. H. Clemons, "The Sources of 'Timon of Athens,'" *Princeton University Bulletin,* XV (1903–1904): 208 ff.; E. H. Wright, *The Authorship of Timon of Athens* (New York, 1910), pp. 8 ff.

[12] *Natural History,* VII, 19.

[13] *Lucian,* tr. A. M. Harmon (Loeb Classical Library; London and New York, 1915), II: 373–375.

[14] *Ibid.,* pp. 377, 335.

[15] Another Italian play on Timon was written in the late fifteenth century by Galeotto del Caretto. See E. K. Chambers, *William Shakespeare* (Oxford, 1930), I: 484.

[16] See *Tutte le opere di Matteo M. Boiardo,* ed. Angelandrea Zottoli (Milan, n.d.), II: 526. (*Timone,* Act V, Scene 4.)

[17] R. W. Bond argues that Shakespeare probably knew Boiardo's *Timone.* He directs attention to what Boiardo's Timon says of his plan to live in the wilds. This, he thinks, is one indication that Shakespeare took something from Boiardo. ("Lucian and Boiardo in 'Timon of Athens,'" *Modern Language Review,* XXVI [1931]: 52 ff.)

[18] The *Silva* has been edited by Justo García Soriano (Sociedad de Bibliófilos Españoles, segunda Época, X; Madrid, 1933). For the chapter on Timon, see this edition, I: 123–125, and for the editor's determination of the date of publication, I: xxxvii ff.

[19] Edition of 1592 (Lyon), p. 78.

[20] For an evaluation of Pliny's influence upon animalitarianism see A. O. Lovejoy *et al., A Documentary History of Primitivism and Related Ideas* (Baltimore, 1935), I: 404 ff.

[21] Edition of 1561, sig. A^v.

[22] Quotations from Alday are from the edition of 1566 (?), sigs. B 2 ff.

[23] Edition of 1592, p. 78.

[24] Quotations from Painter are from the edition of 1566, fols. 57^v ff. The indebtedness of Painter to Gruget has been noted by Douglas Bush, *Mythology and the Renaissance Tradition in English Poetry* (Minneapolis, 1932), p. 35 n.

[25] Without support in Plutarch or Amyot, North does say (edition of 1579, p. 219) that Timon was called a "vyper," but this choice of a rather common epithet does not seem significant.

[26] Edition of 1598, pp. 361, 362.

[27] For dating of the academic *Timon*, see G. C. Moore Smith, "Notes on Some English University Plays," *Modern Language Review*, III (1908): 143, and O. J. Campbell, *Comicall Satyre and Shakespeare's Troilus and Cressida* (San Marino, Calif., 1938), p. 96, note.

[28] Features that are shown in common by *Timon of Athens* and the academic *Timon* have been much commented upon. They are listed and discussed in Bond, *op. cit.*, pp. 64 ff.

[29] *Timon, a Play Now First Printed*, ed. Alexander Dyce (for the Shakespeare Society; London, 1842), p. 65.

[30] *Ibid.*, pp. 4, 89, 91.

[31] *Ibid.*, p. 85.

[32] *Morando, the Tritameron of Love* (1584) and *Gwydonius, the Carde of Fancie* (1584), in *The Life and Complete Works in Prose and Verse of Robert Greene*, ed. A. B. Grosart (1881–1886), III: 79 and IV: 40. Grosart prints these two works from editions of 1587.

[33] *Gwydonius, the Carde of Fancie* (1584) in Grosart, edition cited, IV: 139. For other references to Timon made by Greene, see Wright, *op. cit.*, p. 12, note.

[34] *Wits Miserie, and the Worlds Madnesse* (1596), p. 100.

[35] *Catharos. Diogenes in his Singularitie* (1591), fol. 8^v.

[36] Fol. 69^v.

[37] *Essayes* (1603), p. 164.

[38] See Pierre Villey, *Les Sources et l'évolution des essais de Montaigne* (Paris, 1933), pp. 85–86.

[39] See H. R. D. Anders, *Shakespeare's Books* (Berlin, 1904), pp. 51 ff., and G. C. Taylor, *Shakespeare's Debt to Montaigne* (Cambridge, Mass., 1925).

[40] This section of the chapter has been published, substantially in its present form, as part of *The Beast Theme in Shakespeare's "Timon,"* (University of California Publications in English, XIV [1943]), pp. 49 ff. For representative twentieth-century comments on the beast theme in *Lear* and *Timon*, see Bradley, *op. cit.*, pp. 246, 443; Theodore Spencer, *Shakespeare and the Nature of Man* (New York, 1942), pp. 142, 148, 182; G. C. Taylor, "Shakespeare's Use of the Idea of the Beast in Man," *Studies in Philology*, XLII (1945): 532 ff.; and R. B. Heilman, *This Great Stage: Image and Structure in "King Lear"* (Louisiana State Univ. Press, 1948), pp. 93 ff. and 105 ff.

[41] See Caroline F. E. Spurgeon, *Shakespeare's Imagery and What It Tells Us* (New York, 1935), pp. 194 ff.

[42] James Sanforde, *The Garden of Pleasure . . . Done out of Italian into English* (1573), fol. 99^r.

[43] Ludovic Lloyd, *The Pilgrimage of Princes, penned out of sundry Greeke and Latine aucthours* (n.d.; 1573?), fol. 183^v; Thomas Fortescue, *The Foreste or Collection of Histories . . . dooen out of Frenche into Englishe* (1571; a partial translation of Mexía's *Silva*), fol. 29^v. Both of these sayings are given, with somewhat different wording, by William Baldwin in *A Treatise of Morall Philosophie* (1547), sigs. H 2 and G 8^v. See *Diogenes Laertius,* tr. R. D. Hicks (Loeb Classical Library; London and New York, 1925), II: 7, 53.

[44] Thomas Stanley, *The History of Philosophy* (1655), Pt. VII, p. 24.

[45] *A Dialogue betwene Lucian and Diogenes of the life harde and sharpe, and of the lyfe tendre and delicate,* tr. Sir Thomas Eliot (n.d.), fols. 7^v and 5^r.

[46] O. J. Campbell observes that both Thersites and Apemantus are buffoonish commentators who display some of the characteristics of Jonson's Carlo Buffone (*Shakespeare's Satire,* New York, 1943, pp. 106, 187).

[47] See Antony Stafford, *Staffords Heavenly Dogge: or The life, and death of that great Cynicke Diogenes* (1615).

[48] *The Palace of Pleasure* (1566), fol. 58^v.

Notes to Chapter III

"Macbeth"

(Pages 79–137)

[1] *Notes on Shakespeare's Workmanship* (New York, Holt, 1917), p. 20.

[2] *Chronicles* (1587), "Historie of Scotland," pp. 170–171.

[3] *Ibid.*, p. 174.

[4] *Ibid.*, p. 176.

[5] See Alois Brandl, "Zur Quelle des Macbeth," *Englische Studien*, LXX (1935–1936): 169 ff.

[6] Edition of F. J. Amours (Scottish Text Society; Edinburgh and London, 1906), IV: 278.

[7] Anthony Nixon, *Oxfords Triumph* (1605), sig. B; Matthew Gwinne, *Vertumnus* (1605), sig. H 3ʳ; and Isaac Wake, *Rex Platonicus* (1607), p. 18. See *Macbeth*, ed. J. Q. Adams (Boston and New York, 1931), p. 250; Mrs. C. C. Stopes, *Shakespeare's Industry* (London, 1916), p. 335; and H. N. Paul, "The Imperial Theme in *Macbeth*," *Joseph Quincy Adams Memorial Studies*, ed. J. G. McManaway *et al.* (Washington, 1948), pp. 253 ff.

[8] Edition of 1606, pp. 373–377.

[9] *Ibid.*, p. 366.

[10] *Macbeth*, ed. G. L. Kittredge (Boston, 1939), p. 240.

[11] *Ibid.*, pp. 239–240.

[12] Doubt has been expressed that the Forman notes on *Macbeth* and other plays are genuine. See *Macbeth*, ed. J. Q. Adams (Boston and New York, 1931), pp. 294 ff.; David Klein, "The Case of Forman's Bocke of Plaies," *Philological Quarterly*, XI (1932): 385 ff.; S. A. Tannenbaum, *Shakespearian Scraps and Other Elizabethan Fragments* (New York, 1933), pp. 1 ff. But many scholars accept the notes as genuine, including Kittredge (see note 11 above) and Chambers. Chambers says simply that they "have been questioned, but are genuine" (*William Shakespeare: A Study of Facts and Problems*, Oxford, 1930, II: 388).

[13] P. 266.

[14] Pp. 503–504.

[15] P. 268.

[16] Pp. 507–508.

[17] P. 509.

[18] P. 507. The description remains in that form in later editions.

[19] Edition of 1621, p. 261; edition of 1625, p. 491.

[20] See John Barnard, *Theologo Historicus, or the True Life of the Most Reverend Divine, and Excellent Historian Peter Heylyn* (1683), pp. 94–101.

[21] Edition of 1621, p. 64.

[22] Edition of 1635, pp. 507–508.

[23] See, for example, Francis Douce, *Illustrations of Shakespeare* (London, 1839); T. F. Thiselton Dyer, *Folk Lore of Shakespeare* (London, 1833); Floris Delat-

tre, *English Fairy Poetry: From the Origins to the Seventeenth Century* (London and Paris, 1912); and M. W. Latham, *The Elizabethan Fairies: The Fairies of Folklore and the Fairies of Shakespeare* (New York, 1930).

24 *The Wife of Bath's Tale*, line 860; *The Miller's Tale*, line 293.

25 Thomas Nashe, *The Terrors of the Night* (1594), sig. B 2ᵛ.

26 Edition of S. J. H. Herrtage (E.E.T.S.; London, 1881), p. 113.

27 As is argued by Latham, *op. cit.*, p. 53.

28 Definition of "Lamie" in Sir Thomas Eliot, *Bibliotheca Eliotae* (1548).

29 See G. L. Kittredge, *Witchcraft in Old and New England* (Cambridge, Mass., 1929), pp. 218 ff.

30 Edition of 1597, p. 74.

31 On the close connections between witches and fairies, see the article by J. A. MacCullough in the *Encyclopaedia of Religion and Ethics*, ed. James Hastings (New York, 1925), V: 687 ff. On fairies and witches sailing in sieves (cf. *Macbeth*, I, iii, 8), see T. F. Thiselton Dyer, *op. cit.*, p. 33, and *Shakespeare's England* (Oxford, 1916), p. 543.

32 Edition of 1552, under "VV. ante I."

33 *Ibid.*, under "VV. ante I."

34 *Ibid.*, under "H. ante E."

35 Edition of 1573, definition 343 under "H."

36 Edition of 1611, p. 539.

37 *Ibid.*, p. 184.

38 Edition of 1603, sig. A 4ᵛ.

39 Edition of 1659, under "HA."

40 *Ibid.*, under "HA."

41 Huloet, *op. cit.*, definition of "Ffurye of hel" under "F. ante V."

42 Edition of 1548, under "Larua."

43 Variorum *Macbeth*, ed. H. H. Furness (Philadelphia, 1873), p. 325.

44 *Scotorum Historiae* (1527), fol. cclviiiʳ.

45 Edition of 1587, "Historie of Scotland," p. 171.

46 The argument that Shakespeare's weird sisters are Nornlike powers of destiny is supported by G. L. Kittredge in his edition of *Macbeth* (Boston, 1939).

47 In W. W. Skeat's *Glossary of Tudor and Stuart Words*, ed. A. L. Mayhew (Oxford, 1914), the "weird" in Shakespeare's phrase "weird sisters" is said— rightly, I think—to be "used of the three witches, as foretelling destiny."

48 See "Weird" in the the *Oxford English Dictionary*.

49 Edition of 1606, pp. 376, 377.

50 See Matthew Gwinne, *Vertumnus* (1605), sig. H 3ʳ, and Isaac Wake, *Rex Platonicus* (1607), p. 18.

51 For a discussion of the demonic metaphysics of *Macbeth* in the light of pre-Renaissance Christian theology, see W. C. Curry, *Shakespeare's Philosophical Patterns* (Baton Rouge, 1937), pp. 66 ff.

52 Edition of 1613, pp. 35–36.

53 *The Hierarchie of the Blessed Angels* (1635), p. 442.

54 See C. V. Boyer, *The Villain as Hero in Elizabethan Tragedy* (London, 1914), pp. 192 ff.

[55] Caroline F. E. Spurgeon, *Shakespeare's Imagery and What It Tells Us* (New York, Macmillan, 1935), pp. 326–327.

[56] For a discussion of Macbeth's fear as a passion, see the chapter entitled "Macbeth: A Study in Fear" in Lily B. Campbell, *Shakespeare's Tragic Heroes: Slaves of Passion* (Cambridge, 1930), pp. 208 ff.

[57] F. S. Boas, *Shakspere and His Predecessors* (New York, n.d.), p. 422.

[58] R. G. Moulton, *Shakespeare as a Dramatic Artist* (3d ed.; Oxford, 1897), p. 150.

[59] See *Shakespeare's Holinshed*, ed. W. G. Boswell-Stone (London, 1907), pp. 30 and 33.

[60] See Boece, *Scotorum Historiae* (1527), fol. cclxi^r.

[61] Edition of 1587, p. 172.

[62] Edition of 1598, sig. D 3^r.

[63] Edition of 1596, pp. 86–89.

[64] Edition of 1605, fol. 112. For the conventional Elizabethan tyrant, often fear-stricken, see W. A. Armstrong, "The Elizabethan Conception of the Tyrant" and "The Influence of Seneca and Machiavelli on the Elizabethan Tyrant," *Review of English Studies*, XXII (1946): 161 ff., and XXIV (1948): 19 ff.

[65] *Ibid.*, fol. 52^v.

[66] For stories in which the stain of blood remains upon a murderer in spite of his attempts to remove it, and also for stories in which a murderer is terrified at a feast by an omen of doom, see Beatrice Daw Brown, "Exemplum Materials Underlying *Macbeth*," *Publications of the Modern Language Association*, L (1935): 700 ff.

[67] *The True Tragedy of Richard the Third*, ed. W. W. Greg (Malone Society Reprints; Oxford, 1929), lines 1416–1418.

[68] *Ibid.*, lines 1783–1786.

[69] *Ibid.*, lines 1878–1881.

[70] *The Troublesome Reign of John, King of England*, ed. J. S. Farmer (Tudor Facsimile Texts; 1911), Pt. I, sig. G 4^r.

[71] *Ibid.*, Pt. II, sig. D 2^v.

[72] *Ibid.*, Pt. II, sig. E 2^v.

[73] Domestic murder plays of the sixteenth and seventeenth centuries show this power at work. See H. H. Adams, *English Domestic or Homiletic Tragedy, 1575 to 1642* (New York, 1943).

[74] Percy Fitzgerald, *The Life of David Garrick* (London, 1868), II: 71–72; quoted in the Furness Variorum *Macbeth*, p. 221.

[75] J. Dover Wilson, *The Essential Shakespeare: A Biographical Adventure* (Cambridge Univ. Press, 1932), p. 131.

[76] Edward Dowden, *Shakspere* (in the series of *Literature Primers*, ed. J. R. Green; London, 1877), pp. 59–60.

[77] A. C. Bradley, *Oxford Lectures on Poetry* (London, 1923), p. 328, note.

[78] *Ibid.*, pp. 328 ff.

[79] *Op. cit.*, pp. 120–121.

[80] *The Complete Works of John Webster*, ed. F. L. Lucas (London, 1927), II: 97 (IV, ii, 153–159).

Notes to Chapter IV

"ANTONY AND CLEOPATRA"

(Pages 139–205)

1 Quotations are from the 1579 edition of North's translation of the *Lives*, pp. 970 ff.

2 *The Countess of Pembroke's "Antonie,"* ed. Alice Luce (Litterarhistorische Forschungen, III; Weimar, 1897—a reproduction of the edition of 1592, though the title "Antonie" is taken from the edition of 1595), lines 1794–1801 (Act V).

3 *Ibid.*, line 16 (Act I).

4 *Ibid.*, line 922 (Act III).

5 *Ibid.*, lines 1155–1158 (Act III).

6 *Ibid.*, lines 1240–1243 (Act III).

7 *Ibid.*, line 410 (Act II).

8 *Ibid.*, lines 1629–1632 (Act IV).

9 *Ibid.*, lines 1950–1952 (Act V).

10 *Ibid.*, lines 1758–1760 (Act IV).

11 For some account of these editions, see *The Complete Works in Verse and Prose of Samuel Daniel*, ed. A. B. Grosart (Spenser Society, III; London, 1885), pp. 3–19; H. Sellers, "A Bibliography of the Works of Samuel Daniel, 1585–1623," *Bibliographical Society Proceedings and Papers*, Vol. II, Pt. I (1928), pp. 29 ff; and S. A. Tannenbaum, *Samuel Daniel (A Concise Bibliography)* (New York, 1942), pp. 1 ff.

12 Grosart's edition of *Cleopatra* is based on the edition of 1623. The edition of 1611, which gives very nearly the same text as that given by the edition of 1607, has been reprinted by M. Lederer, *Materialien zur Kunde des älteren Englischen Dramas*, XXXI (1911).

13 For arguments pro and con see *Antony and Cleopatra*, ed. R. H. Case (The Arden Shakespeare, Ed 7; London, 1934), pp. x–xi (Case notes some similarities in phrases and ideas between *Antony and Cleopatra* and the lines added to *Cleopatra* in 1607); E. K. Chambers, *William Shakespeare: A Study of Facts and Problems* (Oxford, 1930), I: 477–478; Johannes Schütze, "Daniels 'Cleopatra' und Shakespeare," *Englische Studien*, LXXI (1936): 58 ff.; and Walther Traub, *Auffasung und Gestaltung der Cleopatra in der englischen Literatur* (Würzburg, 1937), p. 14.

14 See, for instance, Chambers, *op. cit.*, I: 477.

15 Edition of 1594, sig. I 2ᵛ (Act I).

16 *Ibid.*, sig. I 3ᵛ (Act I).

17 *Ibid.*, sig. I 4ʳ (Act I).

18 *Ibid.*, sig. I 4ʳ (Act I).

19 *Ibid.*, sig. I 4ᵛ (Act I).

20 *Ibid.*, sigs. I 4ᵛ and I 5ʳ (Act I).

21 *Ibid.*, sig. I 5ᵛ (Act I).

22 *Ibid.*, sig. K 2ʳ (Act II).

23 *Ibid.*, sig. M 6ʳ (Act V, sc. 1).

24 *Ibid.*, sig. N 3ᵛ (Act V, sc. 2).

25 *Ibid.*, sig. N 5ᵛ (Act V, sc. 2).

26 *Ibid.*, sig. N 8ʳ.

27 North's translation of the *Lives* (1579), p. 1007.

28 Edition of 1594, sig. I 8ʳ (Act II).

29 *Ibid.*, sig. I 3ʳ (Act I).

30 *Ibid.*, sig. I 3ᵛ (Act I).

31 North's translation of the *Lives* (1579), p. 1009.

32 Edition of 1594, sig. I 5ʳ (Act V, sc. 2). The "awry" in the Shakespeare passage, which matches Daniel's "wryes," is Rowe's correction, obviously called for, of an "away" found in the Folios.

33 *Ibid.*, sig. I 2ᵛ (Act I).

34 *Ibid.*, sig. I 5ʳ (Act I).

35 *Ibid.*, sig. N 2ʳ (Act V, sc. 2).

36 *Ibid.*, sig. N 4ʳ (Act V, sc. 2).

37 A collection of correspondences between *Antony and Cleopatra* and Daniel's earlier *Cleopatra* is made by R. H. Case, edition of *Antony and Cleopatra* cited, pp. ix–x. Another collection, independently brought together, is made by H. H. Furness, Variorum edition of *Antony and Cleopatra* (Philadelphia, 1907), pp. 514–515. I have not given all the correspondences that these editors have noted, and I have given some that they have not noted. I have omitted those that seem to me to contribute nothing, or almost nothing, to the argument. I am more indebted to Case than to Furness.

38 North's translation of the *Lives* (1579), p. 983.

39 *Ibid.*, p. 986.

40 *Poeticall Essayes* (1599), sig. Bʳ. The first of these correspondences, between "Egyptian fetters" and "fetters of Egypt," is noted by R. C. Bald, "Shakespeare and Daniel," *Times Literary Supplement*, November 20, 1924, p. 776.

41 See, for example, H. D. R. Anders, *Shakespeare's Books* (Berlin, 1904), pp. 85–89, and H. E. Rollins, Variorum edition of Shakespeare's *Poems* (Philadelphia and London, 1938), pp. 425–426.

42 "Cleopatra and 'That Criticall War,' " *Times Literary Supplement* (anonymous leading article), October 11, 1928, p. 718.

43 *Three Plays for Puritans* (London, Richards, 1901), pp. xxvii–xxviii.

44 *Shakespeare* (London, Longmans, 1929), pp. 188–189.

45 Edition of 1598, sig. Fᵛ.

46 Sir Richard Barckley, *A Discourse of the Felicitie of Man* (1598), pp. 43–44.

47 Richard Reynoldes, *A Chronicle of All the Noble Emperours of the Romans* (1571), fol. 17.

48 Thomas Beard, *The Theatre of Gods Iudgements* (1597), p. 250.

49 A. C. Bradley, *Oxford Lectures on Poetry* (London, Macmillan, 1923), p. 281.

50 M. W. MacCallum thinks that the omission of the Parthian fiasco is a notable indication of Shakespeare's desire to gain sympathy for Antony (*Shakespeare's Roman Plays and Their Background*, London, 1910, pp. 335–336).

[51] No injustice to Shakespeare's Cleopatra is done, I think, in Leo Kirschbaum's presentation of her as a consistent voluptuary, "Shakespeare's Cleopatra," *Shakespeare Association Bulletin,* XIX (1944): 161 ff.

[52] Inconsistencies among modern critics, Schücking and others, who have found discontinuities in Shakespeare's treatment of Antony and Cleopatra are briefly discussed by S. L. Bethell, *Shakespeare and the Popular Dramatic Tradition* (London, 1944), p. 117. Bethell himself thinks that "regarding the play psychologically, one cannot reconcile the vicious, the vulgar, and the commonplace in Antony and Cleopatra with the sublimity with which they are invested, especially as they face defeat and death" (p. 117).

[53] *Antony and Cleopatra,* ed. G. L. Kittredge (Boston, Ginn, 1941), p. 183.

[54] Edition of 1571, fols. 17^v and 18^r.

[55] Edition of 1597, p. 250.

[56] Edition of 1601, pp. 196–197.

"Coriolanus"

(Pages 207–264)

[1] Edition of 1579, p. 237. Quotations from North's Plutarch immediately following are from the same edition: from the "Life of Caius Martius Coriolanus," pp. 237–248, and the "Comparison of Alcibiades with Martius Coriolanus," p. 262.

[2] Pp. 496–497.

[3] Pp. 311–312.

[4] *Le Théâtre d'Alexandre Hardy,* ed. E. Stengel (Marburg, 1884), II: 56.

[5] *Ibid.,* II: 91.

[6] P. 271.

[7] Pp. 361–362.

[8] I accept a change in the Folio text which is usually made by editors. The change puts First Citizen in the place of Second Citizen as the maker of replies to Menenius and Coriolanus. These replies should obviously be given to the leader of the rebellion, who, of course, is First Citizen.

[9] O. J. Campbell makes a thought-provoking argument for the rejection of this praise of Coriolanus as coming from a buffoonish commentator in a tragical satire (*Shakespeare's Satire,* New York, 1943, p. 209).

[10] Fols. 15–18.

[11] See *Coriolanus,* ed. H. H. Furness (Variorum edition; Philadelphia and London, 1928), p. 395, note to IV, i, 4–5.

[12] See Aristotle's *Politics,* III, 7 and IV, 2, 4. Cf. Plato's division of each of his three kinds of government into a good form and a bad (*Politicus,* 302DE and 303A).

[13] Sigs. E 3–F.

[14] Edition of 1586, pp. 579–582.

[15] For comment upon *Julius Caesar* and *Coriolanus* as plays representing steps in a development of democracy, see F. T. Wood, "Shakespeare and the Plebs," *Essays and Studies by Members of the English Association,* XVIII (1933): 68. A general consideration of Renaissance ideas concerning monarchy, aristocracy, and democracy is to be found in J. E. Phillips, Jr., *The State in Shakespeare's Greek and Roman Plays* (New York, 1940).

[16] Edition cited, p. 242.

[17] *Political Characters of Shakespeare* (London, Macmillan, 1945), p. 265.

[18] Edition cited, pp. 243–246.

[19] *Ibid.,* p. 260.

[20] See chapter ii above. See J. W. Draper, "Flattery, a Shakespearean Tragic Theme," *Philological Quarterly,* XVII (1938): 240 ff., and P. A. Jorgensen, "Shakespeare's Coriolanus: Elizabethan Soldier," *Publications of the Modern Language Association,* LXIV (1949): 227–228.

[21] Ludovic Lloyd, *The Pilgrimage of Princes* (1573?), fol. 183ᵛ.

[22] Robert Pricket, *Times Anotomie* (1606), sig. B 2ʳ.

[23] *Memorable Conceits of Divers Noble and Famous Personages of Christendome* (a translation by "I. S." of Gilles Corrozet, *Les Propos memorable des nobles et illustres hommes de la chrestienté*, 1602), p. 273.

[24] Ludovic Lloyd, *The Practice of Policy* (1604), pp. 59–60.

[25] *Memorable Conceits*, edition cited, p. 273.

INDEX

INDEX

Date Due